"This prophetic book offers a paradigm shift in our understanding of persons with disabilities within the life of Christian congregations. Raffety changes the focus from inclusion in the community to leadership of the community, seeing disability not as a problem but as a dignified experience in which God is at work for justice."

—WILLIAM STORRAR, *Director, Center of Theological Inquiry*

"Erin Raffety writes as a pastor to pastors and as an anthropologist to anthropologists in this forceful, fascinating book which lays bare the violence done in the name of inclusion. In prose that is fierce, humble, and precise, Raffety issues a wakeup call to churches and, by extension, the institutions that shape our field. This book offers a stunning example of what an engaged anthropology could look like and where it could lead."

—DANILYN RUTHERFORD, *President, the Wenner-Gren Foundation for Anthropological Research*

"In this powerful book, Erin Raffety calls churches to reckon with limits of inclusion by showing how prevailing practices and paradigms rarely challenge the structures of ableism and inequality that disenfranchise disabled people. This is essential reading for religious communities ready to grapple with entrenched assumptions and embrace deeper possibilities for justice and liberation."

—JULIA WATTS BELSER, *Associate Professor of Jewish Studies, Georgetown University*

"Many, perhaps most, readers of this thoughtful volume will be playing catch-up on matters related to disabled persons. This welcome book is in part instruction, as Raffety helps us to clarify categories of our thinking. It is partly a summons to learn from and pay attention to those too long treated in our society in condescending ways. And it is in part advocacy, as Raffety urges us to move beyond a 'paradigm of inclusion' to full empowerment, recognition of and leadership by disabled persons. This book will go a long way to help us catch up in practice to our best but often ill-informed intentions."

—WALTER BRUEGGEMANN, *William Marcellus McPheeters Professor Emeritus of Old Testament, Columbia Theological Seminary*

SRTD
STUDIES IN RELIGION, THEOLOGY, AND DISABILITY

SERIES EDITORS

Sarah J. Melcher
Xavier University, Cincinnati, Ohio

John Swinton
University of Aberdeen, Aberdeen, Scotland

Amos Yong
Fuller Theological Seminary, Pasadena, California

From Inclusion to Justice

Disability, Ministry, and Congregational Leadership

Erin Raffety

BAYLOR UNIVERSITY PRESS

© 2022 by Baylor University Press
Waco, Texas 76798

Cover design by theBookDesigners
Book design by Baylor University Press

The Library of Congress has cataloged this book under paperback ISBN 978-1-4813-1694-1.

Library of Congress Control Number: 2022940712

For Lucia, a supreme companion.

Series Introduction

Studies in Religion, Theology, and Disability brings newly established and emerging scholars together to explore issues at the intersection of religion, theology, and disability. The series editors encourage theoretical engagement with secular disability studies while supporting the reexamination of established religious doctrine and practice. The series fosters research that takes account of the voices of people with disabilities and the voices of their family and friends.

The volumes in the series address issues and concerns of the global religious studies/theological studies academy. Authors come from a variety of religious traditions with diverse perspectives to reflect on the intersection of the study of religion/theology and the human experience of disability. This series is intentional about seeking out and publishing books that engage with disability in dialogue with Jewish, Christian, Buddhist, or other religious and philosophical perspectives.

Themes explored include religious life, ethics, doctrine, proclamation, liturgical practices, physical space, spirituality, and the interpretation of sacred texts through the lens of disability. Authors in the series are aware of conversation in the field of disability studies and bring that discussion to bear methodologically and theoretically in their analyses at the intersection of religion and disability.

Studies in Religion, Theology, and Disability reflects the following developments in the field: First, the emergence of disability studies as an interdisciplinary endeavor that has impacted theological studies, broadly defined. More and more scholars are deploying disability perspectives in their work, and this applies also to those working in the theological academy. Second, there is a growing need for critical reflection on disability in world religions. While books from a Christian standpoint have dominated the discussion at the interface of religion and disability so far, Jewish, Muslim, Buddhist, and Hindu scholars, among those from other religious traditions, have begun to resource their own religious traditions to rethink disability in the twenty-first century. Third, passage of the Americans with Disabilities Act in the United States has raised the consciousness of the general public about the importance of critical reflection on disability in religious communities. General and intelligent lay readers are looking for scholarly discussions of religion and disability as these bring together and address two of the most important existential aspects of human lives. Fourth, the work of activists in the disability rights movement has mandated fresh critical reflection by religious practitioners and theologians. Persons with disabilities remain the group most disaffected from religious organizations. Fifth, government representatives in several countries have prioritized the greater social inclusion of persons with disabilities. Disability policy often proceeds based on core cultural and worldview assumptions that are religiously informed. Work at the interface of religion and disability thus could have much broader purchase—that is, in social, economic, political, and legal domains.

Under the general topic of thoughtful reflection on the religious understanding of disability, Studies in Religion, Theology, and Disability includes shorter, crisply argued volumes that articulate a bold vision within a field; longer scholarly monographs, more fully developed and meticulously documented, with the same goal of engaging wider conversations; textbooks that provide a state of the discussion at this intersection and chart constructive ways forward; and select edited volumes that achieve one or more of the preceding goals.

Contents

Acknowledgments

It is impossible to truly capture the collaborative nature of book writing, let alone ethnographic research and writing. At the heart of knowledge-making lie real, complicated, heartening relationships with people who make it all so deeply challenging and worthwhile. This book would not have been possible without the eleven disabled persons, their families, congregations, communities, and pastors with whom we spent time, worship, ministry, and months together from 2019 to 2020. I hope we did you justice, but I also hope you can forgive us wherever we fell short. Thank you especially to Jess and Arundel, Pastor Maggi, Pastor Pam, Bailie, Lisa, Mary, and Michelle, for reading through drafts of this manuscript and being so patient with me.

This book would also not have been possible without my research team, Francesca Weirich-Freiberg, Lottie Friedman, Gail Tierney, Maci Sepp, and Kevin Vollrath, whose ethnographic skills, time, analysis, interpretations, and insights anchor this book. Ethnographic work can be so weirdly isolating, like being at a cocktail party that is swirling around you but feeling all alone, and you were true companions on the journey. Students in my Ministry with People with Disabilities class also provided valuable feedback and inspiration, especially on the introduction, in spring 2020. The first Ministry with People with Disabilities class I taught in 2018 at Princeton Seminary, which I very much muddled through, still connected me with students and disabled faith leaders like Emmie Arnold, J. J. Flag, and Anna Gheen, and students and faith leaders living with chronic illness, like Kristen Levens and Madison Trivits, whose insights have all contributed to this work in ways they may never fully understand. Thank you to Stuart Carroll and the students in the CCS program at TCNJ for the learnings they contributed to this book, as well as to Jessica Patchett and Martha Haythorn for their ministry partnership and encouragement.

I'm especially thankful to Abigail Visco Rusert for her willingness to run a conference on disability and youth ministry in 2018 that gave me the opportunity to connect with many of the scholars who have formed my own thinking, ministry, teaching, and writing in disability and theology, and with whom I have the joy of staying connected and in conversation, including but not limited to Ben Conner, Amy Jacober, John Swinton, Miriam Spies, Keith Dow, Laura MacGregor, and, of course, Wes Ellis.

It's almost an embarrassment of riches to mention how many eyes and hands there have been on this manuscript. Thank you to Eric Barreto, Noah Buccholz, Caroline Cupp, Alex Davis, Scott Ellington, Wes Ellis, Terri Elton, Lindsey Jodrey, Laura MacGregor, Hanna Reichel, Miriam Spies, Nate Stucky, John Swinton, Gail Tierney, and Leon Van Ommen for taking the time to read drafts of this book and give your feedback. Wes, you were particularly critical in (hopefully) keeping me out of the realm of heresy and in making me feel like I could become a practical theologian along the way. John, your encouragement and criticism have been vital to this work.

I'm grateful to my colleagues at Princeton Theological Seminary and the Center of Theological Inquiry for their support of my unconventional career and this project. I'm especially grateful to Victor Aloyo, Kenda Dean, Gordon Mikoski, Maria Insa Iglesias, Josh Mauldin, and William Storrar for their collegiality and care. It was a Louisville Institute Project Grant for Researchers and an invitation to a Collegeville writing workshop that also provided critical funding, connection, and more companions for this book, especially Andrew Cornetta, Ruthie Braunstein, Tia Noelle Pratt, and Nicolas de Zamarocszy. Thank you to Beth Scibienski and Stephen Faller, whose mentorship as clergy colleagues has taught me so much. Thank you to Cade Jarrell and John Swinton at Baylor, who have both believed in this book and in me.

Most of all, I'm thankful to my friends and colleagues: reconnecting with Caroline Cupp, Jessica Slice, and Athena Stevens from Davidson College has left me so in awe of the power and graciousness of the disability community. My friends Beth Daniel Lindsay, Christina Jarvi,

Erin Spalinski, Jessie and Jason Lowry, Lindsey Hankins, Natalie Portis, Deborah Jodrey, Kim Copeland, and Anne Moffit have all talked me through numerous ideas and anxieties along the way. Without the amazing care nurses Barry Federovitch and Sylvia Roberts have provided Lucia these last five years, none of this writing would have been possible. I'm thankful for my mom, dad, sisters, and my husband, Evan. And thank you to my daughter, Lucia, who continues to be the best companion I could ask for in life and in teaching me about disability, ministry, and God.

Introduction

INTRODUCING THE PROBLEM

In 1975, disability activist Vic Finkelstein imagined a village in which everyone had physical impairments and used wheelchairs. Because of this, when the people designed their town, they put the ceiling heights at 7 feet 2 inches rather than 9 feet 6 inches and the doors at 5 feet rather than 7 feet 4 inches. Everything was lowered, including the cabinets, the tables, and the beds. One day, when a few able-bodied people, through no choice of their own, came to stay in the village, they kept hitting their heads on the doorways, and they started to stand out because of the big bruises on their foreheads. Doctors, psychiatrists, and lawyers got involved to try to solve the problem of the able-bodied. Special helmets were handed out to the able-bodied to be worn and braces were designed to give relief so that able-bodied people could function at a more normal height. Charities were formed, and there was even talk of creating special homes for the "disabled able-bodied." But one day, when a few able-bodied people got together, it dawned on them that there was really nothing wrong with them—they had simply been disadvantaged, excluded on the basis of their bodily experiences. Maybe they were only made to feel as though they were a problem. Maybe they were not even disabled at all (Finkelstein 1975).

When I use Finkelstein's story in my seminary classes and in my teaching with churches, a lot of people immediately want to push back

1

on his illustration of the social model of disability. They want to argue that even though Finkelstein's illustration helps us to realize that disability is social, or that disability is most certainly an effect of not just an environment but a society that prefers, prioritizes, and privileges people with "able bodies," there is still something invariably tangible, concrete, or different about disabled people. After all, they retort, even if we remove all the physical and social barriers for disabled people, won't some disabilities—for instance, those that are intellectual and developmental—still be there?

Of course, there's some truth to that point. As with any analogy or model, the social model of disability is partial and incomplete. That's why disabled people, especially people in the disability rights movement, even Finkelstein, raised these points many years ago—they acknowledged that there are embodied experiences of pain, movement, and neurological and physical differences that also affect some disabled people.

But it may be more important to ask why so many of us, particularly those of us who identify as non-disabled, so readily push back against this provocative illustration, especially when we've also seen something truthful, valuable, and enlightening in it about ourselves. Are we not seeking to point out that the problem still lies within "them" rather than within "us"? Are we not seeking to maintain some distance between "us" and "them"? What problem are we trying to solve, anyway?

When disabled people come to church, many non-disabled people in the church tend to see problems: our stairs are inaccessible to people in wheelchairs, our hymnals can't be read by blind people, and even our Sunday school curriculum is all geared toward "typical" children—it doesn't consider autistic kids, kids with sensory disorders, kids with learning disabilities, or kids who are medically complex. Some churches quickly become overwhelmed by these problems and give up. Others fixate on them, diligently making concerted efforts to solve the problems that they are encountering. They really care and they're doing their best, but even this perspective and this approach to "solving the problem" of disability in churches still treats people, or at least disabilities, as a problem, an obstacle to be managed or overcome.

Yet even if significant physical and social barriers are overcome for disabled people with respect to church access and inclusion, then what? Is solving the problem of disability the point of ministry with disabled people, or might church people, especially those of us who are primarily able-bodied, need radically new ways of thinking about disability and disabled people? What if our solutions fundamentally misunderstand the problem? What if the church is part of the problem?

REPENTING OF OUR ABLEISM: FROM INCLUSION TO JUSTICE

This book begins from the simple premise that disability is not a problem (Davis 1997, 9) but a dignified, incarnate human experience through and in which God is at work. Although this is a not a radical theological teaching—many scholars have thought it and many churches would affirm it—I also argue that our thinking and practice at the congregational level are still steeped in societal prejudice toward disabled people. Churches unintentionally, yet tragically, embody this prejudice in our eagerness to solve problems for disabled people. This is what it means to be able-bodied and to exhibit ableism in our practices, ministry, and theology. Being able-bodied is a privileged position, because, as Finkelstein helps us see, the world was built with non-disabled people in mind, and not only our architecture but our systems of education, employment, healthcare, and citizenship have historically preferred and demanded able bodies.

Of course, being able-bodied and disabled are false binaries, rather than real, complex experiences (Shildrick 2009; Wendell 2010); they're both constructed by the culture we live in. But just as our culture prefers whiteness, maleness, and heterogeneity, so, too, do we take able-bodiedness as both a false norm and a perfect ideal. If you enjoy able-bodied privileges and you're reading this book, chances are you don't identify yourself that way. Perhaps you have never thought much about your body beyond its appearance or the occasional cold or flu. But for people whose bodies do not conform to or fit the norm—a norm that, as we shall see, goes beyond the physical into the realm of the psyche and the intellect—this is something they think about or are confronted with nearly every day. Disabled people face not just individual but systematic prejudice in America because capitalism demeans people it labels unproductive, beyond rehabilitation, or dependent. In fact, ableism leads us all to believe that we are only valuable if we are these things, so much so that we fail to see ourselves clearly as human beings with human bodies, human needs, and human cares.

In a section of her book entitled "What Does Ableism Look Like?" disability activist Emily Ladau provides snapshots of and statistics on systematic and economic inequality disabled people face in the United States today (2021, 84–85). Excerpts from Ladau's full list below show that disability rights, legislation, and more visibility for disabled people in society today often give the false impression that we are living in a post-ableist society. Instead, Ladau writes, "My hope is that . . . this brief list of examples will awaken you to just how deep-seated ableism is in every part of our society, and that you'll begin to recognize both blatant and subtle ableist patterns" (84):

- In two-thirds of the United States there are statutes in place that allow courts to deem a parent unfit on the basis of their disability, which means their parental rights can be terminated.

- During the 2015–2016 school year in the United States, a mere 16.6 percent of students with intellectual disabilities were included in general education classes about 80 percent of the time. The rest of the time they were segregated.

- Hundreds of thousands of people with disabilities, especially with intellectual and developmental disabilities, are still forced to live in institutional settings instead of in their communities.

- The median income for Americans with disabilities is less than 70 percent of the median earnings of those without a disability.

- Since 2015, more than eight hundred disabled people, world-wide, have been murdered by their caregivers. Media outlets often report on these cases using language that shows sympathy for the killers, framing it as though caregivers were relieving themselves of a burden.

- During the COVID-19 pandemic, many states and countries issued guidelines explicitly calling for disabilities to be taken into account as a reason to *not* provide lifesaving health care to sick people. (Ladau 2021, 84–85)

For these reasons, when I'm referring to these norms and the prejudice they inflict, I use the term able-bodied. When I'm referring to people who are not disabled, I use the term non-disabled to move disability off the periphery and toward the center in a conversation about ministry with disabled people (Linton 1998, 13). Yet readers will see that this book also understands disability as both an identity and an epistemology that challenges and makes meaning in the world as it is, because disabled experiences provide so much critical insight into what could be (Dolmage 2017). Alongside other scholars and theorists, I seek to add a relational quality to the social model of disability (Jacobs 2019; Reeve 2012; Thomas 1999), recognizing disability's intersectional, psycho-emotional, rela-tional, and even spiritual qualities. My approach to disability combines social, relational, and affirmative models of disability, centering disabled persons' interpretations of their own experiences, appreciating their real, embodied experiences, as well as their social experiences of discrimination, and valuing their different ways of being and thinking in the world (Cameron 2007, 2011).

Just because disabled bodies and minds don't conform to societal norms doesn't mean they're less valuable, deficient, or wrong. Finkelstein's parable helps able-bodied people view disability through a framework of social construction, something disability rights activists have been doing for decades. Although disabled persons may have different experiences due to bodily or cognitive differences, these differences are only made "less than" in comparison to some idealized, able-bodied "norm." In thinking about disability this way, disability rights activists and scholars essentially reclaimed the term disability and recovered pride, insight, and beauty in its identity and experience.

But a lot of people, especially people in churches, still think disability is a term to be avoided. They might prefer terms like "differently abled," "special needs," or "different abilities," but disability rights activists and scholars have intentionally chosen to identify as disabled persons. To be disabled offers a different experience of the world, but the term "disabled" also maintains an important critique of prevailing injustice against the validity and value of disabled experiences. For these reasons, this book uses the term "disabled person," foregrounding the critical importance disability makes to people in the world and following the lead of disability activists and scholars. The book largely avoids person-first language, because of its awkward linguistic construction, and because it subtly invokes ableism in insisting that disabled people are people in ways that we do not do with other groups. Of course there is diversity of thought around language and it is always changing, but articulating disabled personhood should be on disabled people's own terms.

But disabled perspectives are not important to this book solely because they bring diverse points of views. They're also important because they call the church to accountability, where the church, like so many other institutions, has not just failed disabled people but failed to follow Christ in its ministry. Because this book is an ethnographic study, I take the church as both an empirical reality and a theological certainty. As an empirical reality, the church as we know it exhibits able-bodied privileges, preferences, and prejudices; therefore, when this book invokes "we" language, it is referencing the corporate oversights, problems, and sins of the able-bodied church. Rather than forcing a separation from non-disabled people or assuming disabled people aren't in churches, this language acknowledges the fact that our churches operate by able-bodied norms and privilege able-bodied ministry and leadership. Disabled and non-disabled are not parallel identities in society or the church, because ableism undermines our relationships with one another.

However, the church as a theological certainty means that Christ's death has liberated all of us from sin and death: even when we fall short, Christ is there among us, calling us to fellowship, ministry, and justice with him. Therefore, in this book I argue that one of the primary problems in ministry with disabled people (and ministry in general) is that the able-bodied human experience, rather than the Christ-centered human experience, forms the norm for how we enter into human relationships and how we conceive of the church. It is not enough to welcome disabled people into the space of the church; rather, able-bodied people need to be confronted by and transformed from the ways we have consistently, albeit often unintentionally, prioritized the able-bodied experience. In fact, I would argue that churches cannot possibly offer welcome to disabled people unless there is true repentance regarding the sin of ableism within and on behalf of the church. This repentance cannot be a one-off apology but must take the form of a confessional ministry, in which the church commits to being transformed from this worldly conforming that has been so invisible yet insidious (Rom 12:2). Simply put, ableism, not a lack of ramps or sound systems or braille hymnals or special education teachers, is the biggest obstacle in ministry with disabled people in churches today.

The first part of this book draws on congregational research with churches that exhibited a preference for inclusion as their prevailing paradigm for ministry with disabled people. Inclusion, the stated goal of providing equal access and rights for disabled people, frames legislation with respect to citizenship, education, and employment in the contemporary United States. However, drawing on Disability Studies scholars, I show that inclusion rarely critiques, exposes, or dismantles the unequal power dynamics between able-bodied and disabled people in society. Instead, my research shows how inclusive ministry in congregations often serves to entrench ableism further within structural practices of ministry. Accordingly, I offer interpretations of scripture that help able-bodied people grapple with their tendencies to treat disabled people as problems or ministries, and invite able-bodied people to listen well in congregational ministry with disabled people. I show how listening makes it possible for the church to lament ableism and injustice faithfully alongside disabled people, making the church a compelling and repentant witness to injustice as the foundation for receiving and amplifying the ministry and leadership of disabled people.

Second, beyond an anti-ableist stance, this book looks to scripture, ethnographic evidence, and personal experience to show how Jesus calls and is calling disabled people into ministry. Too many theologies of disability and approaches to ministry with disabled people stop with the conviction that disabled people are made in the image of God and that all are welcome. But this book makes it clear that Jesus calls disabled people into ministry and that the Spirit amply unleashes herself to make each and every one of us ministers. Drawing on Jesus' call to Bartimaeus in Mark 10:46–52, I demonstrate how the church can enter into dignifying dialogue with disabled people by nurturing and amplifying their calls to ministry. Alongside practical theologian John Swinton, I charge pastors and lay leaders to consider how the ministry of disabled people transcends the boundaries of pastoral care or Christian education within which disabled people typically find themselves in the church, inviting us to new modes of pastoral care, worship, ministry, and leadership (Swinton 2020a). This is why this book focuses so broadly on congregational ministry: ministry with disabled people is not limited to one segment of church ministry, and the congregation must not be the barrier that stands in the way of disabled people's call to ministry. Even as disabled people and theologians of disability have been circling around these truths for decades, able-bodied people still see disabled people primarily as a ministry rather than as ministers.

Accordingly, a third purpose of this book is to showcase and demonstrate the lessons disabled leadership can impart to the church universal—to acknowledge the valuable critiques ministry from disabled people offers to practices of worship, pastoral care, and congregational ministry so churches can grow in faithfulness to God and others. We testify too frequently about gifts for ministry among disabled people without precision and specificity. We advocate for more disabled people in leadership, but we fail to appreciate the critical insights different practices of leadership may demand from all of us. We extol the rush of the Holy Spirit in Pentecost and we say we want the kingdom of God to come near, but would we even know it if it came to us? Or would we protest the upside-down kingdom, because it's so different from the world we imagine? The book draws on ethnographic research to present "glimmers of the kingdom" from churches that are boldly receiving the ministry of disabled people and being transformed by the Spirit so that our collective theological imagination can be stretched and prodded. Rather than a systemic theology or theoretical model, I offer and analyze empirical examples of disabled leadership that has been there all along so that able-bodied people can begin to behold it and receive it.

CONFESSIONS OF AN ABLEIST PARENT[1]

When our daughter, Lucia, experienced early onset of a progressive, genetic disease of the brain as an infant and was diagnosed with multiple disabilities at thirteen months, all people could say to us was "I'm so sorry." I have written elsewhere (Raffety 2016) about how chafing to us those three little words were, how revealing that although congratulations and joy were reserved for whole and healthy babies, sorrow and mourning were the primary ways people now found to relate to our daughter and our family. Even as people in our church family surrounded us with love and acceptance, some of their comments belied that they struggled to accept Lucia as she was, subtly maintaining hope in a future for her that looked like everybody else's. One Sunday, when I explained Lucia's brain disease and developmental delays, a kind woman at church said to me, "But you never know. Maybe she will get up and walk. Maybe she will be able to eat and talk like other kids . . . maybe someday she will be normal."

As a parent and as a minister, it was a watershed pastoral care experience to begin to view the world of disability from the inside out, to gain a glimpse of how other people viewed the baby who I knew was made in the image of God. As I began to read more in the field of Disability Studies, I found a community that embraced disability as not just as social critique but as a dignified way of interpreting and inhabiting the world. It spoke to my sensibilities as both an anthropologist and a person of faith to illuminate that medicalization and normalization were just one (limited) cultural way of interpreting disability, and that the human experience of disability, the experience of being with, raising my daughter, and pastoring alongside her helped me behold and understand things about ministry that I never could have without her.

But deep in my heart of hearts, and something I only admitted to a few people along the way, was a worry of my own. For a person like me, for whom a resounding great adventure of my life has been being loved by and learning to love God, I worried that while Lucia might be able to receive love, she may never truly be able to give it or express it to others.

---

[1] Portions of this section were presented at keynote lectures at Princeton Theological Seminary and Furman University in 2018.

This really broke my heart. Not because I had expectations that Lucia should be able to "love me back" or tell me so, but because to me, what it means to be human (I realized) is not just to receive love but to be able to give it. I have long told many agnostics and atheists, especially in academia, that the reason why I'm a Christian is not so much about the afterlife or the cosmic power of God, but about what God is doing right here, right now on earth, which I feel so blessed to be a part of. I'm a Christian because this dynamic relationship with God makes life so rich and profound. I realized that I wasn't worried about Lucia's ability to give and express love so much as I was worried about Lucia's ability to, well, *be like me*.

These may seem like sincere things for parents to worry about and wish for their child. In some humble sense, they still are. But time, revelation, and, I believe, God's ministry through my own daughter have taught me that beneath their good intentions, they were also self-conscious, self-centered fears that, oddly, said so much more about me than about God or the person to whom I gave birth. What I've been completely flabbergasted by as my daughter nears eight and a half years old is how decidedly unhindered she is when it comes to showing love to people all around her. I realize now that buried in my fears for her were these normative, self-referential ideas of what I thought it could or would or should look like to give or receive love, but what's happened in loving and learning alongside Lucia is that *my* preconceived notions of what love looked like have been powerfully disrupted by her different and good ways of being in this world.

To love Lucia has involved a call to advocacy in a world that does not support her way of life. Even though Lucia is only eight, our family has fought countless battles with insurance companies, congressional leaders, school districts, and private companies to get and maintain her access to medicine, medical treatment, nursing care, affordable healthcare, education, and supportive equipment. Although many Christians pride themselves on not being political, loving our daughter means that our family has never had a choice. Lucia has opened up my eyes to the hope for justice for disabled people in this world, and I simply cannot love her as Jesus did without repenting of my own ableism and advocating for a vision of justice that doesn't just include her but dignifies and centers her.

In short, much of my parenting and ministering experience has been a process of unlearning, of becoming attuned to my own ableist biases, unearthing and ferreting them out and sharing them, so that I can help churches and pastors gain glimpses of different and valuable perspectives on God and the world. As a person who identifies as temporarily able-bodied, I'm constantly engaged in cross-cultural translation when it comes to my scholarship and ministry with disabled people. My daughter has been a valuable cultural broker in that work (Fadiman 1997), helping me to experience the world critically and with particular attention to the confines of ableism. Throughout this text, I interweave experiences in ministry, fieldwork, and parenting, and as an ethnographer and a pastor, I strive to share particular stories and experiences of my interlocutors and congregants, with their permission, of course.

LISTENING AND ASKING BETTER QUESTIONS:
TOWARD A NEW PARADIGM OF CONGREGATIONAL MINISTRY

The data from this fieldwork is based on two ethnographic studies I conducted, one in the summer of 2018 with families with disabled children who are nonverbal (Raffety et al. 2019), funded by the Templeton Foundation through the Yale Center for Faith and Culture's "Joy and the Good Life" study. The second I conducted over approximately eight months between 2019 and 2020 with eleven churches and families with persons with disabilities in the New York, Philadelphia, and greater New Jersey area through a Project Grant for Researchers through the Louisville Institute (Raffety 2020b). From 2015 to 2020, I also served as the associate pastor at a local Presbyterian Church U.S.A. (PCUSA) congregation in New Jersey, and I draw on these experiences, as well as my teaching experience at Princeton Theological Seminary, my parenting experiences, and my relationships with disabled congregants and pastors in this book. This book is an amalgamation of that learning—the personal, the pastoral, and the ethnographic—but although it begins with lived human experience, it doesn't end there. In fact, the book is premised upon the audacious claim that the experiences of disabled people are vital not just to cultural understanding but to theological understanding that disabled people help us behold God, ministry, and leadership in important and different ways.

When we were recruiting churches in the summer of 2019 for our research, I recall a series of hesitant conversations with a suburban Presbyterian church and its staff. One youth pastor, Pastor Brad, asked whether most churches that had indicated interest in the project "had it together" when it came to disabled people. "Are they doing it well, or are they struggling like us?" he asked cautiously. And then he went on to tell me that he was afraid that if we spent time with the families of disabled people in his church, we might see that everything they were asking for was warranted, and if the church could just provide it, things would be better. But if we came back and offered that advice, he was sure that the church would never be able to live up to the needs of these families.[2]

My heart warmed listening to Pastor Brad. Implicitly, he was concerned with the very question of this book, that of what good ministry with disabled people looks like. But it was also clear that he was trapped in a paradigm for ministry that undermined his confidence as a pastor and his instincts about what it meant to care for his flock. He cared so deeply, and yet he saw ministry with disabled people as a project, one at which he and his church were failing. He cared about these families, but he felt certain that if the church weren't already failing them, it was going to fail them. It was simply a matter of time. He'd rather fail in private, he seemed to be indicating, than fail so that others could see.

Even bracketing the particular context of disability ministry, these concepts of success and failure in ministry need more unpacking. The idea that the pastor is someone who works to "solve the problems" of the flock sets up a critical, oppositional relationship between leader and congregation that is both transactional and hierarchical. And yet, having taught at a seminary, where we emphasized logic, critical thinking, and problem-solving as tools for ministry, I can see how this slippage happens. I may even be responsible for it. I can see how easily congregations and people can become objects rather than subjects in pastoral ministry. And when it comes to disabled people, funneling them into a program is usually the way pastors and congregations "deal with them."

Ironically, the churches Pastor Brad was worried about, those that seemingly "had it together" and thus had thriving worship or social ministries with disabled people, were quick to admit that they had also made many mistakes along the way. Not only were some of their programs challenging to sustain, they also grieved that having these programs operating on the perimeter of church life meant that something was still broken in their churches and their communities. Simply put, it wasn't necessarily the case that more inclusive programs led to more inclusive churches, or that more inclusion made church ministry better or more just.

Although I set out to write a book about ministry with disabled people, I have realized that disabled leaders are asking students, pastors, and congregants to shed a problem-solving orientation to ministry

---

[2] Fieldnotes, May 4, 2019.

and to come a bit closer, to listen a bit deeper, to notice what it is God is doing. This is really a book that identifies and rejects transactional models for congregational ministry in favor of confessional and collaborative ones. This is a book that forsakes problem-solving in order to ask better questions that seek understanding. Indeed, throughout the book the reader will notice that disabled ministers and leaders are reframing approaches to ministry, listening, pastoral care, worship, and leadership. This is a book that highlights the importance of listening to congregations in theological education. And this is a book that will not settle for congregational ministry that is not anchored in seeking the type of justice that turns the world upside down.

As an able-bodied person speaking to an able-bodied church, I acknowledge the limits of this text. It is important to recognize that disability is an incredibly varied embodied, cultural, societal, and global experience, and writing about disabled persons tends to collapse these important differences. Writing from an able-bodied perspective, despite the wisdom and contributions of my disabled interlocutors and the breadth of disabled leadership, still misses some of the cultural nuance, much as the best-trained ethnographer never presents or can present any view other than her own. Like Finkelstein's analogy, this text will be incomplete, one-dimensional, and insufficient at times. Even as a cultural critique, this text will likely exhibit, refract, and even reflect ableism at times, as it's embedded in and bound up with it. I certainly hope the reader can help me identify and learn from my mistakes.

But, if the work of ethnography is worthy (and since it's my life's work, I certainly hope that it is) in any way, it is for its admission that we need one another to see the world more critically and more clearly, that we learn from other people—and while we do that imperfectly, it is still worth doing. As a parent of a disabled child, a pastor, and an ethnographer, my viewpoint is necessarily different from that of a disabled minister, a disabled congregant, or a non-disabled congregant, and so the story I tell, the book that I write will be inflected with my learnings, even as it features the voices of many others who are different from me.

But if it can tell my own story and that of a few other churches of recognizing and reckoning with our own ableism, maybe it can begin to make a difference to the persons in the pews. If it can find its way toward affirming, illustrating, and amplifying the important role disabled people have in ministry, perhaps it can help us to behold the world with just a little more humility and awe and openness. Perhaps it can help us listen with just a bit more compassion and with a bent toward justice. Perhaps it can enable ministry to flourish where it has always and already been, because others can finally behold it. But this time the others are not necessarily disabled people—they're you and me. And what a privilege it is to be invited to experience God differently.

CRITICAL INSIGHTS OF DISABILITY SCHOLARS AND ACTIVISTS

Finkelstein's story at the beginning of this chapter was penned during the heyday of the disability rights movement, which achieved significant momentum from the 1960s into the 1990s in both the United Kingdom and the United States, ushering in legislative advancements with respect to employment, accessibility, and antidiscrimination. The independent living movement, which stresses the autonomy of disabled individuals, prioritized de-medicalization and de-institutionalization in order to grant disabled people more control over their own lives. The social model of disability, a phrase associated with the work of disabled scholar Michael Oliver in 1983 but in circulation since the 1960s, is a response to the predominant medical model of disability that looks at impairment or disability as originating as a problem within the body of the disabled person. The importance of the social model is that it takes the focus off the individual, noting the ways in which social, physical, and political environments provide the primary disabling factors for individuals.

Many will be familiar with the major pieces of modern disability-related legislation in the United States, both the Americans with Disabilities Act (ADA), passed in 1990 and revised in 2008, and the Individuals with Disabilities Education Act (IDEA), also passed in 1990 and revised in 2004. These legislative achievements, and their many predecessors, are the hard-earned work of disability rights activists whose cry of "Nothing about us without us" and acts of civil disobedience have created significant interventions in accessibility and freedom for disabled people in nearly every aspect of modern society. The definitions of disability and discrimination offered in the ADA and IDEA, regarding both the presence of a "qualified disability" and discrimination based on the perception thereof, reference the significant way in which the social model of disability has shifted the global conversation regarding the limiting nature of impairments and the debilitating presence of widespread discrimination.

An outgrowth of the disability rights movement was the interdisciplinary field of Disability Studies, which emerged in both the UK and the United States, as well as other countries, in the 1980s. Although academics had long studied disability from a clinical perspective, Disability Studies scholars employed the social model as a critical lens through which to examine history, theory, anthropology, sociology, the arts, religion, and education. The first U.S. Disability Studies program was established at Syracuse University in 1994, and since that time scholars such as Lennard J. Davis, Simi Linton, Paul Longmore, Robert McRuer, Rosemarie Garland-Thomson, Tom Shakespeare, and Irving Zola (to name just a few) have continued to push the boundaries of the categories of disability, race, gender, class, and their intersections. Such scholars have also problematized the once-severe boundaries between impairment and disability instantiated by the social model and gone in search of new models for disability that lend increased understanding and insight to the diversity and varieties of human experience.

Written by a disability rights activist and a disabled woman herself, theologian Nancy Eiesland's book *The Disabled God: Toward a Liberatory Theology of Disability* (1994) laid the groundwork for the field of Theology of Disability. Eiesland argues that Jesus' (incarnate and resurrected) disabled body affirms the divine wholeness of other disabled bodies, critiquing disabled prejudice, as well as demanding and ushering in societal and spiritual transformation. From Jesus' wounded body, Eiesland famously also envisioned God in a "sip puff" wheelchair. Her scholarship was revolutionary both for disabled people and for theologians who wanted to explore not just the challenge but also the import and insight of disabled experiences for theological study.

And although she has been criticized for a lack of theological rigor in her work, thanks in no small part to Eiesland, Theology of Disability has flourished, with disabled and non-disabled scholars taking up limits, ethics, eucharist, vulnerability, friendship, and time as fruitful vantages from which disability provides valuable theological insight (Betcher 2007; Creamer 2008; Reinders 2008; Reynolds 2008; Swinton 2016). Biblical scholars have also drawn on Disability Studies to provide a critical and contextualized examination of key texts, especially those concerning purity, exclusion, healing, eschatology, and resurrection (Black 1996; Fox 2019; Schipper and Moss 2011; Yong 2011). And as more disabled persons are active in Christian congregations, ministry, and education, a host of accessibility inventories and assessment tools, along with curriculum and program literature, have arisen to assist churches in improving and expanding their practical programs for disabled people (Carter 2007; Newman 2016; Webb-Mitchell [1994] 2009; 2010).

THE REAL PROBLEMS OF ABLEISM, INCLUSION, AND INJUSTICE

Yet, as a cultural anthropologist, I would argue that despite the explosion of this theological and ecclesial literature, there has not been a cultural shift in perceptions, acceptance, or practical experiences of disabled people in society or in churches. In the United States, we continue to see disability treated as a liability and a deficiency rather than an aspect of diversity, like race, class, or gender in both institutional and private settings (Davis 1995). Even when disability is treated as a difference, that difference is frequently sought to be rehabilitated, corrected, or absorbed through medical treatment, behavioral or physical therapy, or cultural assimilation. In other words, that difference is rarely treated with value, dignity, or respect. Accommodations for disability are regularly treated as an inconvenience, an imposition, or a charity, rather than as rights that are specified by law and integral to the greater good of all society. Disabled people continue to live within an environment and a society that is not merely physically inconvenient, but ethically, morally, and spiritually uninhabitable and unsuitable to their human flourishing.

And it should be no surprise to us, then, that rather than buck the trend, Christian churches often follow suit. Indeed, practical theologians working at the intersection of lived human experience, ecclesiology, and theology note that families with disabled children are far less likely than families with typical children to attend church, given persistent stigma and issues of accessibility (Carter 2007; Conner 2012, 2018; Jacober 2010; Whitehead 2018). Theological institutions have yet to teach explicitly to the needs and gifts of disabled people in their curricula, there are still few disabled people attending seminaries, and students attending those seminaries don't feel equipped to minister to disabled people once they leave (Annandale and Carter 2014; Conner 2018). Denomination-wide statements and individual church mission statements preach welcome and acceptance, but all too often the church is not a refuge for disabled people—it's a reflection of the common culture.

What we need is not a robust valorization of difference but a reckoning in which disability is decolonized from ableism, its hegemonies, and even our theologies. Because we live in a world where ableism reinforces capitalism, whiteness, and heteronormativity, without decolonization from these forces, there can be no justice. These accusations sound radical, because they are. The church has been fed a false narrative about disability in making difference into either a savior or an enemy. Rather, it is the disempowering of disabled people by non-disabled people that has created alienation from one another and from God. Hence, the church is called apart from the world to repent of its ableism, disown its power, abandon inclusion, and pursue justice alongside disabled people. Despite the wealth of literature, tools, and ministries that consider disabled persons and perspectives, no Christian text has taken up the sin of ableism as the paramount problem of disability or the decolonization of justice as the antidote to inclusion.

This book therefore begins with the critique that churches and theologians have moved too quickly toward ecclesial and theological solutions before we've adequately grasped the problems with the way disability has been treated in society and in the church. Furthermore, this book makes several interventions and contributions to the scholarly literature. First, I return to the important critical perspective of Disability Studies, anchoring and critiquing disability ministry through an anti-ableist framework. Second, I provide empirical evidence for disabled ministry and leadership both in and outside of the church. Third, I move the theological conversation with respect to ministry with disabled people beyond welcome, belonging, and friendship and toward justice, nurturing, and receiving their gifts for ministry and leadership.

Although there are many resources for congregations that focus on better theologies, better worship, and better programs, there are none that focus on the role ableism plays in undermining ministry with disabled people. Indeed, most texts that are written by able-bodied people to able-bodied churches shy away from the challenges of the privilege, power, and limitations of their authorship and readership. However, drawing on critiques of normalcy and ability in Disability Studies, this book takes disabled persons' embodied, personal, relational, and political experiences seriously as a starting point for understanding disability. This book thus identifies ableism as a primary challenge for the church in ministry with disabled people. By identifying examples of the author's own ableism in parenting and pastoring, as well as drawing on ethnographic examples and ableist readings of scripture, the book helps congregants identify and confess their own ableism, alongside the church's complicit sins in ableist ministry.

This is a radical new starting point for ministry with disabled people in the church. Although many books reference the social model of disability and the myriad barriers faced by disabled people in society and churches, the literature lacks a theology for grappling with the everyday relational politics of this ableism. Thus, the first half of this book takes the time to set up the problems of ableism in churches today by showing how entrenched they are in not just our attitudes toward disabled people but also in our interpretations of scripture, our worship, even our ministry. In the first half of the book I show that inclusive ministry often subtly maintains disability as a problem to be managed by keeping able-bodied people and churches in charge of ministry and disempowering disabled people. Yet, because the book argues that disabled people are called by Jesus and empowered by the Spirit to be leaders and ministers, inclusion must not stand in the way of God's ministry.

Second, although this book is written by an able-bodied scholar and minister, the commitment to ethnographic knowledge represents not just my disciplinary sensibilities as an anthropologist but also my desire as an able-bodied scholar to take seriously what Nancy Eiesland called "the speaking center" (1994). Although the phrase is somewhat problematic for its priority on speech, in emphasizing the importance of disabled perspectives in the church and church leadership Eiesland anticipated some of the circumstances in which the church and the academy currently find ourselves. Much practical theology and theology proper is not grounded in fieldwork with disabled people, but rather in anecdotal experience of the church, scripture, or theological scholarship. Although these perspectives are valuable, if this book wants congregations to identify their own ableism, who better to teach them than their disabled siblings in Christ? If this book wants to showcase disabled leadership, who better to do so than disabled leaders themselves? In offering a broad view of disability, denomination, and racial/ethnic makeup in our study, I hope to expand the far-too-confined boundaries of this "speaking center," offering glimpses of a more thorough vision of ministry and leadership for the church today.

Finally, it was this ethnographic material that organically and prophetically led this book to a focus on disabled leadership. It was the compelling and diverse ministry and leadership of disabled people in congregations that helped our research team see that the theological literature was woefully impoverished when it came to its modest goals for disabled people in the body of Christ. In championing leadership we are both responding to the ministry we witnessed God doing through disabled people in real congregations and intentionally confronting the recent popular and scholarly turn to Christian leadership that is far too insular in its call for transformation (Raffety 2020a). In looking to critique and refine paradigms of leadership, the church needs to start by unearthing biases that have prevented or excluded certain people from leadership in the first place.

OVERVIEW OF THE BOOK

It is with the creativity, wisdom, and insight of disabled leaders that I return to seemingly staid scriptures in this book, offering fresh insights as to how we must move beyond able-bodied interpretations of transformation, including those we impute to Jesus. Alongside disabled leaders, I seek to read scripture "on the slant," against the grain, noting that just as prophecy offers both critique and creative vision, scripture often offers different insights depending on where we're reading from. Therefore, throughout the book I highlight how disabled leaders helped me behold and grapple with my own ableism in and through scripture. It is the rediscovery of Jesus' ministry through disabled characters and disabled experiences that this book offers the world. The Spirit interprets scripture as a fellow interlocutor in my ethnographic study, a dialogue partner who does not work so much to solve problems as to teach us to ask better questions.

The first chapter introduces the key scripture text that forms the backdrop of the book, the healing of blind Bartimaeus, through which I foreground the theological argument of the book: that disabled people are not just made in the image of God but called by Jesus into ministry and transformed into leaders by the Spirit. This Trinitarian reformulation of disabled ministry identifies the rough outline of the book, as the first three chapters identify the problem with inclusion, the next three chapters reorient readers to Jesus' call to ministry for disabled people and the role of the church in following Jesus toward justice, and the final three chapters provide a critique of Christian leadership models, examples of disabled leadership, and calls for Spirit-led advocacy in the church. The overall shift the book seeks to make is from a paradigm of inclusion to a paradigm of justice, moving churches from the methods and practices of solving problems to asking better questions, listening, lamenting, perceiving injustice, and advocacy. The book attempts to decolonize disability, decolonize Jesus, and decolonize the Spirit as necessary work toward repentance and transformation.

Therefore, although some chapters employ theory and theology to explain and analyze disability and ministry, many chapters, such as chapters 2, 3, 4, 6, and 8, center around the stories of disabled people in the church. Indeed, more theoretical or theological readers may want to focus in on chapters 1, 5, 7, and 9, in which I flesh out the biblical, theological, and theoretical rationale for my arguments, while those seeking practical strategies for ministry may want to attend to the former chapters in more detail and make use of their practical approaches. With the exception of the introduction and the first chapter, each chapter begins with a scriptural epigraph and interprets disabled ministry and leadership primarily through the lens of a scripture not readily associated with disability, as an intentional move toward attesting to the broad insights of disabled ministry and leadership for congregational ministry.

The book is intended to be read as a practical theology of disabled ministry and leadership, as well as an ethnographic invitation to reform in theological education and congregational ministry. The vision of disabled ministry and leadership on the page comes from real people in the pews and the pulpits, but it is still thin given the sins of ableism prevalent in the church that make it inhospitable for so many disabled people. Although the vision for disability justice cast by activists and leaders is compelling, it is still primarily a vision. However, it is clear that there are glimmers of the kingdom in the ministry and leadership of disabled activists if the church is willing to receive them. It is to a new kingdom on earth and in heaven that disabled ministry and leadership are calling the church.

1

The Problem of Inclusion

⁴⁶They came to Jericho. As he and his disciples and a large crowd were leaving Jericho, Bartimaeus son of Timaeus, a blind beggar, was sitting by the roadside. ⁴⁷When he heard that it was Jesus of Nazareth, he began to shout out and say, "Jesus, Son of David, have mercy on me!" ⁴⁸Many sternly ordered him to be quiet, but he cried out even more loudly, "Son of David, have mercy on me!" ⁴⁹Jesus stood still and said, "Call him here." And they called the blind man, saying to him, "Take heart; get up, he is calling you." ⁵⁰So throwing off his cloak, he sprang up and came to Jesus. ⁵¹Then Jesus said to him, "What do you want me to do for you?" The blind man said to him, "My teacher, let me see again." ⁵²Jesus said to him, "Go; your faith has made you well." Immediately he regained his sight and followed him on the way.

—Mark 10:46–52

INTRODUCTION

Cultural scripts on congregational ministry with disabled people often posit two seeming extremes: on the one hand, there are churches that call themselves inclusive, claiming to be welcoming to everyone and anyone, and then there are churches that aren't concerned with disability issues because they simply don't have any disabled people in them. Of course, none of the churches in our study satisfied these ideal types, but we can learn a lot about disability ministry from the way people imagine it, and from the way these two examples often serve as foils for one another.

For one, these examples are posited as extremes. One church has no disability ministry while another church has a thriving ministry, and the answer to the problem is simply more inclusion. But in our study even churches that had thriving worship or social ministries with disabled people were fast to admit that they had also made many mistakes along the way. Not only were some of their programs challenging to sustain but they grieved that having these programs operating on the perimeter of church life meant that something was still broken in their churches and their communities. It wasn't necessarily the case that more inclusive programs led to more inclusive churches, or that more inclusion made church ministry better or more just. Meanwhile, if churches didn't yet have disabled programs or ministries, who was to blame? It would be too easy to blame disabled people themselves for these ministry struggles, and yet, as this book also makes clear, that is something churches often implicitly do. Alternatively, it is tempting to scapegoat our broader culture and society and point out the lack of support for disabled people in general that undermines church ministries. This is certainly a reality, as well.

However, in this book, I try to draw on lessons from our ethnographic data to offer a third explanation. I argue that all the churches in our study, regardless of the particular shape of their ministries, drew on the paradigm of inclusion to measure the successes or the failures of those ministries. But why inclusion? What is the nature of inclusion and what are churches striving for when they talk about creating a more inclusive environment, worship, and ministries for disabled people? Should it be the benchmark of excellence when it comes to ministry with disabled people? Or is there something that looks a bit more like the gospel when it comes to ministry with disabled people?

In this chapter, I provide background on the ethnographic study we conducted with eleven disabled persons in their ministry contexts and congregations in the Philadelphia–New Jersey–New York City tristate area from June 2019 to January 2020. I show that this ethnographic data offered three major findings. First, there is good news: disabled people really want to belong to congregations and congregations really want to include them. This was abundantly clear given the breadth of ministries we observed and the attention we saw being given to disabled people in congregational contexts throughout our research project. I couldn't have written this book without everything we learned from congregations that were willing to share their time, members, families, worship, and ministry with us.

However, the bad news is that congregational ministries with disabled people are also trapped within this container of inclusion, causing them to treat disabled people as problems to be managed through programs, which leads ministry to become transactional, a mere distribution of goods and services. By championing inclusion and maintaining power over disabled people, congregations often reinforce rather than deconstruct ableism. This is not just a ministry problem but a larger church culture problem that we can see more clearly when we look at ministries with disabled people. But it's also a theological problem, because it puts normalcy and the status quo at the heart of the gospel, rather than repentance, justice, or even Jesus. (But more on that later.)

For now, it's important to note that the data from this project also shouted another piece of good news from the rooftops for struggling churches everywhere: despite our corporate sins of ableism in the church, Jesus is lifting up and the Spirit is using disabled leaders among us to disrupt and transform ministry and leadership in our congregations today. It is a confession of the ableism in our own research team that we did not expect to be arrested by the dynamism and insights of disabled leaders, but it is a gift from God that the Spirit allowed us to behold such ministry and leadership even when we didn't have it all together.

So yes, it is the case that able-bodied people, like the crowds that surround Bartimaeus, often stand in the way of Jesus' ministry with disabled people, but it is also the case that the Spirit often finds ways to break through those barriers to reach all of us, even in our sins and shortcomings. That is the good news of the gospel not for able-bodied or disabled people, but for all of us.

Another argument this chapter is making is that while ethnography presents a useful tool for listening to congregations and disabled people, especially with respect to theological education, it's also imperfect. Just as ministers often find themselves trying to solve problems rather than serve people, identifying problems often leads ethnographers and educators into the same traps. Rather, good ethnography helps us to ask better questions alongside our informants: as we enter into genuine dialogue, our assumptions and our prejudices are laid bare. Asking better questions involves deep humility because we can't ask them without admitting what we do not know or how what we thought we knew foreclosed the truth.

Throughout the book, I draw on ethnography as a tool and a metaphor for ministry and pedagogy, and I try to be transparent about my own prejudices and learning as an able-bodied person in ministry and relationship with disabled people. The good news is that I think I am now asking better questions than when I began this project and that the church, too, can move from problem-solving to asking better questions. The hard truth is that this ministry is not for the weary. And the audacious hope is that God is using disabled ministers and leaders to usher in the kingdom. I hope the reader gets a glimpse of all that on these pages.

LEARNING FROM CONGREGATIONS AND DISABLED PEOPLE

In early 2019, I assembled a research team made up of five students from Princeton University and Princeton Theological Seminary, and we circulated an announcement via denominational mailing lists and social media inviting families and churches to participate in our study. The original focus of the research was on better connecting disabled persons, their families, and congregations in order to improve pastoral care with disabled people. In a prior study entitled "Lonely Joy: How Families with Nonverbal Children with Disabilities Communicate, Collaborate, and Resist in a World that Values Words," we identified that families with disabled children who were nonverbal were lonely, because the cultural scripts circulating about disability as tragedy (Cushing 2010) made joy an impossibility (Raffety et al. 2019). We argued that disabled joy must stand in resistance against such scripts, but also against the church or other institutions that perpetuate these scripts, which only reinforces families' loneliness. Therefore, we hypothesized that as much as churches desired to be welcoming and inclusive, somehow they were missing the lived human experiences of families with disabled people. Hence, we were resolved not just to study congregations and how they do ministry but also to spend time with disabled people in order to understand what was missing from such congregations and their ministry.

The design of our study, with its emphasis on disabled people's experiences, especially in congregational settings, makes two important contributions to literature on theology, ministry, and disability. First, we value disabled people's knowledge and experience as integral not just to better ministry but to better understandings of people and God. The study was designed to receive the insights as well as the critiques that disabled subjects offer regarding church contexts so that we could perceive their hurt, their pain, and their frustrations. This posed somewhat of a challenge in that able-bodied congregations and leaders were sometimes afraid of what disabled people might be sharing, or in other cases, disabled persons and their families had become estranged from congregations altogether due to some of these challenges. Some disabled subjects told us they were afraid to share their real thoughts with us, while some were eager to have their names included in the study. In order to protect the privacy of disabled persons, congregations, and parachurch organizations, we offered anonymity to all subjects, but the church world is still small. People talk. Therefore, the potential cost of vulnerability to these research subjects should not go overlooked.

Second, our study sought to understand the relationships between disabled people and their church communities by also studying their experiences in church settings. Congregations and parachurch organizations contributed generously and significantly to our study and understanding of ministry with disabled people. Indeed, it was the time spent with congregations that quickly convinced me that we could not just study pastoral care, as we had originally planned to, apart from other ministries. In expanding the study to include myriad other congregational ministries with disabled people, we experienced a fuller sense of how churches were engaging with disabled people on their own terms.

For example, for many churches, worship was a primary site at which they engaged and interacted with disabled people, but for others, youth group, fellowship nights, Sunday school, or support groups were the places where they ministered with disabled people. Here the strength of ethnographic research, its flexible, malleable, "go everywhere" nature, is also its greatest weakness in that with a research team of six individuals and approximately six months of funding for active research, we could never attend every event we wanted to attend, so we always had to settle for less fieldwork than we wanted.

But we also realized that the reason this expansion beyond pastoral care in the study was so important was because disabled people were prompting the church to critically examine basic ecclesial practices of ministry, worship, and leadership. Hence, although this book does not offer a full ecclesiology of disabled ministry, it does use our research insights to question, redefine, and reimagine practices of ministry less as matters of problem-solving, program management, or service provision and more as participating in God's action in the world. Relatedly, it seeks not to make worship more "inclusive" but to return liturgy and worship to the people, especially to disabled people, testifying more fully to who Jesus is, scars and all. It seeks to move Christian leadership out of the realm of technical expertise and toward the advocacy of the Spirit, who is disruptive, expansive, collaborative, and creative. And while this chapter and many chapters reckon with the sins of ableism and the able-bodied biases pervading the church, the book also offers hope for the church in the movement for disability justice and the wildly expansive vision of the kingdom of God and human flourishing evident in disability communities.

The disabled people and the churches we studied were particularly diverse in experience of disability, age, geographic location, and denomination. We intentionally prioritized this diversity of experiences of disabilities in our sampling: we wanted to understand a variety of experiences of disability in the context of pastoral care. Hence, the sample expresses the most diversity in disability experiences and geographic context, whereas there is less diversity in terms of racial/ethnic background or denominational experience, because those were not the priorities of the study. Relatedly, although we wanted to build on previous studies of disabled children and their families, we also wanted to take adult experiences of disability in the church seriously. Too often churches find it easy to include disabled children when they are children, but as they grow and no longer fit in with children, it is much more difficult to find a place for them in ministry (Raffety 2018). Finally, in order to attend to a broad experience of disability, we ended up including a variety of church permutations and traveling to the suburbs of Philadelphia, the Jersey shore, and the Bronx, which provided contextual diversity.

Because the study majored in the particulars versus the general, our research was anything but uniform. This meant that some of the disabled people we spent time with did not belong to typical congregations but were in transition or primarily participated in parachurch organizations like InterVarsity and Young Life. Although we had originally conceived of the research as comprising units in which both the disabled person and the congregation had to give their context for consent, we gradually relaxed this requirement in order to sample a wider range of disability and experiences of Christian ministry and community. In some cases we got to know the individual better, in other cases the churches, in some both. We also added some interviews with other disabled leaders and disabled communities to supplement our learning throughout the process.

Research Participants

Context/Congregation	Primary Research Participant(s)	Disabilities Represented	Location	Denomination	Racial/Ethnic
Co-Op City	Unnamed older adults; Pastor Arnaldo	Physical, dementia, mental illness	Bronx, NYC, urban	UMC	Majority Latinx
Living Waters Evangelical Church*	Jeb; Jamal*	Adult, Physical, I/DD	Central N.J., suburban	Evangelical	White dominant
First Assembly of God/King's Table special needs ministry	Cata family; Pastor Jeff	Adult and children with physical disabilities, mental health, I/DD	Freehold, N.J., suburban	Assemblies of God	White dominant
Presbyterian Church of Ralston*	Pastor Brad; Michelle, Frank, Jonah, and Amos*	Youth with autism, I/DD	Ralston, N.J., urban	Presbyterian (PCUSA)	White dominant
Resurrection Lutheran Church/ Joyful Noise	Pastor Maggi; Arundel, Jess, J'den, and Morrigan Clarke	Autism, Mood Disorder, children with I/DD	Hamilton, N.J., urban	Evangelical Lutheran Church in America (ELCA)	Clarkes are Black and Latinx; congregation is white

Context/Congregation	Slackwood Presbyterian Church	St. Bartholomew Lutheran Church	St. John Chrysostom	St. Thomas	Tree of Life/Our Community Cup
Primary Research Participant(s)	Bailie Gregory (under care with ordination process)	Unnamed older adults	Father Edward J. Hallinan, Pastor; Mary Chollet, Director of Parish Ministry and Communications; Beth and Michael; Lisa O'Malley (also Rod Powell, friend of Lisa); Joanna; Jim	Linda and Jason*	Pastor Pam; Mike; Spencer and Sam*
Disabilities Represented	Bipolar 2, PTSD, anxiety	Physical, dementia, mental illness	Blindness, adults and children with autism, I/DD	Autism, I/DD	Adults with physical and I/DD
Location	Trenton, N.J., urban	Trenton, N.J., urban	Philadelphia, Pa., suburban	Brick, N.J., suburban	Philadelphia, Pa., urban
Denomination	PCUSA	ELCA	Catholic	PCUSA	PCUSA
Racial/Ethnic	White dominant	White dominant, some Black, Latinx	White-dominant; Rod (nonmember) is Black	White dominant	White dominant

Context/ Congregation	Primary Research Participant(s)	Disabilities Represented	Location	Denomination	Racial/Ethnic
Young Life Capernaum/ InterVarsity	Kat Walker	Kat is a little person w/arm deformities; YLC ministers to youth with I/DD; InterVarsity is a nondenominational ministry where Kat serves in leadership	Central N.J., urban	Evangelical/ nondenominational	White dominant, some Black, Latinx

*Indicates pseudonym used

Ethnographic studies, like that of the eleven individuals and their ministry contexts and congregations in our study, are often far too small to be considered representative samples of larger populations, but that is not their aim in any case. Instead, ethnographic studies, in which researchers come alongside people in their regularly scheduled lives, taking seriously what they say and what they do, are valuable in getting at the particular qualities of human experience—what it feels like and what it means to be cultural beings. By paying deep, sustained attention to particular people and stories, ethnographers capture the felt experience of patterns of culture, experiences we do not have access to through statistics, surveys, or quantitative data. Therefore, in order to understand what congregational ministry and pastoral care often felt like from the perspective of disabled people and their families, we came in close, spending time in their homes, accompanying them in their daily activities, attending church alongside them, as well as connecting with their clergy and other church leaders.

As mentioned, our research was particularly limited by time, distance, and the lack of racial/ethnic and denominational diversity in our sample. Although our student research team brought a range of experiences to the table, none of them identified as disabled themselves, and having disabled perspectives on the team would have been invaluable. We were unable to pay our informants for their time, but we did offer "celebration of research" presentations at which we discussed the findings with the participating individuals and congregations, and we workshopped ideas and hypotheses, and revised multiple chapters of this book, in collaboration with participating research subjects.

But the research itself, as the reader will see, is also bound by some of the same inequalities inherent in ableism and endemic to inclusion. There are many things I would have and have done differently in subsequent studies: my recourse is to tell the truth of what we learned and how we learned it with as much transparency and humility as possible. As with any ethnographic study, my research team and I are indebted to our interlocutors in insurmountable ways. Therefore this book, written from an able-bodied perspective to an able-bodied church, adopts a confessional mode with respect to narrative and ethnography (Whitmore 2021). By illuminating my ableism, I hope not only to help congregations see theirs more clearly but also to receive disabled persons and their ministry and leadership more fully.

This is yet another important epistemological feature of ethnographic research—that it demands accountability by way of reflexivity, asking researchers, as the instruments of knowledge, to reflect on how their particular power and privileges influence the data. Throughout the book, I take that commitment seriously not just as an ethnographic exercise but as a knowledge-making opportunity. My contention is that when research, scripture, and ministry hold up a mirror to able-bodied privilege, truth-telling is the bridge not just to knowledge-making but to understanding and repentance.

DISABLED PEOPLE WANT A SEAT AT THE TABLE

The value of spending time with families with disabled people, their pastors, and their fellow congregants is that we got to experience ministry from multiple angles, and it was very clear that disabled people really want to belong to congregations and congregations really want to include them. Of course, the individuals, congregations, and clergy who participated self-selected into our study and we therefore cannot generalize about the desires of these churches as representative of all churches. Indeed, at the sampling stage, many churches self-selected out of our study because, as mentioned in the introduction, they "didn't have any people with disabilities" or didn't have any (specialized) ministry to people with disabilities. But even when it comes to churches and leaders in our study who were somewhat hesitant, they were not hesitant because they did not care, but rather because they were convinced they had so much to learn.

At InterVarsity and Young Life Capernaum, our researchers shadowed Kat Walker, a little person with arm deformities, who as a college grad was coming to see that she had not just been changed by ministry but called into it. She and the other leaders at Young Life Capernaum, a ministry for disabled youth, particularly those with intellectual and developmental disabilities, sought to be a bridge between disability and the church, providing opportunities for young people to connect with Jesus and one another through camps and clubs. In Freehold, New Jersey, our researcher met the Cata family, who have been fostering disabled children with medical complexities for decades, and their worshiping community, King's Table, an Assemblies of God Church that offers care, respite, and fellowship to families caring for disabled children. King's Table was not waiting to learn how to be in ministry with disabled people; rather, they just did it. In Trenton, at St. Bart's Lutheran, and in the Bronx at Co-Op City, our researchers experienced the challenges facing older people and mentally ill people in urban, under-resourced contexts. Often fighting heavy traffic at the end of the work week, our researchers never knew what they would experience at Our Community Cup, a weekly fellowship night hosted by Tree of Life Presbyterian Church just outside of Philadelphia for disabled adults. One night, yoga therapy goats arrived out on the lawn; most nights, karaoke on stage attracted regulars; and every Friday night, disabled folks gathered around tables to talk and just be in a world that makes so many demands on them.

These are just a few snapshots of the many contexts, communities, and challenges this research lifted up. In fact, several of the above do not appear by name on the subsequent pages of this book, because there was simply too much nuance and too much data to share. But the overall point is that in every context and organization that we studied, much as you can see above, disabled people wanted a seat at the table, and congregations were eager to include disabled people. Despite the stories that we heard of frustration with and a disconnect from church, disabled people resiliently sought to connect with congregations, participate, and lead. Indeed, the language of welcome and inclusion permeated discussions of church life and ministry so much that we couldn't help but dig deeper into it. What did it mean for churches to be inclusive? After all, the diversity of contexts and approaches to something like "inclusive ministry" glimpsed above is apparent. But if the church does the including, what is it that disabled people have to offer? Who is the church in inclusive ministry? Who is God in inclusive ministry? And is inclusive ministry worth striving for?

ACCOMMODATIONS DO NOT DO JUSTICE

Whenever I teach a class on disability in the United States, I begin with an "ADA Scavenger Hunt" in order to acquaint learners with this major piece of legislation that frames disabled civil rights and experiences in the United States. As they pore over the legal document, students frequently comment on at least three things. First, disability is defined rather broadly: the ADA makes provision for persons with physical and mental impairments, those with a record of impairments, and even those perceived as having impairments, or having experienced discrimination on the basis of a perceived impairment. Disability, according to the ADA, does not need to be permanent to qualify, and the ADA even makes provision for mental health conditions that limit major life activities of bodily function to be included.

Second, students are often surprised to read that the discrimination acknowledged against disabled people in the document is also framed as an economic burden versus simply an injustice. It is notable that the findings of Section 12101 outline countless forms of discrimination endured by disabled people, justified in the census reports (6), and including segregation (2), as well as (3) discrimination in the areas of "employment, housing, public accommodations, education, transportation, recreation, institutionalization, health services, voting, and access to public services" (Sec 12101 Findings). Subsection 5 goes on to say that exclusion is not always outright but includes "the discriminatory effects of architectural, transportation, and communication barriers, overprotective rules and policies, failure to make modifications to existing facilities and practices, exclusionary qualification standards and criteria, segregation, and relegation to lesser services, programs, activities, benefits, jobs, or other opportunities." Yet, whereas Subsection 7 names the goals of granting "equal opportunity, full participation, independent living, and economic self-sufficiency" to disabled individuals, Subsection 8 specifies that Congress finds that

> the continuing existence of unfair and unnecessary discrimination and
> prejudice denies people with disabilities the opportunity to compete

on an equal basis and to pursue those opportunities for which our free society is justifiably famous, and costs the United States billions of dollars in unnecessary expenses resulting from dependency and nonproductivity. (Sec 12101 Findings)

Students are right to question why disabled people are positioned as a financial burden to the nation in order to justify their rights to that nation. Although the Findings Subsection is meant to provide justification for equal opportunities for disabled people, it ends up invoking the economic hardship of the United States, "resulting from [disabled people's] dependency and nonproductivity" as collateral for disabled rights. Even though economic opportunity and self-sufficiency are an important part of disabled rights and access, the positioning of disabled persons as a burden on the nation in the very document that purports to extol their rights and value is egregious and demeaning.

Third, moving past the preamble, in Title I, "Employment," the ADA outlines qualified disabled people's rights to "reasonable accommodations" from "covered entities" so long as they do not pose "undue hardship," such as significant difficulty or expense to the covered entity. According to the section on Employment (12111), reasonable accommodation may include making facilities accessible or providing job restructuring, modifications, or supports for disabled persons. In the same section, undue hardship to an employer is evaluated given the nature and cost of accommodation, the financial resources or facilities respective to the accommodation, the overall financial resources or facilities available, and the type of operations of the covered entity. Clearly, the law allows much flexibility in interpretation as to what counts as a reasonable accommodation and an undue hardship.

In Titles II and III, the law also, importantly, outlines the burden on public entities, such as transportation and public accommodations, with respect to commercial facilities (employment), to provide ADA-accessible services and facilities. Although these titles have had an enormous impact on disabled individuals in terms of daily living and travel, it is important to note that given the above definitions of reasonable accommodation and undue hardship, the effect of the ADA is that it puts the onus on disabled persons, rather than the covered entity, to pursue legal action if they cannot access not just employment but other activities of daily living, such as trying to enter a store that is fundamentally inaccessible. In other words, the ADA offers a legal pathway for disabled individuals and their allies to *pursue* accessibility, not a *promise* of accessibility across the nation. Not only are such lawsuits dependent on further access to time and resources, but the vast majority of ADA lawsuits do not allow for financial remuneration or settlements. Instead at the end of the road, individuals may or may not receive their reasonable accommodations without much other compensation for their time and labor.

Even though both the ADA and the IDEA, the Individuals with Disabilities Education Act, have been instrumental in improving the lives of people with disabilities in the United States, relying on individual accommodations to promote justice for disabled people is problematic for several reasons. First, this process empowers institutions to serve as the arbiters of access for disabled individuals. Although these institutions are beholden by law to provide necessary accommodations to disabled persons and are legally prevented from inquiring during hiring processes into applicants' disability status, they are ultimately in charge of whether and how they interview, hire, or accommodate disabled individuals. As so many scholars have noted, the high rates of unemployment among disabled individuals, the disproportionate poverty of disabled people in America, and the lack of representation of disabled individuals in positions of authority throughout the public and private sectors make clear that accommodations are not being equitably distributed.

Second, individual accommodations often subject disabled persons to medicalized processes of verification, inhibiting their privacy and undermining their authority and capacity to represent themselves. In other words, the processes used in schools and workplaces for securing accommodations, despite our widespread understanding that disability is not primarily a medical but a social phenomenon, attempt to bracket that social element of disability by defining disability purely in terms of medical deficits and abnormalities. At the heart of processes of accommodation, with respect to employment and education, is an attempt to make the individual more "normal" so that they will fit better into the typical environment. Although there may seem to be nothing untoward about that process, it reinforces the idea that it is people with disabilities who present the problem, rather than the environment. It is easier to accommodate individuals on an ad hoc basis rather than to examine why the environment is inhospitable in the first place.

This is the final reason why individual accommodations for disabled persons are a poor substitute or step toward justice and equity. Indeed, they continue to operate in a way that reinforces normalcy and able-bodied power by atomizing individuals who need accommodations from those in power. Even though cloaking the processes of accommodations in secrecy is meant to protect disabled individuals' privacy, it has the unintended effect of obscuring how power works, keeping disabled people disempowered by positioning them as the benevolent recipients of accommodations, and maintaining systems, institutions, and the status quo at all costs. Meanwhile, the structure of accommodations presumes disabled people are counted out rather than counted in. For them to count in, able-bodied institutions and able-bodied people must provide adaptations. As they do so, they are congratulated for these accommodations, even as providing them is a form of maintaining their own supremacy. Disabled people who are accommodated are assimilated to the means and desire of able-bodied power. Disabled people who receive accommodations remain objects of charity, which is ironic, since accommodations are a right under the law.

Are accommodations necessary for disabled participation? Certainly. Do they contribute to social change and justice for disabled people in the United States? Absolutely not. Not only do disabled people disproportionately live in poverty today in the United States, undermining the economic goals of the ADA, but the meager supports of the law and the myriad exceptions from it provided to private businesses, institutions, and even churches (as we shall see) at disabled people's expense further stymie access for disabled folks to healthcare, education, citizenship, rights, and freedom.

This is why inclusion is often presented as a more robust vision for disabled participation that goes beyond legal requirements like accommodation and toward justice and equality, purporting to integrate disabled folks at all levels of society. In the next section, I describe the approaches and goals of inclusion as a movement within society, institutions, and the church.

INCLUSION AND "JUSTIFIABLE EXCLUSION"

When institutions aspire to or assert that they are "inclusive," what is it that they mean? And when inclusion is positioned as the goal for greater justice and equity, just what is it we are striving for? Shockingly little has been written on inclusion as a cohesive political movement (Ravaud and Stiker 2001), but the reason for giving credence to the disabled people's movement in the introduction to this book and even the legal implications of the ADA above is to recognize that the roots of inclusion notably come from the cries of disabled activists, pushing for broad civil rights and claiming, "Nothing about us without us." However, if we follow inclusion from bold and idealistic activists to its practical implications, we may be surprised by what we find. A legal definition of inclusion emphasizes disabled people's rights to full participation in all aspects of society, as well as the provision of appropriate supports so that people with disabilities can be fully integrated into existing environments.

As the previous analysis of the ADA suggests, these modest goals for inclusion are not only far from realized but may actually run counter to the goals and concerns of disabled people today. In this section, I examine the concept and practice of inclusion through the lens of children's education, accessibility, neoliberalism, and exclusion in contemporary America. In so doing, I question the value of inclusion in showing that it functions to articulate visions of accessibility while simultaneously practically undermining them. When it comes to church politics, disabled persons are often publicly welcomed while they are "justifiably excluded" (Titchkosky 2011), suggesting that, at best, inclusion is a false witness and at worst a concealer of sin and ableism in our very midst.

In her book *Claiming Disability*, activist and author Simi Linton describes inclusion within the environment of education, arguing that true inclusion goes beyond merely mainstreaming disabled students who can keep up with the traditional educational environment (1998, 63–65). As Linton puts it, full inclusion is unique because "it is not an education plan to benefit disabled children. It is a model for educating all children equitably" (61). She explains,

> The pedagogical practices and curriculum are designed to reach a broad range of children, and integration and active participation are goals that the school is committed to. Whereas the practice of mainstreaming has been restricted primarily to children with physical disabilities and sensory impairments, the inclusion model incorporates all children, no matter their disability, in a general education classroom. . . . This is a startling idea for many people, particularly if they have never seen it in action. In classroom environments such as these, the criteria for demonstrating competence may not be the same for all children, but together the group tackles the subject matter and each child engages with it consistent with his or her aptitude and needs. Goals and standards are shifted not downward but out, to a more flexible and broader means of demonstrating competence. The burden to "keep up" is shifted off the individual student, and the whole classroom environment shifts in its overall procedures and expectations to maximize learning for all. (1998, 60)

Linton penned these words in 1998 but was quick to point out that she did not want to overromanticize inclusive education (62). Indeed, she noted that integrating schools without proper training for teachers and students could result in rejection for disabled children. A few decades later, not only is the inclusive education Linton describes far from the norm in schools in the United States but the Individuals with Disabilities Education Act (IDEA) also goes about ensuring the rights of disabled students to education by isolating and atomizing their needs from those of their classmates and communities. Although the IDEA, importantly, guarantees the rights of all students to a free, public education in the least restrictive environment (meaning that general education classrooms are preferred for students unless they are not the best fit), educational plans are individually negotiated by parents, therapists, teachers, and administrators. Very little about how we do general education in this country makes use of Disability Studies' critiques, principles of universal design, or insights of disabled educators themselves, and special education still operates as an appendage to the educational apparatus.

But what about inclusion in other public environments? What does it mean to seek inclusion for disabled people? Writing over a decade after Linton, Tanya Titchkosky talks about her experience grappling with inaccessible washrooms (despite the display of accessible signage) in her workplace and the "stories-at-the-ready" explanations that were given for this situation (2011, 71–76). Titchkosky describes these comments, writing,

> "Justification" is one dominant type of comment. People say, *because* of the past, *because* of the passage of time, *because* of ten, twenty, thirty years, *because* it won't make a difference, *because* we don't know what to do . . . the washrooms remain inaccessible. Or . . . *in order to* fight for ramps, *in order to* balance costs and benefits, *in order to* take care of who belongs, or *in order to* make plans for the future while living with the harsh paradox of the inaccessible labeled accessible . . . the washrooms remain as what is—inaccessible. (2011, 76)

By taking the time to probe the explanations given for lack of access, Titchkosky determines that "*giving* reasons determines the ordinariness of inaccessibility; all such reasoning relies upon and sustains the common-sense explanation of *disability as excludable*" (77). In this way, Titchkosky draws our attention to the paradoxical ways in which disability is allegedly included, yet justifiably excluded, by way of such reasonable explanations. One need only look to the paradigmatic image of access, the wheelchair symbol itself, to recognize the conceit of access and inclusion: "The existence of a universal sign for *access* is reliant on an exclusive and exclusionary physical and social environment. In order to point towards access, there must be an assumption of a general lack of access" (2011, 61).

Titchkosky's pointed critique of the politics of access coheres with both Sara Ahmed and David Mitchell and Sharon Snyder's arguments regarding the relationships among neoliberalism, ableism, and inclusion. Coining the term "inclusionism," Mitchell and Snyder argue that neoliberalism (and neoliberal institutions) works to preserve itself and to avoid having to change by virtue of including some disabled persons, only those who fit or pass or are not "too disabled" (2020, 187). They write, "Inclusionism requires that disability be tolerated as long as it does not demand an excessive degree of change from relatively inflexible institutions, environments, and norms of belonging" (187, italics removed). Under inclusionism, disability still remains a problem, but it's tolerated or celebrated in such a way that its justifiable exclusion becomes invisible.

Although writing about racism and diversity in *On Being Included* (2012), many of Sara Ahmed's observations about the rhetoric of diversity and its silencing effects can also be applied to inclusion. In her research Ahmed observes that institutional statements of commitment, like being for antiracism, for diversity and equality, or for inclusion are opaque, because institutions are so often not doing what they are purporting to do, and such statements can even be used to block recognition of racism or ableism within the institutions (116). Titchkosky's experience, for instance, with finding the accessible sign in front of inaccessible washrooms, backed by justifications for why inaccessibility is understandable in these cases, comes to mind. Ahmed concludes that such statements of commitment are intentionally "non-performative": "The failure of the speech act to do what it says is not a failure of intent or circumstance, *but is actually what the speech act is doing . . .* naming can be a way of not bringing something into effect" (117, emphasis original). Yet, when people attempt to point out ableist experiences, structures, or rhetoric in institutional spaces, they are often met with what Jay T. Dolmage calls ableist apologia. Ableist apologia defends institutions from ableism on the basis of ignorance, thus both excusing and ignoring that ableism is happening ("I didn't know that I was being ableist"), or surrenders the institution as ableist ("Of course the institution is ableist"), implying that there's not much to be done about it (2017, 35–39). As with inclusionism, these apologies critically reinforce neoliberal policies or the institution at the expense of the individuals who continue to find the institution inaccessible.

This is why, when it comes to the space of church, it is concerning that two poles of disability visibility often amount to the platitude, "But we have no disabled people in our church," or to the statement of radical inclusion, "We are inclusive: all are welcome at our church." Yet the naming of both of these extremes paradoxically erases disabled people. In the first, even as disabled people, who make up the largest global minority group, must statistically be present, their presence is undermined by able-disabled people who somehow do not know about or recognize their disabilities. It functions as ableist apologia: there's no need for me to be concerned with ableism, despite the fact that if no disabled people were present in the congregation, it would be a direct result of ableism, and if people are present and they are not comfortable being open about their disabilities, that is still a function of ableism. In one fell swoop, "There are no people with disabilities in our church" demonstrates the justifiable exclusion of disabled people from Christian congregations. Dolmage argues that, much like the steep steps of academic buildings that function not just to exclude disabled people but to elevate spaces, a statement like, "There are no disabled people at our church" functions not just to exclude but to project a desire for eradication, or at least a lack of desire for integration (2017, 45). Clearly at such churches, there are not just no disabled people now; there will not (and perhaps should not) be disabled people in the future, either.

Meanwhile, many have pointed out how the statement of radical inclusion, "We are an inclusive church: all are welcome," critically obscures exactly who is being welcomed from view while simultaneously maintaining the perception that the church itself is inclusive, despite contrary experiences. Of course, such statements are well-meaning in that they function as signals to folks who have been discriminated against, and they are often aspirational rather than realistic. However, the question remains as to whether the statements really exist to welcome so much as they exist to maintain and support the institution as it is. Indeed, we know that disabled people are disproportionately less likely to attend church, serve on leadership councils, or be ordained, and we know this is due to ableism, yet statements of inclusion do little to address the practical problems in our institutions. Relatedly, we know that Christians actively fought to obtain a loophole from the ADA that leaves inaccessibility excusable with respect to church buildings even under the law in the United States today (Dingle 2018). Despite the fact that some Christians advocated for church inclusion in the ADA, the antiquated arguments and language of Christians was added to the ADA, the exception has been preserved, and churches can often hide behind this exception made by the law rather than pursue accessibility for disabled persons.

CONCLUSION

I am concerned that, despite the intent of inclusion, it often functions to silence exclusion, even as it obliterates disabled bodies, lives, and ministries from view. Furthermore, the sin of ableism, inherent in exclusion, must be grappled with if justice is to be possible. This book takes up that concern with respect to interpretations of scripture, lived experiences of disabled people in the church, congregational ministry, leadership, and theology. And despite the critique offered above, I mentioned that our fieldwork gave us much reason to hope. Indeed, our fieldwork invited us to have a more honest conversation about both inclusion and exclusion, primarily because disabled leadership pointed toward a vision of justice that didn't undermine disabled experiences of injustice but rather featured them as necessary truth-telling and ministry in pursuit of something like justice.

At Resurrection Lutheran Church in Hamilton, New Jersey, Jess Clarke and her family created an opportunity for families to worship in an environment where their children's differences wouldn't be criticized but rather embraced. At St. John Chrysostom, a Catholic parish just outside of Philadelphia, Lisa O'Malley, a blind lector, boldly articulated her claim to assist in all aspects of ministry and leadership or go elsewhere, so deep was her call to lead and to serve. And at Princeton Theological Seminary, Bailie Gregory, a bipolar student pursuing ordination, imagined a church that listened to her and to others with mental illness as witnesses and authorities for transformation, rather than persons simply in need of care. The Clarkes', Lisa's, and Bailie's visions for ministry and leadership exposed that our research team's visions were far too limited by our own ableism. But God had thrust ministry and leadership from disabled persons into our faces, compelling not just us, but the church and the world, to a far better paradigm of justice for congregational ministry led by disabled people.

In the tenth chapter of Mark, Bartimaeus is not just accidentally but intentionally overlooked and silenced by the able-bodied crowds and disciples who hear him crying out for mercy. He's by the roadside, he's not even anywhere near the temple, but the disciples and the crowds still conspire to keep him from Jesus. Yet the ableism of the crowds is only part of the story, because Bartimaeus' radical pursuit of Jesus, his faith, has something to teach all of us. Bartimaeus reminds us that disabled people will not and should not come to the church quietly. They have every reason to speak up, to lament, to grieve the injustices they are suffering, to make themselves visible to the church, if not hold the church accountable for them. The question that Bartimaeus raises is not just whether the church will have ears to listen; it's whether the church will throw down its cloak and pursue Jesus alongside Bartimaeus. Will the church have the faith to let go of its problem-solving programs and ask better questions? Will the church have the humility to repent of ableism, injustice, and even inclusion? Will the church have the courage to nurture those who are called to minister and lead?

2

The "End" of Inclusion

[1]On one occasion when Jesus was going to the house of a leader of the Pharisees to eat a meal on the sabbath, they were watching him closely. [2]Just then, in front of him, there was a man who had dropsy. [3]And Jesus asked the lawyers and Pharisees, "Is it lawful to cure people on the sabbath, or not?" [4]But they were silent. So Jesus took him and healed him, and sent him away. [5]Then he said to them, "If one of you has a child or an ox that has fallen into a well, will you not immediately pull it out on a sabbath day?" [6]And they could not reply to this.

[7]When he noticed how the guests chose the places of honor, he told them a parable. [8]"When you are invited by someone to a wedding banquet, do not sit down at the place of honor, in case someone more distinguished than you has been invited by your host; [9]and the host who invited both of you may come and say to you, 'Give this person your place,' and then in disgrace you would start to take the lowest place. [10]But when you are invited, go and sit down at the lowest place, so that when your host comes, he may say to you, 'Friend, move up higher'; then you will be honored in the presence of all who sit at the table with you. [11]For all who exalt themselves will be humbled, and those who humble themselves will be exalted."

—Luke 14:1–11

LETTING GO OF THE TABLE

A few years ago, as the associate pastor at a small church, I attended one of our worship committee meetings—a bunch of folks sitting around a table talking about hymns and scripture and bulletins. Gradually conversation drifted toward a certain developmentally disabled adult who's a member of our congregation. We had disabled people who sang in the choir, ran video equipment, and served as ushers in our congregation, but everyone began to fixate on this one woman's behavior during worship. "She's always getting up or crying out, and it's distracting," they complained. "She needs to be taught what's right and wrong," someone else chided. "She needs to be disciplined."

Later that evening I texted my clergy colleague and told her I was gutted about how that conversation at the worship team meeting had gone. Initially she pushed back a little bit. "People were just airing their frustrations," she texted back and admitted that even she struggled with this particular person.

On his way to a meal at the leader of the Pharisees' house, Jesus confronts the religious leaders about healing on the sabbath. Defiantly healing a man with dropsy who stands between him and this banquet dinner, Jesus appeals to their shared Jewish ethics: "If one of you has a child or an ox that has fallen into a well, will you not immediately pull him out on the sabbath day?" Once at the banquet, Jesus continues confronting widespread ancient conventions about honor feasts by imploring guests to take the lowest seat as those who exalt themselves will be humbled, while those who humble themselves will be exalted.

I can't imagine the Pharisees received these lessons with open arms. Both out on the street on the sabbath and in the home of the chief religious leaders at the holy banquet, Jesus' words and actions spoke truth to power, as he attempted to usher people toward a fuller, yet revolutionary interpretation of the law. In healing this man with dropsy on the way to the banquet and then chiding the Pharisees for taking the seats of honor, was Jesus suggesting that these banquets were not a holy observance but rather a tool of injustice? Was Jesus suggesting that these tables were missing guests—the humble, the lowly, even disabled people? Or was Jesus suggesting something far more radical? After all, Jesus was clearly speaking in this chapter to religious leaders and to those in power. He wasn't necessarily asking them to use their power, around those tables, for good. Was that even enough?

Maybe Jesus was really asking them to let go of the table.

INTRODUCTION: INCLUSION—A GOSPEL MANDATE?

From 2000 to 2010, theologians embraced the goals of inclusion with respect to disabled people, analyzing scriptural analogs both for inclusion and for what it would look like to really welcome disabled people into the church. For instance, Jennie Weiss Block in *Copious Hosting: A Theology of Access for People with Disabilities* (2002) argues that, far from a secular paradigm, "the gospel of Jesus Christ is a gospel of access; creating access for those on the margins is a Christian mandate" (120). Likewise, Brett Webb-Mitchell, in his book *Unexpected Guests at God's Banquet* ([1994] 2009), uses the banquet feast in Luke 14 to emphasize that "the presence of people with disabilities in these stories sheds light on how inclusive the Kingdom of God is in welcoming and accepting those who are disabled as God's chosen" (85). Alongside Weiss Block, Webb-Mitchell argues that it is the congregation's gospel mandate to "invite, welcome, and finally accept and celebrate the presence of 'unexpected guests,' and as people discover that we are all members of Christ's community" (99).

It is difficult to provide a comprehensive definition of inclusion, given the breadth of institutions and actors that espouse it as a goal and its pervasive cultural currency. However, inclusion, as articulated in the Americans with Disabilities Act (1990) and the Individuals with Disabilities Education Act (2004), emphasizes peoples with disabilities' rights to full participation in all aspects of society, as well as the provision of appropriate supports so that disabled people can be fully integrated into existing environments. Given the cultural and institutional emphasis on inclusion across legislation, schools, transportation, and employment, it is not surprising that American churches as institutions that are active in the world also tend to embrace and reflect this priority for inclusion in their ministry with disabled people.

Many of these goals of inclusion are also in line with what the church believes about the diverse nature of the body of Christ and Christ's ministry in scripture and in the world. However, especially within the last decade, many theologians of disability have also been critical of inclusion as a model for disability ministry, because they argue that its worldly priorities and practices do not go far enough. John Swinton, in his article "From Inclusion to Belonging: A Practical Theology of Community, Disability and Humanness" (2012), acknowledges the importance of legislation in both the UK and the United States that has been implemented to protect disabled people from oppression and discrimination. But he also writes,

> As societies, we are, apparently keen on the *inclusion* of people with disabilities. However, as we have seen, legislation does not really tell us what disability is or offer quite as much protection as is often

claimed. . . . The law is important and can be central to the process of inclusion. However, while law can change structures it simply cannot change hearts. *The law can legislate for inclusion, but it cannot help people to belong.* (2012, 182)

For Swinton, the main problem with inclusion is that it does not go far enough—it may give disabled people a seat at the table and allow them to participate, but it does not integrate them into the fabric of Christian community. No one notices when they are missing, and, therefore, they do not belong. In other words, inclusion may be a beginning, but it should not be an end in ministry with disabled people.

Indeed, evidence from empirical studies would seem to suggest that models of inclusion have not accomplished what Weiss Block and Webb-Mitchell had hoped for: "In their national survey of people with and without disabilities, the National Organization on Disability (2010) identified a substantial gap in the extent to which people with and without significant disabilities attended a church, synagogue, or other place of worship (i.e., 43% versus 57% attended at least once per month, respectively)" (Carter, Boehm, et al. 2015, 374). A follow-up study of 433 parents or caregivers of youth and children with developmental disabilities found a paucity of supports within congregations evident, striking and inexplicable (Carter, Kleinert, et al. 2015). In turn, theologians like Swinton, Hans Reinders, and Thomas E. Reynolds have developed theologies over the past decade that assert discipleship, friendship, and vulnerability over inclusion as the essence of Christian community and Christian ministry with disabled people.

But none of these theologies takes stock of the ways in which theological and congregational preferences for inclusion may have undermined and continue to undermine practices of ministry with disabled people. Meanwhile, scholars in the field of Disability Studies who analyze neoliberalism and intersectionality have troubled the extent to which the inclusion of "disability" as a category of diversity actually invites cultural and structural transformation. Scholars like critical theorist Sara Ahmed, queer theorist Robert McRuer, and Disability Studies activist Mia Mingus point out that the inclusion of disabled people in existing institutions and environments rarely disrupts the status quo. As McRuer argues, the confines of neoliberal diversity enlarge the space for certain persons, certain bodies—namely those who are heterosexual and able-bodied—to transform and shift flexibly, while people who are minoritized are tokenized and stereotyped as those whose otherness defies transformation (2006, 18–19).

Neither inclusion nor neoliberal diversity has brought the change each seeks, because both operate within, perpetuate, and extend, rather than undo, worldly structures of injustice. This is because, as disability scholars point out, within inclusion and neoliberalism there is still a hierarchical and embedded "norm" of a white, able-bodied, male, heterosexual subject whose presumptive hegemony cannot be denied. In his critique of inclusive ministry, theologian Thomas E. Reynolds points out that inclusion, paradoxically, tends to deny difference, assimilating a "them" into "us," "assuming the rightness of its own position as an inside, all the while masking the fact that the inside itself is a construction based upon othering an outside" (2012, 219). Reynolds' critique of inclusion, alongside Disability Studies' critique of neoliberal diversity, helps explain how our worship committee could tout its ministry as inclusive, all the while maintaining its normative, able-bodied center. Church ministries have been taught to achieve or project inclusion, but ironically this merely performs "diversity," maintaining the boundaries of power between "us" and "them."

Thus, drawing on scholarship from Disability Studies, this chapter identifies ways in which ministries of inclusion may be not merely ineffective but outright harmful to disabled people. This is because such ministries often unknowingly perpetuate able-bodied biases, and in so doing, fail to recognize that their very practices are bound up with the injustices they seek to curb. If they cannot recognize able-bodied biases, they cannot repent of able-bodied culpability in injustice, let alone receive or empower disabled leadership. I argue that the church has moved too quickly beyond ministries of inclusion to other practices and theologies without critically reflecting on some of the damage done by well-meaning inclusion. I demonstrate some of the ways in which inclusion has been internalized as it continues to pervade interpretations of scripture that threaten the development of genuine relationships with disabled persons, let alone the ability for the church to perceive Christ's calling or the Spirit's work in disabled people's ministry or leadership.

By emphasizing empirical and personal examples of how inclusion obscures disabled ministry and leadership, I usher the able-bodied church toward practices of listening, lamenting, repentance, and confession, which I take up in subsequent chapters. But in this chapter I ultimately probe the double meaning of inclusion's "end." It seems safe to say that inclusion is not an end but rather perhaps a mere beginning in ministry with disabled people—but might Christian faithfulness signal another end to inclusion as we know it?

INCLUDING AND SILENCING DISABLED PEOPLE

> [46]They came to Jericho. As he and his disciples and a large crowd were leaving Jericho, Bartimaeus son of Timaeus, a blind beggar, was sitting by the roadside. [47]When he heard that it was Jesus of Nazareth, he began to shout out and say, "Jesus, Son of David, have mercy on me!" [48]Many sternly ordered him to be quiet, but he cried out even more loudly, "Son of David, have mercy on me!" [49]Jesus stood still and said, "Call him here." And they called the blind man, saying to him, "Take heart; get up, he is calling you." [50]So throwing off his cloak, he sprang up and came to Jesus. [51]Then Jesus said to him, "What do you want me to do for you?" The blind man said to him, "My teacher, let me see again." [52]Jesus said to him, "Go; your faith has made you well." Immediately he regained his sight and followed him on the way.
>
> —Mark 10:46–52

From Anonymity to Identity: Calling Forth a Ministry

When we had only about two months of ethnographic research project remaining, one of the congregations we were working with just outside of Philadelphia, St. John Chrysostom, contacted our research team about being interviewed for a news story about their ministry with disabled people and the study we were doing.[1]

I fumbled around a bit with the initial invitation. All research with human subjects needs to be cleared by an ethics board to make sure it does not cause undue harm to the people who participate in the research. It is standard procedure in ethnographic studies, especially studies with minors and vulnerable persons, to guarantee anonymity to research subjects. So when we originally cleared the study with an Institutional Review Board (IRB) and negotiated consent with families and churches, we had indicated that all research participants would be anonymized.

But by the time Mary Chollet, the Director of Parish Ministry and Communications at St. John's, contacted me about the story, she had already begun reaching out to all the families and persons who were involved in the study. They enthusiastically emailed back saying they

---

[1]   Portions of this section were previously published in Raffety 2020b, "From Inclusion to Leadership: Disabled 'Misfitting' in Congregational Ministry," *Theology Today* 77, no. 2: 198–209.

were eager to go "on the record." Without prompting, Mary wrote, "Beyond the Princeton 'angle,' I see this as another opportunity to highlight the need for pastoral care for our adults and children with disabilities. Too many Catholic parishes still are not getting the message."[2]

What did it mean that disabled people were asking to have their names and churches included in the study? Was standard procedure, protecting the anonymity of the research subjects, the right thing to do? Or had we stumbled into new territory with this invitation? Should "we," the research team, maintain control over the identities of disabled persons, or were we being asked to reevaluate what we thought we knew was right?

Seeing beyond the Crowd

In Mark 10:46–52, it is the presumably able-bodied disciples and crowds that stand in the way of Jesus' ministry to Bartimaeus and Bartimaeus' ministry to his community. At the outset of the scripture it is Bartimaeus who sits on the roadside, blind and begging; when he hears that Jesus of Nazareth is leaving, he cries out loudly, "Jesus, Son of David, have mercy on me!" The scripture does not specify whether it is the disciples or members of the crowd who silence him, but the next verse reads, "Many sternly ordered him to be quiet, but he cried out even more loudly." (Mark 10:48). A dramatic shift in the mentality of the "many" is evident after Jesus stands still and calls Bartimaeus to him. At this point those who had previously silenced Bartimaeus' disruptive presence call to him, encouraging him: "Take heart; get up, he is calling you." A reading, therefore, that focuses on Jesus' "healing" of Bartimaeus, who is blind, often eclipses the healing the crowd undergoes.

Indeed, the shift in the mentality of the able-bodied crowd from silencing Bartimaeus to perceiving his agency, and perhaps even his ministry, is truly profound. It is hard to know exactly how this shift occurs, but textual evidence reminds us that although others "shushed" him, Jesus stood still and called Bartimaeus to him. These seemingly trivial actions serve to nurture the hearts of the crowd, transforming their relationship to Bartimaeus. Whereas at the outset of the passage, the "many" can only see Bartimaeus as a disruption to Jesus' ministry, after Jesus stands still and calls him, they seem to reverse their narrow interpretation of those with whom Jesus may associate. Both Bartimaeus' faith and

[2] Fieldnotes, email communication with Mary Chollet, October 16, 2019.

agency and Jesus' pastoral leadership participate in the transformation of the crowd's attitude to Bartimaeus.

Jennie Weiss Block, in a chapter on scriptural exegesis, makes the distinction, as many have, between curing and healing in the Gospels. Expanding the definition of healing to take on a spiritual dimension, Block also points out that "much of Jesus's active ministry on earth was aimed at the restoration of spiritual wholeness, which he offered to the entire community, not just those who were sick or disabled" (104). Similarly, Brett Webb-Mitchell argues that the invocation to welcome "the poor, the crippled, the blind, and the lame" to the banquet feast results in a transformation of the entire community. In a chapter entitled "God's Banquet Feast and the Church," Webb-Mitchell identifies a number of games and activities (primarily able-bodied) congregations can do together to understand the needs and perspectives of persons with disabilities. The activities include brainstorming harmful terms used to describe disabled people (112), and several simulations that allow able-bodied people to "experience" disability by putting cotton in their ears, wearing bandages (112–14; 116), or whispering or dimming the lights during worship (122–23). Webb-Mitchell argues that

> in these activities and discussions, people have learned a great deal about their own reaction to and perception of people with disabilities. They also are open to perceiving the world anew when looking through the experience of those with disabling conditions. The true teachers in these settings are often the people with disabling conditions who become the instructors, through experience, for the able-bodied learners. (129)

Although the elevation of the disabled person to teacher in such activities seems promising, the disabled person only becomes a teacher insofar as the able-bodied congregation needs to learn and dispose of their prejudices and limitations. Furthermore, disabled people are not actually included as teachers in these scenarios; rather, they are reduced to perceptions of their disabilities by able-bodied participants.

Disabled activists and scholars have widely rejected such simulations, because they not only center able-bodied peoples' judgments of disabled people rather than disabled people but also provide highly inaccurate and reductive renderings of disability (see, for instance, Silverman, Gwinn, and Van Boven 2014). Although Webb-Mitchell acknowledges that many of the proposed activities will be awkward for congregations, he does not seem to consider that they may actually be hurtful or harmful (especially the generating of offensive names!) for disabled people present. Perhaps tellingly, in the passage quoted above, Webb-Mitchell uses the default "people" to refer to able-bodied persons, while the humanity of "those with disabling conditions" is reduced to the lessons their conditions offer other "people."

Likewise, to reinterpret Mark 10:46–52 as primarily a narrative about the social healing of the crowd threatens to make Bartimaeus instrumental merely to able-bodied transformation. As Sharon V. Betcher puts it, "Disabled persons have often been read . . . following [disability scholar Lennard J.] Davis' literary analysis, as stock characters in biblical narratives, as bodies that aggravate and then illustrate the redemptive plot line" (2007, 81). For Betcher and other disabled scholars and persons, the healing narratives may appear "reputedly redemptive" but upon further interpretation are "effectively colonizing," in that they work to resolve a fear of the abnormal (2006, np). Betcher's contention is that reading such narratives as "the normal set against the abnormal, even so as to counter-suggest inclusiveness does not . . . undo the hegemony of normalcy, nor does it participate in transvaluation" (2007, 87). What Betcher highlights is that, despite its winning reputation, inclusion as a desired end in ministry with disabled people has an underside. This is because rather than participating in "transvaluation," as Betcher puts it, inclusion tends to maintain rather than disrupt power dynamics.

When we talked with churches and families about our study on disability ministry and the church, I always framed our desire through research to enhance church ministry. I often used this as another benchmark for ongoing consent, saying, "If the project begins to be something that is a hindrance or a deterrence to your ministry, that's a good indication that we need to stop and talk, that we may even need to discontinue the study." When Mary and the families from St. John Chrysostom emailed to say that this increased visibility would, in fact, enhance their ministry, I began to realize that since the inception of the study, nearly every family, disabled person, or church with which we'd come into contact had been gently yet clearly saying to us, "But you can use our names, we don't mind."[3] In that seemingly trivial way, disabled people had been drawing us to their ministry and leadership, a theme that was coming up over and over in the study, but that we were struggling to perceive

---

[3] Email communication with Mary Chollet, October 16, 2019.

clearly, because it's not the dominant way researchers or pastors do ministry with disabled people.

In laying groundwork for a previous project's methodology, I noted that one of the reasons disabled subjects are often omitted from studies or at the very least anonymized is because of the history of prior injustices committed against them (Raffety et al. 2019). U.S. Research Regulations provided by the Department of Health and Human Services have been informed by abuses to disabled persons exposed in the Nuremberg Doctor's Trial in Germany in 1947 and subsequent abuses in the United States. But these regulations do not list disabled persons as vulnerable populations, instead specifying only pregnant women, prisoners, and minors. Hence, regulation of studies involving disabled subjects is monitored by individual IRBs, which may not possess much knowledge of working with disabled people.

However, contemporary literature, including works by Eric G. Yan and Kerim M. Munir (2004) and Ruth Northway, Joyce Howarth, and Lynne Evans (2014), makes clear that the exclusion of such populations from research may also reproduce inequalities and disadvantages, and meaningful adjustments can and should be made to include people with developmental disabilities in ethical human subjects research. Indeed, it is often the perception that disabled persons cannot understand or do not communicate, let alone comprehend the structuring of consent to be included or named in research, that undermines their inclusion in research studies. What our experience in this current project reminds us of is that IRB conventions for research, like nearly all standards in university and institutional settings, are patterned upon a typical, able-bodied subject who consents in written ways, anonymity being the clear mode for protection of such a subject. But by failing to interrogate such methods and merely embracing them, we did not invite insight into how the ethics of our project may have actually been limited by employing "one size fits all" methods.

What I began to wonder with Mary's invitation and the consent given by the families and individuals with disabilities at St. John's to speak to the press was whether we were unintentionally silencing our research subjects by maintaining their anonymity. What good is research about critical perspectives on inclusion and receiving the gifts, ministry, and leadership of disabled people if those disabled leaders remain obscure and anonymous? What good is research that profiles how churches have ministered with disabled people but discourages networking or broader ecumenical partnerships because it does not name those congregations? Is there something about anonymity itself that undermines God's ministry, especially God's ministry with disabled people?

I thought back to the story of Bartimaeus, how important and noteworthy it is that this man who was born blind is named in the healing narrative in Mark, even as he remains unnamed in the other Gospels, and as nearly every other person with a disability appears as but an anonymous object of healing in ministry in the New Testament. As such, I realized that Bartimaeus' very naming is part and parcel of a move toward dignity, a call from God to ministry for disabled persons, a clue in the story that Jesus is not the sole protagonist of this healing but that Bartimaeus is a partner, a minister in his fate. I thought about all the people we had met to that point in our study, and how, if they are ministers like Bartimaeus, each and every one, then God, at the very least, is asking us to call them by name.

I am embarrassed to admit that when I met with my research team to discuss the intervention St. John's was inviting us to consider in the way we negotiated anonymity and consent in our research, it was only then that we realized that many disabled people had been asking us all along to use their names as we wrote about them, and that we had failed to hear them. As the lead researcher, I had likely placed such importance on the ethnographic commitments to informed consent, confidentiality, and anonymity that the research team was not able to push back or adjust sooner. The net result was that we had failed to listen. Like the able-bodied crowds in the presence of blind Bartimaeus, we had doggedly gone on with what we perceived to be *our* ministry, without letting Jesus open us to the ministry that he wants to do and is doing through disabled people.

As a result of this learning, we went back to each of our informants, giving each family and congregation the option to have their names used in the publication of the research, should they choose. As such, this publication uses some names of informants who have signed the consent addendum to have their identifying information printed, whereas others, according to their wishes, may remain anonymous (see table in chapter 1). In opening up further to the insights of persons with disabilities with respect to the very methodology of our study, I believe we finally began to enter into a more genuine dialogue with our research subjects.

But our bias as to what a research study should look like, who should be in control, and how they would be best served by the study threatened to preserve the status quo and thus prevent us from perceiving the ministry and leadership of disabled people. And yet, disabled people were certainly *included* in our study: the entire study was framed as an effort to listen to and learn from them, their families, and their churches. Yet, to use Betcher's words, while the study was "reputedly redemptive," it threatened to be "effectively colonizing" in prioritizing the power, control, and insights of the researchers over those of the research subjects (2006, np). Even as the study purported to look for the transformative, it served to preserve the normal against the abnormal, undermining itself and its findings. Because of the way the study tacitly confirmed ableist conventions of research, consent, and control, it struggled even to perceive disabled ministry and leadership right in front of our very eyes.

For someone who cares deeply about ethics, research, and ministry, it is hard to tell this story and to admit the ways in which our own politics of inclusion undermined the efficacy of our research. Indeed, looking back, I see so many things I would do differently: this study fails in so many respects truly to do the work the book names that is central to nurturing the ministry and leadership of disabled people. But not to tell it would certainly do more harm than good. To tell the full story is one step toward identifying how ableism presents such an obstacle in both research and ministry with disabled people. I am part of that obstacle, whether I care to admit it or not.

In the next section, I consider how, at the level of congregational ministry, the politics of inclusion may not only fail to help churches register injustice but serve to shore up power in the hands of the able-bodied. This runs directly counter to Jesus' teaching, of course. The question is both how did we get here, and what do we do about it?

REREADING THE BANQUET TEXT

[12]He said also to the one who had invited him, "When you give a luncheon or a dinner, do not invite your friends or your brothers or your relatives or rich neighbors, in case they may invite you in return, and you would be repaid. [13]But when you give a banquet, invite the poor, the crippled, the lame, and the blind. [14]And you will be blessed, because they cannot repay you, for you will be repaid at the resurrection of the righteous." [15]One of the dinner guests, on hearing this, said to him, "Blessed is anyone who will eat bread in the kingdom of God!" [16]Then Jesus said to him, "Someone gave a great dinner and invited many. [17] At the time for

the dinner he sent his slave to say to those who had been invited, 'Come; for everything is ready now.' [18]But they all alike began to make excuses. The first said to him, 'I have bought a piece of land, and I must go out and see it; please accept my apologies.' [19]Another said, 'I have bought five yoke of oxen, and I am going to try them out; please accept my apologies.' [20]Another said, 'I have just been married, and therefore I cannot come.' [21]So the slave returned and reported this to his master. Then the owner of the house became angry and said to his slave, 'Go out at once into the streets and lanes of the town and bring in the poor, the crippled, the blind, and the lame.' [22]And the slave said, 'Sir, what you ordered has been done, and there is still room.' [23]Then the master said to the slave, 'Go out into the roads and lanes, and compel people to come in, so that my house may be filled. [24]For I tell you, none of those who were invited will taste my dinner.'"

—Luke 14:12–24

When we questioned pastors of churches about what theological rationale they might give for the importance of ministry with disabled people, many of them cited Matthew 25, framing disabled people as "the least of these," unto which the church is commanded to provide care, or 1 Corinthians 12, in which disabled people are "the weaker parts," or at least perceived to be the weaker parts of the body, even though they have importance. In each of these theologies, the church maintains its role, and also its power and hegemony, as that which welcomes, includes, or ministers, while disabled people are perceived as those in need of welcome, inclusion, or ministry. The story of the rich host and the banquet meal in Luke 14 is one that churches have readily embraced as a rallying cry for inclusion of disabled people. But what would it mean to take Jesus' story of the host and his friends in all their flaws seriously, rather than dismiss them as allegorical characters? What might it mean to reconsider not just the ministry but the ministers in this passage, the politics of the banquet, and its place in ministry?

In the earlier verses of Luke 14, we find Jesus, who has been teaching and healing on the sabbath, headed to the house of one of the leaders of the Pharisees to eat a sabbath meal. After performing another healing on the sabbath before he even gets to dinner, Jesus arrives, only to contest the way the guests have taken their seats. Making the declaration that guests should always sit in the lowest seats so that they may not be disgraced but rather may be invited to move up, Jesus reinforces a reordering in which the humble will be exalted and the exalted will be humbled (14:11). In verse 12 he continues his teaching on humility to the host, the leader of the

Pharisees, instructing him not to invite to dinner those who can repay him, such as his friends, brothers, relatives, or rich neighbors, but rather those who cannot repay him—those to whom Jesus refers to as "the poor, the crippled, the lame, and the blind" (v. 13). Jesus further tells the leader of the Pharisees that for doing so he will "be repaid at the resurrection of the righteous" (v. 14). After one of the dinner guests replies, "Blessed is anyone who will eat bread in the kingdom of God!" Jesus tells a story of a host who does precisely what Jesus has said *not* to do: he throws a banquet, and the many he invites—seemingly those who can repay him, given that they have land, oxen, and marriage status—decline, telling his slave they are too busy tending to their households. When the host then becomes angry, he tells his slave, "Go out at once into the streets and lanes of the town and bring in the poor, the crippled, the blind, and the lame" (v. 21b). When the slave tells the host that there is still room, the host asks the slave to compel people to come in so that the house may be filled. Verse 24 concludes with either Jesus or the parable's host saying, "For I tell you, truly none of those who were invited will taste my dinner."

Traditional interpretations of this parable don't really concern or take up the experience of disability. According to biblical scholar Louise Gosbell in *The Poor, the Crippled, the Blind, and the Lame* (2018), this parable was almost exclusively read allegorically by early scholars like Augustine, Jerome, and Bede, and as an eschatological parable up until the nineteenth century, comparing the inclusion of the poor, the crippled, the blind, and the lame to the inclusion of Gentiles in the heavenly kingdom. Scholars have argued that when the host tells the slave to go out into the streets and the lanes of the town, those dwelling in these inner city places represent Jews who are marginalized within the community. When the slave tells the host that there is still room, the host goes beyond the Jewish community to that of the Gentiles, widening the scope of Luke's table and the breadth of the gospel.

As scholars began to consider parables within historical and eschatological context, however, the lens of disability became a critical category with which to trouble and challenge these allegorical interpretations. For instance, disability scholars have taken issue with the allegorical interpretation in which the host is God, especially because God's inclusion of persons with disabilities appears as an "eschatological afterthought," as disabled people are only included after the host becomes angry that the table is empty (Ferrari as translated and qtd. in Gosbell, 178). As disability scholar James Metzger remarks, "God as snubbed host" is an "ableist, capricious, paternalistic God" (Metzger 2010, 23.1). Disability Studies scholar Markus Schiefer Ferrari notes that the parallelism between the familial relations and "the poor, the blind, the crippled, and the lame" reinforces the otherness of those with disabilities, which is further exacerbated by the fact that those who do the inviting are noted to be blessed and included in the heavenly kingdom, while the passage says nothing about the inclusion of the poor and the disabled in the eschaton (Ferrari as translated and qtd. in Gosbell, 178–79).

As Gosbell summarizes,

> By allegorising the poor and people with disability mentioned within, not only are the poor and those with disability once again deprived of agency and value in their own right, but, interpreters do not have to grapple with the implications of this parable for the most marginal members of society. A disability reading of this parable seeks to interrupt ablest interpretations which consider the poor and people with disability as only referents to others and consider the truly countercultural message given to the earliest members of the [sic] Jesus' movement: that all people are invited and should have access to the eschatological banquet celebration. (2018, 227)

Indeed, this emphasis on the breadth and transformation embedded in Jesus' invitation echoes the interpretation Brett Webb-Mitchell seeks to offer of Luke 14 in his book *Unexpected Guests at God's Banquet*. Webb-Mitchell, like Gosbell and others, makes the argument that Luke was intentionally building on the genre of banqueting, evident in Second Temple and Greco-Roman culture (Gosbell, 204), as well as Old Testament scriptures. Therefore both Gosbell and Webb-Mitchell helpfully assert that Luke is doing something provocative in reinterpreting how meals reflect the social order for a messianic purpose.

However, Webb-Mitchell's insistence that the grand host of the feast is God, the servant Jesus, and all of us the poor and disabled guests (2009, 88–89) moves the interpretation of the parable back into allegory, and threatens to undermine some of the perplexing and important context embedded within the parable. Meanwhile, Gosbell, in her thorough assessment of Second Temple and Greco-Roman sources, helps provide a nuanced interpretation in noting that it was custom in Greek tradition to invite disabled guests to lavish banquets, as their monstrous features would be mocked as entertainment for the privileged (2018, 205–8). She notes that the *akletoi*, those who could not repay the host, were also invited for the purpose of entertainment, for mockery and derision (209). Thus, given these cultural customs, Gosbell argues that an allegorical reading is misleading and inappropriate. Furthermore, she asserts that a radical inversion takes place in the parable, in which those who are poor and disabled are elevated from the role of entertainers for the enjoyment of the upper class to full inclusion in the Jesus movement and the future kingdom of God (226).

The problem with Gosbell's reading, however, is that, like Webb-Mitchell's, it tends to dismiss the importance of the audience to which the parable was addressed and thus makes assertions about full inclusion where inclusion may be what is actually being unearthed and even critiqued. Perhaps tellingly, this parable is also followed by Jesus revealing to the crowd that one must hate one's father and mother, carry one's cross, and sell all of one's possessions in order to follow him (14:25–33). Hence, in light of the greater context of Jesus' highly contested ministry of sabbath healings, his elaboration on table etiquette that comes before the story (14:1–11), and the commands to give up one's comfortable life that surround the Luke 14:12–24 pericope (see 14:25–33 again), as well as the context of extreme wealth and status conjured within the passage itself, I believe we can faithfully read Jesus in this parable as purposefully speaking truth to power. Given that the hearers in the crowd and the hearers at the banquet were likely implicated in the trappings of wealth and power, and that Jesus tells this perplexing parable *after* issuing the command to invite those who cannot repay, we must also resist any reading that renders the meaning of the passage reducible to mere generosity of spirit. After all, few scholars seem to trouble themselves with the ultimate, summarizing line of the parable, "For I tell you, truly none of those who were invited will taste my dinner."

We know from ancient history, from the broader context of scripture, and from the makings of injustice that these two groups of which Jesus speaks in the parable, namely "friends, brothers, relatives, or rich neighbors" and "the poor, the crippled, the lame, and the blind" are hardly exchangeable opposites but rather actors whose social and political fates are deeply intertwined. The evidence that these groups are not so much opposites as adversaries is hidden in the second story in plain sight—the host invites a group of people with possessions and social status, who, on account of these very things, can't be bothered with the banquet. When the host becomes angry and seeks to fill his banquet hall, the slave need go no farther than the streets and lanes, because it is there that those without status live, forced into a life of humiliation, begging and languishing.

At first glance, Jesus' grouping together of the poor, the crippled, the blind, and the lame seems yet another example of objectification and pacification of marginalized people. But as Betcher points out, there is historical evidence to show that debt slaves and prisoners of war were often humiliated in the ancient world; masters poked their eyes out and beat them, disfiguring them in order disable them and hold them captive (2006, np). Thus, in Jesus' invocation of "the poor, the crippled, the blind, and the lame," there may just be a hidden critique of power, a call to prophetic justice that would have been convicting to hearers who knew why these persons were grouped together, as objects of empire colonialism and violence.

It is highly significant that on the heels of the command to invite those who cannot repay, Jesus tells a story that thrusts injustice, human excess, and subsequent insult into the faces of his first audience and into our faces, and yet we look away. Alongside Gosbell or Webb-Mitchell, we prefer to fixate on some ethereal banquet to which all are welcome, but I don't think that's the point of this text. Instead, for those of us in power, I think there is a summons in this text to come face to face with the consequences of our domination, participation in injustice, and the nominal, conforming politics of inclusion that shores up power at the table in the hands of the able-bodied. Although the vision of the banquet is invoked throughout the Gospel of Luke as a vision of the heavenly order, a vision of the second coming of Christ, the host's conviction that "none who are invited will taste my dinner" communicates the radical notion that the parable of the host is at best a cautionary tale, and at its most extreme an anathema against banquets as the ancient world knew them. After all, at the next banquet, the Last Supper at Passover in the book of Luke, Jesus is betrayed unto death by one seated next to him at the table. It is not until the final banquet, when Jesus breaks bread with them, that the disciples recognize him as the risen Christ on the road to Emmaus. My point is that the messianic banquet texts in Luke are by and large broken banquets, in which disciples, leaders, rich hosts, and curious crowds fail to glimpse the full vision of justice that Jesus' kingdom work seeks.

As Betcher sums up, the problem with neoliberal practices of inclusion, in which the church today is deeply implicated, is that at their center lies neither a truly disruptive Christian ethics nor politics of Jesus, but a "hegemony of normalcy" (2006, np) in that our "sentimental sponsorship of the oppressed" (Chow 1993, 112) requires "respectability, propriety, and civility" (Betcher 2006, np) as the colonizing practices even at the Christ table. Betcher writes, "Rather than 'saving' or 'healing' the other, our 'love' may then actually end up insisting upon its own way, insisting upon our own psychopathological orientation to normalcy, that is" (2006, np). Here Betcher is making reference to the way in which the countercultural, other-worldly work of Jesus' healing ministry has been narrowly interpreted as the redemptive colonizing of discordant bodies and social ways of being, all the while calling for a "transvaluing Spirit from guarantor of miraculous remediation towards the recognition of persons living the variability and vulnerabilities of bodies with real presence to life" (2006, np).

We not only need new texts to consider, we also need new lenses for interpretation. But as we continue to borrow those lenses from culture or tradition, we fail to participate in the truly transformative politics that Jesus seeks to usher in. Further, before moving on to new texts and ministries, able-bodied congregations and pastors need to be willing to admit the ways in which we have been unable or unwilling to see our own complicity by insisting on our own ways. In the conclusion to this chapter, I offer a challenging perspective from my own ministry and usher able-bodied Christians toward repentance and confession as resources in receiving Jesus' ministry through the ministry and leadership of disabled people.

CONCLUSION: LETTING GO OF INCLUSION

The failure we noted in our church's practices of welcome and inclusion helped us to see that we needed disabled people not just present in worship and ministry, but leading at the table. After the worship team's conversation about the disabled woman's disruption in worship, the leadership team at the church issued an invitation to a disabled person to serve not only on the worship team but also on the session, the governing representative body of the congregation. Of course, it felt like the rectifying move, the going out into the lanes and the streets that Jesus speaks of, the kind of generous hosting that Jesus was asking of the church. But I can't help but feel that even in our seeming innovation, we were merely leaping from one form of inclusion to the next. Although the session gained one disabled person, our move to ministry seemed more like an effort to right past wrongs and sweep them under the rug rather than truly face them and understand them, let alone take responsibility for them, repent of them, and change.

As I look back I can't help but wonder: What if that conversation around the table had helped us to see our ableism and our sin in plain view? What if faithfulness for primarily able-bodied churches in ministry with disabled people involves picking apart our ministries of welcome, hospitality, and inclusion and seeing them clearly for what they are? What if the way forward is not better, more theologically sound ministries, but ministries that are able to admit their sin, their complicity in the worldly project of inclusion? We in the church often fail to see that the equity of the messianic meal is not dependent on the mere inclusion of the oppressed: they're already included. Behold, they're the friends, relatives, and neighbors of God!

Rather, this messianic meal calls for the repentance of the righteous. For the church, letting go of our paradigm of inclusion may just be the only thing that beckons Jesus and his friends to host a feast of true transformation for the world. If Jesus is out begging in the roads and the lanes, it will not do merely to invite him and those like him to "our" tables. If we truly want to sit at table with Jesus, we must consider that he is asking something far more radical of the church when it actually comes to being church. Jesus wasn't just talking about rearranging chairs. He was upending the table itself.

3

Listening beyond Inclusion

[38]Now as they went on their way, he entered a certain village, where a woman named Martha welcomed him into her home. [39]She had a sister named Mary, who sat at the Lord's feet and listened to what he was saying. [40]But Martha was distracted by her many tasks; so she came to him and asked, "Lord, do you not care that my sister has left me to do all the work by myself? Tell her then to help me." [41]But the Lord answered her, "Martha, Martha, you are worried and distracted by many things; [42]there is need of only one thing. Mary has chosen the better part, which will not be taken away from her."

—Luke 10:38–42

INTRODUCTION: MARY, MARTHA, AND INCLUSION

In early May 2019, I spoke over the phone with a young pastor at a large, urban Presbyterian church with a thriving youth group program. He talked about the conflict he had in connecting with a family at the church who had two sons, one neurotypical (Amos) and one who is autistic with intellectual disabilities (Jonah), particularly regarding Jonah's inclusion in youth group. Pastor Brad and Michelle, Jonah's mother, would exchange numerous phone calls and texts, have an occasional in-person meeting, but still feel as though they were talking past one another. When Pastor Brad and I talked through the possibility of their church's participation in the study, he had wearily asked me whether there were other churches that were doing this ministry well or if all churches were struggling as much as his was. "We can't do what the school can," he

63

protested, when it came to Jonah's inclusion in youth group. But he also worried that if their church participated in the study, our response to Michelle would empower her to ask for more. She would become an even larger thorn in Brad's side.

Michelle was deeply frustrated. She felt misunderstood and beaten down despite the multiple conversations between her and Brad. She stressed that the youth group needed to be inclusive; she felt that their unwillingness to acquiesce to this explicit purpose was a form of injustice. She was afraid that at youth group, Jonah was being left out or made fun of at worst, bewildered at best. She also hoped Jonah would have the positive experience she'd had growing up in church, of a close-knit, supportive youth group. She idealized the church of her youth and had joined this church with the hope that her children would have a similar experience to hers. She tearfully told me that her dream for Jonah was that when he was an adult, and she and her husband Frank were no longer there, there would be enough people in his life who cared about him that he would not be alone. She had worked hard to ensure that Jonah was close to his extended family, and she hoped the church would be another group of people who cared about Jonah in his adult life.

Brad told me he felt positively overwhelmed by that statement—how could the church take care of Jonah after Michelle and Frank were gone? In general, Brad expressed tremendous stress around the interactions he had with Michelle and Frank and the requests that the family made. "They keep moving the goal posts," he protested, with respect to the church's need to make accommodations toward Jonah's involvement in youth group. Even when Brad seemed to be able to do everything Michelle and Frank wanted for Jonah, he felt that they were still unsatisfied.

Listening to Michelle, Frank, and Brad, I was reminded of the story Jesus tells of his visit to Martha and Mary's house. As Martha busies and distracts herself with the many tasks of hosting, Mary sits at Jesus' feet, listening to what he is saying. In biblical times, Jesus's audacity in visiting a woman's house and Mary's audacity in sitting at Jesus' feet would have undermined his authority as a teacher, precisely because her behavior designated her as a disciple. In those times, rabbis would not have discipled women. In the story, Martha doesn't do anything wrong, but she also maintains her cultural role: she busies herself playing the role of host. Yet Jesus boldly tells her this is but a distraction: "Mary has chosen the better part, which will not be taken away from her."

Michelle and Brad were busy, too: no one could doubt that they were both working hard to find ways for the church to accommodate Jonah. But they were locked within a paradigm of inclusion—every time Michelle asked for inclusion for Jonah and Brad refused to provide it, Michelle thought the church was giving up on Jonah, and Brad felt like he, too, was failing. Brad was probably right that the church couldn't live up to the standard of inclusion provided at Jonah's school, but he also didn't question whether inclusion should be the gold standard for ministry. Michelle knew what inclusion looked like for Jonah at school and she knew what church had looked like for her as a child, and so she asked and advocated for what she thought her family needed. But putting herself and her family in the position of constantly asserting their rights to Brad was proving exhausting, distancing, and actually disempowering. With every interaction, with every request, she actually gave Brad and the church more power. Michelle and Brad became locked in a transactional relationship that made it impossible for them to see themselves on the same side—to listen to one another, let alone listen to Jonah or to Jesus.

What Michelle and Brad couldn't see at the time was that the paradigm of inclusion actually prevented them from listening to one another and from doing ministry together. In this way, Michelle and Brad's struggle is instructive for so many of us who know that things are not as they should be for disabled people, but who are also realizing that the church can't resolve this injustice by creating better ministries and services for "them." Rather, the church has to become an instrument of resistance and transformation against mere inclusion in the world, because Jesus' ministry, as illustrated by the story of Mary and Martha, seeks to uproot injustice, even injustice that looks like Martha's well-intentioned, busy-minded ministry.

But if able-bodied people like Michelle and Brad are often the Marthas, not the Marys, in the story, how do we become more like Mary and Jesus? How can we get to Mary if not through more and better ministry? What Jesus shows us in this passage is that ministry begins with really listening at the feet of those we seek to love and serve. It means being transformed by the hurt and the pain of the disabled people and their families who have somehow still, by the grace of God, made it into our pews. And it means lingering there, not for the sake of wallowing, but for the sake of witnessing to injustice in the world, beholding and lamenting the wrong in the powerlessness of disabled people, rather than sweeping it under the rug. Jesus reminds us that paying attention to disabled people's pain is key to understanding and loving Jesus.

The very first time I spoke to Michelle, I happened to be sitting in my office, and she called me up on the telephone in tears. She told me that she had been at a disability advocacy meeting where one of my seminary students told her about my studies of ministry with disabled people and she was desperate for my help. When Michelle, her family, and the Presbyterian Church of Ralston joined our research study several months later, Michelle's frustration and pain, not just at Brad but with the multiple ways in which she, her family, and her son were constantly misunderstood, continued to flow in every phone conversation, email, and in-person meeting.

As Michelle oscillated between anger and tears, I often felt overwhelmed and confused about what to do. Try as I might to help Michelle and Brad meet in the middle, they kept putting me in between them and then talking past one another. In some ways I felt prepared as a researcher to do this translation work, to help represent the best of each of them to one another. But the pastor in me shuddered. I was being triangulated, and in so doing was unlikely to do any good in this situation. Eventually I kind of gave up, or gave in, to simply sitting with them, especially with Michelle, in her pain. Even if there were nothing I could do, she was still willing to talk to me. She was eager to have me listen.

In the chaos and the overwhelm, I gradually started to realize that there was something quietly holy and sacred about the way Michelle had let me in. I never felt that I deserved her confidence, especially when the church had failed her so many times. As Brad had noted, Michelle was also resilient and persistent: even though she was often overcome with tears and despair, the texts came at all hours of the day, the emails bursting with emotions, suggestions, ideas, and insights: she never ceased to keep trying to connect with the church on her son's behalf. She believed it was possible. She kept reaching out, she kept sharing her hurt with me: whether it was because I was another mother of a disabled child or a scholar striving to help the church, I did not know, but she kept putting her pain and frustration out there to be held, and because I couldn't really do much else, I uneasily bore it with her.

If Michelle had been my congregant, I probably would have messed up these holy moments by saying more. I probably would have tried to offer her solace, fix her problems, or, at the very least, defend Brad or the church from wrongdoing. But because I was a researcher trying so hard to understand, I mostly just listened. There were times when I tried to affirm that the church did care, but because I didn't really have words of wisdom, I began to speak the language of emotions. My emotions began to mirror Michelle's. I expressed sorrow alongside her that things were going so poorly for her and her family. This was her reality, whether Brad or the church shared it, and I could see that it came from deep, real frustration and pain. What's more, I had the background to know that the inclusion Michelle was fighting for hadn't come easily to her family, I could see that supporting Jonah and getting him what he needed was a constant struggle, but I could also see how much Michelle loved and cherished her son. All I could do was grieve with her that things were so messed up.

Yet, even though I was serving as a parish pastor and a seminary professor in 2019, looking back on doing that research and those moments of sitting with Michelle "in the suck" felt like the most valuable ministry I did all year. But those things aren't ministry because they solved Michelle's family's problems by mending the brokenness in relationships and society, or because they fixed the issues with the approaches to ministry at Michelle's church. They are ministry because God helped me see and value Michelle's pain for what it was. They are ministry because God attuned my heart to Michelle's not just to behold but to feel some of her pain alongside her. They are ministry because Michelle invited me into the faithful practice of listening, and, as a pastor, the most faithful thing I could do was listen to her.

In Romans 12, the apostle Paul compels the early church not to be "conformed to this world, but be transformed by the renewing of your minds, so that you might discern what is the will of God—what is good and acceptable and perfect" (v. 2). How do we do this? After several verses of explanation regarding the body of Christ and its varied gifts, Paul exhorts that body to the following: "Let love be genuine," Paul writes in verse 9, "hate what is evil, hold fast to what is good." On the topic of suffering and pain, Paul furthers, "Rejoice in hope, be patient in suffering, persevere in prayer" (12), concluding somewhat repetitively in verse 14, "Rejoice with those who rejoice, weep with those who weep."

It seems almost remedial that in exhorting the body of Christ, Paul tells us that the mark of genuine love is to be mere mirrors of one another's emotions. But how often, in our discomfort with pain and our zeal for hope, do we trample upon, minimize, or discount the suffering of others? How infrequently are we "patient in suffering," and how infrequently do we ally ourselves with the suffering, do we "weep with those who weep?" How often do we trade pain for problem-solving, so eager are we to resolve this pain, sweep it under the rug, and move forward? Paul's words are remarkably simple, yet ardent and compelling. There is no way for the church to do authentic ministry with disabled people if the church cannot behold the pain and the suffering disabled people and their families have felt and continue to feel in their daily lives.

But how can weeping with those who weep be a plausible, meaningful strategy for ministry with disabled people? Especially in the face of injustice and pain, weeping seems irresponsible and ineffective. If we weep with those who weep, might it come off as trite sympathy and cheap pity—or, even worse, will we be overcome and immobilized with grief ourselves? In this chapter, I draw on ethnographic research with congregations, families, and disabled people to demonstrate further the need for a new paradigm for ministry with disabled people that moves beyond inclusion and toward justice. However, in moving beyond inclusion, I urge the church not to busy itself but to begin and remain with disabled people in the important work of listening. Listening sounds simple, but this chapter works to anchor it in strong foundations of pastoral, biblical, and practical ministry that have often been left behind and forgotten in the face of "inclusive ministry" with disabled people. What this chapter does is help congregations understand that their ministry cannot be transformed by Jesus until they sit at his feet. Their ministry cannot be servant-led without empathetic and active listening. Their ministry must find the humility to listen if it hopes to be an instrument of justice and transformation in the world.

RECOGNIZING TRANSACTIONAL MINISTRY

Nearly every family in our study mentioned circumstances of feeling uncomfortable or unwelcome at church; many mentioned that they eventually became so frustrated that they gave up and stopped coming. Beth, a Catholic mother of two, tells the story of her and her husband trying to take their baby and their disabled son to mass when they were both very little. "I'll never forget, we finally sit down in the pew, and this older man behind me goes s-h-i-t!" "So we used to church hop," she continues. Michael, who was nonverbal, was often very loud in worship, so they would go anywhere with a crying room, "or we would go to separate masses," she says referring to her and her husband and their two kids, her eyes getting wide, about which she remarks, "That killed me."[1]

Linda, mother to Jason, now a young adult with developmental disabilities, said she had talked to numerous families with children and young people with disabilities who wanted to go to church but for whom it was not possible to sit through the long services. Although he could go to Sunday school when he was young, as Jason got older, that required Linda to go too, to offer assistance, and sometimes she

---

[1] Fieldnotes, August 27, 2019.

preferred to stay in worship. But she didn't like who she became when she was there, as she felt that she was constantly goading Jason to keep quiet or stop moving, and neither of them could really enjoy the service. She recalled one time in worship during a particularly meditative moment when Jason burst out with his booming voice, "Have to be quiet. No make noise. God won't like it!" The congregation responded to the outburst by laughing, but Linda just felt sad.[2]

In late February 2020, the state of New Jersey was abuzz after a story broke of a Catholic parish denying first communion to an autistic boy on the basis of his inability to "distinguish between right and wrong" (Burke 2020). Unfortunately, these types of exclusions are actually not all that uncommon and are very painful. As Eric W. Carter (2007), Amy Jacober (2010), and Andrew L. Whitehead (2018) all document in their empirical research, families with disabled children are far more likely to refrain from participating in church activities or even leave church permanently due to the perception of being unwelcome. As practical theologian Brian Brock writes, "By radiating a passive lack of welcome, the church, like most places in modern society, becomes another social space people with special needs feel they should avoid" (2020, np).

Carter's research identifies five barriers to ministry, including architectural, attitudinal, communication, programmatic, and liturgical barriers (2007). But the last one, particularly unique to church, should give us pause. Although liturgy in the Greek actually means "common work" or the work of the people, too often liturgy remains under the power and control of the clergy. As practical theologian Don Saliers writes, "What is done in our public worship of God rehearses who we are to be in our life relationships. Issues of justice and power are symbolized in worship services, whether we are aware of this or not" (1998, 30). Excluded from the heart of Christian ministry, many disabled people and their families have slowly retreated from church life, because their presence was treated by the church as another problem to be managed.

According to Michelle, the Presbyterian Church of Ralston had made significant, successful efforts in including Jonah in church as a young child. Michelle remembers how Jonah used to just scream and scream at first when they went to church, but the Director of Christian Education arranged for the janitor to open the church on off hours so Frank could bring Jonah, and their younger son, Amos, to play and get acquainted with the sanctuary space when no one was there. Eventually, Jonah felt

---

[2] Fieldnotes, October 29, 2019.

comfortable going into the worship service. Michelle remembers feeling overwhelmed by Jonah's behavior issues when he was younger, which was why it was so significant that both the Director of Christian Education and the Hand Bell Choir Director reached out to her. The Director of Christian Education met with Michelle to talk about what she could do to best include Jonah in Sunday school classes, and the Hand Bell Choir Director invited Jonah to play. Although Michelle wasn't sure Jonah could do it, the Director invited a high schooler to stand next to Jonah and help him know when to play, and both boys have been enjoying playing hand bells at church for years.

But this rather seamless inclusion came to a screeching halt when Jonah got into middle school and joined the youth group. Michelle explains,

> Up until that point, I hadn't asked a lot of the church, but when I had asked, [the church] had offered very tailored, easy solutions. So I had in my mind when Jonah joined youth group it would be the same, informal responsiveness, because that all made a big difference for his participation, so that was my expectation with youth group.[3]

Michelle recalls consulting the Presbyterians for Disability Concerns resource group to develop concrete suggestions for how the church could help support Jonah in youth group. Based on those conversations, she first suggested to Brad that he help her identify a small number of youth "buddies" for Jonah at youth group; she then suggested that she speak directly with the youth group assistants about Jonah's disability; finally, she suggested that she, Michelle, observe the youth group in person.

However, the reason Michelle made these requests is that she and Frank wanted Jonah to have the experience of growing in independence as a youth at church, and they also wanted to make sure church could provide the safe space necessary for Jonah to do so. When Michelle spoke to me about Jonah, she emphasized that he was in a self-contained classroom at school, and that over the years they'd struggled even to get information about what went on at school, because Jonah could not communicate it to them verbally. On one occasion, Jonah had completely missed a field trip to Philadelphia, because of that lack of communication; on another occasion, a peer had been bullying Jonah, even suggesting he kill himself, and Michelle and Frank only found out a year after the comments were made. Michelle and Frank had had to fight hard for safety and inclusion when it came to keeping Jonah protected and

---

[3] Fieldnotes, May 14, 2019.

supported. So while Michelle had shed tears on the phone with me, she stood up for Jonah when she advocated for him with Brad. If she could provide clarity about what Jonah needed, like in other institutional settings, she could make this work.

Yet Brad was reluctant to implement these suggestions because he was determined to make youth group a parent-free space in order to offer young people freedom of expression, and he felt that Jonah did not necessarily need the level of support that Michelle wanted for him. In general, he seemed overwhelmed by Michelle's requests: his goals were to sustain the large youth group model and grow the youth group during his time at the church. He thought that the level of support Michelle and Frank were asking for was simply not possible. Brad tellingly fixated on the comments Michelle had made about hoping that the church could offer support and care to Jonah as he became an adult, thinking that she was asking the church to provide long-term services and supports for Jonah. When Brad spoke to me, he alternated between two versions of the conflict with Michelle and her family: on the one hand, he argued, Michelle was asking too much; on the other hand, he argued, the church was incapable of providing what Michelle was asking for. To Brad, it was a lose-lose situation.

Reflecting on the series of conversations, Michelle realized that they were not really conversations at all. When Michelle had issued requests, Brad had denied them, emphasizing the church's role as gatekeeper of social services. But neither Michelle nor Brad wanted the church to be primarily a social service provider. How had their relationship reached such a stalemate? And what could possibly be done about it?

Jim, the father of an adult disabled son at St. John Chrysostom Catholic parish, talks about not telling people how his family is really doing, because he knows they don't really want to hear it—although, of course, that just makes him feel more isolated. "It's like a façade," he says about his life:

> So . . . with autism you have certain educational needs and supports you're looking for . . . some of them are incredibly rare, you don't have sufficient knowledge or programs, so within your own family you're isolated, so people will ask how's Jonathan doing, well, he's the same, but that's not really very good. Well how are you doing, not very good but I don't really—no one wants to hear that—that's going to take an hour and someone's going to say well you ruined the party because you told the truth, well, why even ask the question then, because it's not

very good dealing with five seizures in a day or two hours sleep. So that sense of isolation. . . . [4]

Jim's description of his isolation is cloaked with the language of inclusion: he himself makes it seem as though that isolation from his family and friends is a direct consequence of a lack of "educational needs and supports" or "[in]sufficient knowledge or programs." But pastors and congregations must recognize that disabled people, and especially their parents and families, have been taught to speak the language of inclusion: society has taught them that if there were just better services and programs (and if they were just better advocates!), their family members' lives would be more worth living, and they would all feel less alone.

But if I dig further into Jim's comments, I start to hear his emotions come through. I start to hear that isolation, so often misinterpreted as a synonym for exclusion or a need for more programs and supports, is actually a code word for hurt and pain. The heart of what Jim is saying is that his son and his family are "not really [doing] very good," but as he clearly points out, "no one wants to hear that." In fact, no suggested services or solutions help get at the "truth" of Jim and his family's experience. Jim knows he will, as he says, ruin the party just by speaking, so he typically doesn't share how he really feels. Jim knows that pain that doesn't move toward a solution is not welcome at parties. And it may not even be welcome at church.

Because the social isolation disabled persons and their families feel in contemporary society is so well documented, it is the tendency of both pastors and families to assume that the problem of isolation can be solved by providing services to disabled people. When disabled parishioners and their families name the isolation they feel to pastors and other church members, we tend to intellectualize that isolation—we try to dig to the political, social, economic, and practical roots of the problem—assuming that disabled people are holding that isolation out as a problem they want us to solve. The typical approach of inclusion to isolation is to "solve it" by better integrating families into congregational life or connecting them with services. But in mobilizing our congregational problem-solving skills, we fail to pay attention to what is at stake for God's people at the heart of that isolation, and that is the experience of sadness, rejection, pain, and hurt. We also fail to pay attention to the fact that while the world may make inclusion its ministry, God is calling us to something more.

[4]   Fieldnotes, August 27, 2019.

The reality, of course, is that disabled people do need *both* social services and supports *and* for pastors, churches, and friends to bear witness to their pain and suffering. However, the problem with the paradigm of inclusion and with the practice of transactional ministry is that we've traded the gospel for inclusion and ministry for goods and services. One of the biggest consequences of the paradigm of inclusion is that it forces people like Michelle to become advocates for accommodations rather than people. As Michelle assumed the role of pushing for services and supports for Jonah, Brad saw her as nothing more than a social worker, strategically advocating for things the church was not resourced to provide. It didn't matter whether Michelle's asks were reasonable or not; the relationship that inclusion created, wherein Michelle did the asking and Brad did the gatekeeping, was broken, dehumanizing, and disempowering. It was disempowering for Michelle, because her requests weren't being heard, even as they were being dismissed. It was dehumanizing for both Michelle and Brad, because they began to relate to one another as transactors locked in a struggle for resources. And it was broken in that the church maintained a position of power over Michelle, Jonah, and her family that Brad didn't actually want to be in. Brad's point all along was that the church could not provide what Michelle was asking for, but with every denial of her requests, he subtly maintained the church's power and control by playing the role of gatekeeper when it came to access and inclusion for Jonah. Lines were drawn. Michelle's family was on one side, the church on the other.

Advocating for accommodations in a world that refuses to provide them is arduous and tiresome: there is really no way to advocate without complaining, without listing one's demands, but this is what we require from disabled people and perhaps most especially their parents, time and time again, to ensure that they have equal or at least reasonable access to rights, education, and social services. Indeed, the very enforcement of the ADA and the IDEA falls to disabled people themselves bringing lawsuits against entities and institutions that fail them. But, especially when it comes to disabled people, the government is not a protector or a guarantor of rights: rather, the government is more like the judge in Luke 18:1–8 who has neither fear of God nor respect for people, but upon being bothered by the persistent widow, ultimately gives her what she wants in order to avoid further interaction with her. Jesus uses such a parable to demonstrate the fallenness of the world's concept of justice, the faithfulness of the widow in contradistinction to the indifference of the judge, and the necessity of prayers that do not cease. But in putting the work of prayer, justice, and persistence firmly on the shoulders of disabled people and their allies, the church becomes none other than the unjust judge itself. Michelle's insistence exasperated Brad. If he were to give in, it would have been simply to get her off his back—not to pursue justice, let alone minister to her.

But over time I realized that Brad was not the only one who failed to listen. Due to the global pandemic, it was nearly two years later when I reached out to share a draft of this chapter with Michelle, and the emails came flooding in again. She relayed that rereading my account of the misunderstandings between her and Brad had been triggering and upsetting. "I'm left wondering, what's the point of the church, like what is their purpose?" Michelle asked. She marveled how such a small ask of Brad and the church could have turned into such a huge issue.

But her emails also implicated me in her pain. "I'm worn out by not being believed or listened to," she wrote.

> Harold [senior pastor] seemed to also take the stance, similar to the portrayal of me in the chapter, that Brad was the victim of our family's unreasonable demands, he was working super hard to help, and we could never be satisfied. Harold chose to do nothing to intervene in the situation.
>
> I told you and Harold the truth. I was clear in my description of what happened. People choose not to hear or to believe for whatever reason they have. I can't change that. All I can do is tell the truth as clearly as I am able to. But it is up to others to listen and believe.[5]

As Michelle had talked about her son Jonah's disabilities, she had shuddered that she had often needed to spell out what Jonah could and could not understand, because his disabilities were mostly invisible. Brad did not seem to understand or believe that Jonah was disabled or needed support, and it put Michelle in the awkward position of speaking about Jonah's disabilities largely in terms of deficiencies to emphasize his support needs, rather than his gifts or his strengths. I was disturbed to hear Michelle talk this way about Jonah, too. It sparked judgment in me, because my daughter often has the opposite experience. People look at her, seemingly nonresponsive, nonverbal, and in a wheelchair, and assume she cannot communicate.

---

[5]   Email communication, March 27, 2021.

I've spent her lifetime trying to convince people otherwise. In fact, I recall an experience doing fieldwork in a previous project in which one of my informants, another mother of a disabled child, bemoaned her visit to the very school my daughter was attending at the time. "The kids there were really horribly disabled, though, not like *my daughter*," she shuddered. "I could never send her there."

It was only after Michelle sent the above email and patiently spoke with me in the spring of 2021 over Zoom that I realized Michelle and I, in our experiences of parenting disabled children, were not on different sides of the aisle but rather were in the same boat.[6] I didn't want to be the widow, like Michelle, of course. In writing the first chapter draft, I'd strived to not take sides, because I didn't want to be drawn into transactional ministry alongside Michelle and Brad. I wanted to remain above the fray.

But by doing so, and in my heart of hearts (and Michelle could see this), I'd questioned her family's pain. I'd done something far worse than engage in transactional ministry: I'd seen with my own eyes the pain and the hurt behind words like isolation and advocacy and injustice, and yet I'd given Michelle the impression that she and her family had somehow brought that fate upon themselves. Like Job's friends who come by to comfort him in his pain and end up needling him for what he did wrong, like the judge who pronounces judgment, I didn't want to see my fate as intertwined with Michelle's, because to do so would admit not only that that could happen to me and to my family, but also that I could end up hurting someone else. Instead of seizing the opportunity to move toward Michelle and her family in her pain, to weep with those who weep, I had distanced myself from her.

I realized that Michelle had not silenced Jonah; the church had done that by imploring her to talk about him in ways she would not otherwise have done and by reinforcing the paradigm of inclusion. Transactional inclusion in ministry has the effect of obscuring the very people it seeks to serve: although it may seem to keep them front and center, it does so by rendering them perpetual recipients rather than agents of their own ministry. I was participating in transactional ministry, because, despite Michelle's constant invitations, I had refused to let her in, I had refused to really listen and empathize with her experience as if it had been my own. I had stood aside as a judge who was not merely cruel but undiscerning. And my writing had the effect of silencing Michelle.

---

[6] Fieldnotes, May 2, 2021.

LISTENING WITH HUMILITY

Joanna, a Catholic mother of a son on the autism spectrum, talks about how, after finding her way to St. John Chrysostom, a church known for its masses of inclusion and its openness toward disabled people and their families, she began to worry about how her son would make his first confession. She knew he might be overcome with anxiety, that he wouldn't be able to form the words properly, that maybe he would need to do it differently. She talks about how the parish held a special meeting for parents of kids with disabilities:

> I thought it was gonna be a big meeting and I'd sit in the back of the room and like write down what I had to do, but it was like a table like this and Father Ed just said, 'What makes it hard to come to mass and what do you all need from us to change that?' And it was, like, amazing, and that's when they started talking about the mass of welcome and inclusion, and I started talking about, like, loud organ music makes my son run out . . . [7]

In Joanna's response, it is clear that she'd assumed that in whatever accommodations the parish would make for her son, they would maintain the power over such provisions. Her vision of inclusion, like Michelle's and Brad's, is institutional and transactional: in exchange for attending a big meeting with the powers that be, taking notes, and then toeing the line, her son would be granted his first communion.

But the meeting that she ended up attending surprised her because she was not just given a seat at the table—rather, she was asked about what her experience had been like in worship and shown the willingness of the church leaders to listen to it. When I asked Mary Chollet, the Director of Parish Ministries and Communications, about this willingness to listen, she and others were quick to attribute it to the parish pastor, Father Edward J. Hallinan:

> [W]hat prompted the whole thing was our pastor, Father Ed, saying that he would see families with a loved one with a disability at mass and not see them again and he started to track them down and say, "Why aren't you coming to mass?" And they're like, "Because people yell at us, because it's too much trouble, because, because, because—." So he is the rare pastor who listens as the beginning and the end of his pastoral leadership, so he just set up these listening sessions for families

[7] Fieldnotes, August 27, 2019.

and to this day it's, like, tell us what you need, we're here to do whatever you say you need.[8]

Mary makes Fr. Ed Hallinan's leadership sound so simple and exemplary. But throughout our conversation that day with families and disabled persons in the Parish House at St. John's around another small round table, Mary was doing something else in the conversation that was striking. Although the story families and disabled people were telling about their ministry together at St. John's was one of cultural change, hope, and gratitude in terms of worship and leadership, Mary did not shy away from the hurting parts, or paint over the pain in those stories. If anything, she amplified it.

As we sat together, Mary not only invited each family or person to share but subtly affirmed and amplified their experiences. First, she began the conversation by acknowledging the "bad old days" at St. John's when there was "a complete denial of the need for disability ministry."[9] Second, although she mentioned that many families now flocked to St. John's from other parishes because of that ministry, she acknowledged that they made a lot of mistakes, were still learning, and their ministry was far from perfect. And finally, throughout the conversation, as individuals spoke, Mary made distinct nods to acknowledging their hurt and pain.

For instance, Beth introduced a friend to Mary, who had been to two or three parishes with her disabled daughter and was feeling so rejected she told her she was giving up on the Catholic Church. As she got to know them, Mary recalls saying to them, "I can't believe you guys are willing to give another parish a chance." "I would feel like the mom at this point," she explained that afternoon to the families with children with disabilities around the table, "just feel so burned and so hurt on the child's behalf, that I wouldn't want to try again."[10] When Beth fills in the rest of the story, again emphasizing the woman's tears and statement that she felt like she was dying being at these other parishes where her child was ridiculed, Mary replies, "And who could blame her?!" and then quickly transitions to reminding everyone that things have not always been so good at St. John's, and they are still learning.

---

[8] Fieldnotes, August 27, 2019.
[9] Fieldnotes, August 27, 2019.
[10] Fieldnotes, August 27, 2019.

It was clearly a transformational intervention when Fr. Ed Hallinan and St. John's began to hold these small-scale listening sessions and ask questions around the hurt that families were feeling and to try to understand what might make worship and ministry a better fit for them. But it was also the way they listened and have continued to listen that has helped them become important witnesses, not well-intentioned wishers-away of pain. In providing the listening sessions and in Mary and Fr. Ed's allying themselves with the families, St. John's made an important move. They have emphasized that the same church that has inflicted pain on them is also willing to be there to witness to their suffering, to listen to it and behold its pain and validity.

This primary move of listening as allies makes it clear that although Mary and Fr. Ed may be willing to help, they aren't willing because they know better or have all the answers. They are willing to come close to the suffering and the pain even if it is something they themselves cannot explain, experience, or heal. In so doing, they show that the pain of these families is not insignificant—rather, they foreground it as an important part of ministry. These stories at these listening sessions, whether corporate or private, are given credence and credibility, and Mary shows that they're never silenced, but rather amplified—even after they've been heard time and time again.

What is clear is that for St. John's, the listening sessions are not a means to an end; rather, they *are* the ministry, and therefore there is no effort to move beyond them, curb them, or even reconcile them. St. John's has not stopped holding listening sessions just because they now have braille resources, ASL translators, a fellowship ministry for intellectually disabled adults, and a mass of inclusion. Rather, they continue to hold listening sessions as an expression of the church's confessional posture toward disabled people. They continue to hold listening sessions because the church's vocation is to listen to those who suffer, and really listening is a form of prayer.

It has helped that St. John's has retained listening as a primary vocation in ministry with disabled people, even as the parish develops other ministries in partnership with people in the pews and nurtures disabled persons into leadership. We can glean a couple of key points from how St. John's clergy and leaders practice listening to disabled people that can be implemented in other contexts. First, clergy and leaders should not outnumber disabled people and their families. Because the primary goal of the listening session is to listen to disabled people, it is important that people feel safe, they have an opportunity to listen to one another, and that clergy not be there to control, critique, or steer the conversation. Second, gathering around a table in small numbers is important to set the tone for sharing, being on the same level, and gathering for the purpose of listening. Third, asking simple but straightforward questions is key—questions like, "What have your experiences of church been like?" "What do you want us to know about you and your family?" "What isn't working for you and your family at church right now?" "What is working?" "What do you wish would change?" Also key is reminding people that clergy are here to listen, and their feelings will not be hurt by the families sharing how they really feel. Finally, responding with simple affirmations like, "Thank you for sharing that," "I really appreciate what you are sharing with us today," "I'm really sorry to hear that was your experience," "I'm sad to hear how you've been hurt by the church," "I'm sorry that didn't work for you," reflects that clergy and leaders are truly listening and offering care and companionship, rather than working to move beyond the pain or fix things.

But what about children like Jonah, or those who cannot speak for themselves? Having children present at listening sessions may or may not be appropriate, depending on families' preferences and experiences. For instance, if the Presbyterian Church of Ralston were to host a listening session, Michelle would likely want to share how much it had hurt her to be forced to speak about Jonah primarily in terms of his deficits, and this conversation would not be edifying for Jonah to hear. In these cases in which churches are not yet capable of creating brave or safe spaces in which disabled voices can be centered, holding separate listening sessions initially for parents, disabled children, and even disabled adults is important. It is far too easy for these sessions to be dominated by able-bodied parents of disabled children, who are hurting and have needs—but these needs cannot be heard at the expense of others or in ways that perpetuate ableism. Admittedly, churches cannot avoid encountering ableism even among well-intentioned parents, relatives, and allies of disabled people, but the best witness churches can give in these circumstances is to curb listening sessions that become unfaithful by making disabled people the object of ire and frustration, and make sure to offer sessions that center disabled voices, thus modeling the kind of listening that needs to happen in households and other institutions, even if it is not happening just yet.

It is vital that churches demonstrate listening to young people, especially young people with disabilities, in ways that affirm and amplify their communication and contributions. When I spoke with Michelle in early

May 2021 about her experiences at the Presbyterian Church of Ralston, she reiterated feeling at times like Jonah was in school, because church, under Brad's leadership, was like a black box. How was Jonah doing? Was he okay? She had no idea, because Brad would not give her any information.

"I just want to know that someone is noticing him," she said with emotion in her voice.

"God notices him," the pastor in me instinctively responded, and I could tell, given her tireless efforts, that Michelle believed that. But she didn't have any evidence from the church that that was the case. Early on in the research, Brad had told me that the strangest thing about the conflict for him was that Jonah was actually doing really well in youth group. Michelle acknowledged that she said he liked it, so she kept sending him and tried not to worry.

"*How* is he doing well?" I had asked Brad, and he had given me several examples of how Jonah followed the rules meticulously while other kids goofed off and that was really great to see, how Jonah had volunteered to participate in leading a game, and how when he looked over to see him sitting at dinner, Jonah was never alone; there were always other kids sitting with him.

"Have you shared any of these examples with Michelle?" I asked.

"No," Brad quickly responded. He replied that he didn't think the stories were particularly noteworthy. I encouraged him to share them with Michelle.

"I think she knows," Brad had argued. "They're a great family, everyone loves having them here."

"Have you told them that?" I asked.

"Told them that we're glad you're here?"

"Yes," I replied.

"Sure, I'm sure we've said it."

"You can't say it enough," I responded. "You need to tell them every time you see them, no matter the quality of the interaction, good or bad, 'We're so glad you're here.'" The reason, I explained, is that families with disabled children are getting the message from every institution in society that they are a burden, that their presence requires extra labor, extra money, extra attention, and that their kids aren't worth it. Brad had given Michelle and her family this impression over and over as he painstakingly protested that they couldn't meet Michelle's demands. Even if he was indicating that they couldn't meet those demands not because Jonah wasn't worth it but because the church didn't have the resources, what do we think Michelle likely took from those interactions?

The only interactions that Michelle and Brad were having regarding Jonah were about resources, but Brad had the opportunity to shift the conversation—to listen to Jonah by noticing him.

By the time Brad and I spoke, however, the damage had been done. Brad had let Michelle and Jonah imagine that the church didn't want them, because all they heard from him was protests. Even if Brad had been skeptical that they could accommodate Jonah, he needed to start with listening, and listening involves active reflection. In the case of listening to disabled people, listening involves actively confronting the cultural script that disabled people are not wanted, valuable, or important, by both saying and doing otherwise. It was not only Mary who sat at Jesus' feet; it was Jesus himself who, time and time again, listened to people who were on the margins of society. Jesus came close to them, because they were in pain, because they were suffering. Although Jesus offered physical healing in some circumstances, he always offered dignity by attuning himself to the cries of those in need. The church can do this work if it only has ears to listen. But it clearly involves awareness, humility, repentant hearts, and confessional postures. In this last section, I begin to develop a paradigm of justice in congregational ministry with disabled people that I extend in the following chapter and throughout the book.

The thrust of the approach, however, is that it's not just Brad and I who have made mistakes in ministry with disabled people. Rather, all of us living and inhabiting an able-bodied world have fallen short of not just affirming disabled people's humanity but also listening to their pain, nurturing their ministry, and amplifying their leadership. Listening will thus involve not just active reflection but also introspection, repentance, and confession if the church is to move toward in doing justice with disabled people. If the church is to rekindle ministry with disabled people, it must be willing to listen, and to listen well—not just to Michelle but to Jonah, and perhaps most especially when the going gets tough, to listen even unto rebuke and criticism; not just to hurt and pain but to anger and indignation.

LISTENING TO DISABLED PEOPLE

One of the reasons listening sessions are so powerful is because they bring together able-bodied family members and disabled persons themselves to offer further insight and understanding into their varied experiences. In listening sessions, able-bodied family members must not speak for disabled people; rather, ideally, disabled people are present to share their experiences firsthand. For instance, throughout the conversation at St. John's, Mary Chollet is quick to say that they have made a lot of mistakes in disability ministry along the way, that they don't have it all figured out. When, toward the end of the conversation, I ask Mary if she can elaborate on some of the things they've learned the hard way, she turns to Lisa, a blind lector, and asks if she would be willing to share her experience.

"Gladly," Lisa replies. Lisa is self-assured and well-spoken: she has several graduate degrees but told us earlier in the afternoon with a chuckle that she's looking for work right now. When she speaks, there is strength and conviction in her voice, but the story is one that also produces grimaces from the other parishioners seated at the table that afternoon. Lisa remarks that at her prior parish, St. Cecilia's,

> I wasn't allowed to do [the processional] because I went into do that one Easter and I was told that I was an insurance liability because I could fall and sue the church, so I told [St. John's] that if I was going to be allowed be a lector it was going to be all of it or none of it. So . . . even though the day I got installed I tripped over my own feet because of a communication breakdown with the person helping me, um we were able to get past that . . . and for the first couple times all I was able to do was walk and read.[11]

Lisa speaks so quickly that at first I wonder if I heard her correctly—she tripped the first time she was trying to read scripture during mass at St. John's? At first glance, things at St. John's don't seem much better than at St. Cecilia's, given that Lisa actually fell at St. John's, which was precisely what St. Cecilia's was afraid of!

So what is Mary asking Lisa to share here, and what is Lisa offering?

Remarkably, Mary asks for Lisa to remind St. John's of what hasn't worked, what they're still learning, and perhaps most importantly, what her critical voice and insight offer to this community. It would have been easy for Mary to gloss over the learning curve at St. John's, pawn the lessons off as "strengths in the making," or even hide them. But she asks Lisa to share not just because she knows Lisa feels at home and uplifted at St. John's, but because Lisa demanded "all or nothing," St. John's couldn't quite provide it—and yet, for some reason, Lisa stayed. The brief story Lisa tells is not about St. John's provision or even her own prowess; it's clearly not scripted, and it's messy.

But like Joanna's and Jim's, Lisa's is a story that is welcomed, not just tolerated, at that table. To witness Lisa's story is to sit in the discomfort

[11] Fieldnotes, August 27, 2019.

and critical edges of it, much as to witness Michelle's story calls forth no platitudes or redemption. At St. John's, they may have been telling an overall story of hope when it came to disability ministry, but they were also intent on letting Lisa and others tell how painfully and imperfectly they got there.

Too often able-bodied people think about listening sessions as a necessity for letting disabled people vent and share, and of course, they do offer that important opportunity. But listening sessions are as much for the listeners as for the speakers. As listening sessions become a form of prayer, in which the church hears the cries of those who are hurt, there is also an opportunity for hearts to be changed by the Spirit of God. As a pastor, Old Testament Professor John Goldingay of Fuller Theological Seminary discovered that the same psalms he once thought "stupid" provided him solace and connection when his wife was suffering from multiple sclerosis. But this also caused him to ask what it is we are doing when we are reading the psalms but they don't necessarily correspond to our own thinking and being and feeling (Goldingay 2016, np).

Goldingay says that he realized two things. First, churches that pray and read the psalms can be shaped by who God is as they encounter God in the psalms, even if the psalmist's emotions don't correspond to their emotions. And second, whether it is the praise or the lament psalms, to pray them offers people an opportunity to "rejoice with those rejoicing and weep with those who weep." Goldingay also alternatively calls the lament psalms the protest psalms, which makes clear that lament, something we will discuss at length in the following chapter, is also a form of protest. He points out that many Christians are uncomfortable with the protest psalms because they often ask God to destroy their enemies, but he also argues that this is a relatively contemporary discomfort. Even Jesus, in the New Testament, quotes the psalms, so what is it that we contemporary Christians are so concerned about?

Goldingay goes on to contextualize the psalms and the voices coming from them as those coming from the underside of power, Israel crying out and implicating empire and their oppressors in their plight. He suggests that one of the reasons the pleas for the psalmists' enemies to fall make us so uncomfortable is that we who are in power may be those enemies against whom God is going to act (2016). Yet the psalms offer the Israelites tremendous freedom to cry out to God with the fullness of their hearts, and Goldingay suggests that we Christians, if we minimize those emotions, lack the very freedom to which God is inviting us. In hosting listening sessions, the psalms are fitting prayers with which to open and close, because they make clear that the fullness of our hearts does not make us unfaithful. But they also make clear that in listening and praying alongside those who are hurting and angry, we may feel uncomfortable, and that the discomfort may also be a gift from God. It may have something to teach us about our relationship to suffering. If we can truly listen with our hearts, it may be offering us an invitation to pray with those who suffer.

But before congregations can lament alongside disabled people, they must listen carefully to their words, their actions, and experiences. They must learn not just how to listen but how to make space for people like Jonah and Lisa to be noticed, to speak freely, to lament, to grieve, and to criticize. Therefore, this chapter focuses on giving congregations the tools to recognize and reject transactional ministry in order to move away from a paradigm of inclusion in congregational ministry with disabled people and toward a paradigm of justice. As congregations begin to listen faithfully to disabled people in their pews, it is vital that they turn their focus away from themselves as listeners and toward what disabled people really have to say.

Too often in our reading, for instance, of the story of blind Bartimaeus, we choose to highlight the able-bodied crowd's change of heart at the expense of paying attention to how off-putting the crowd found Bartimaeus' cries, how distinctively the able-bodied crowd misinterprets them, and what he was really saying—he was crying out to Jesus! But there would be no story of transformation without Bartimaeus' crying out. There would be no transformation without Bartimaeus' pushing and prodding of Jesus. In fact, throughout the scriptures, we see a host of protagonists like Bartimaeus—Job, the widow in Luke 18, and the Canaanite woman (just to name a few)—who, despite the protest of the hearers of their laments, will not back down. These scriptures help us realize that the problem isn't so much that disabled people aren't speaking up, but that the church is not listening.

This is a problem, not just for churches but for all of us, and it is why in the face of the lament of disabled people, churches cannot afford to sell the gospel for inclusion but must do the risky work of turning toward God by not turning away from disabled people's hurt, pain, and even critique. It is also important to be clear that what warrants lamenting is the way in which the church has participated in the isolation and exclusion of disabled people, alongside other experiences for such people in the world. What is not being lamented is disability itself. This is where, as much as Michelle, Joanna, and Jim's laments do compel the church to listen for the pain and hurt of isolation, the church cannot settle for their voices; rather, the church must listen well for the voices of those who are not speaking, who are being spoken over, or who cannot speak for themselves.

Indeed, able-bodied parents, despite their own valuable experiences living life alongside disabled persons, have often been unreliable allies, even obstacles to disabled people's dignity (Carey, Block, and Scotch 2020). As we have seen throughout the previous chapters and in this one, even when able-bodied people read the scriptures, we have a tendency to gloss over lament, discomfort, and pain and dismiss the cries and insights of disabled persons. Parents like me who have the best interests of their children at heart can express internalized ableism and cultural inclusion in ways that undermine their children's experiences, infantilize their children, or supersede their voices and experiences.

If we have not learned the value of lament as faithful Christian practice, we will not be able to receive the claims made on us by disabled people as calls not just to listen but to engage more fully with God. If we have not practiced listening beyond the cloak of inclusion, resisting the siren call of inclusive ministry and remaining with disabled people in their seemingly insurmountable, unpalatable, unbearable pain, sadness, and anger, we will not ever be able to lament with them, drawing closer to God and one another. This ministry will also take time, patience, and repentance. We will get it wrong, and when we do, we must have the courage to hear the critical witness of lament from leaders like Bartimaeus and Lisa calling us to new knowledge and new ministry with God.

It must not be the case that listening and lamenting perpetuate the biases of ableism by perceiving and receiving only the shape of laments coming from inside the church, from parents and families, from those whom "we" find palatable to see and hear. Tellingly, even after studying the Bartimaeus scripture, it took years for me to recognize and behold it as lament. Like so many, I had been beguiled by ableism and seduced by a gospel of inclusion. In the next chapter, I argue that Bartimaeus' cries must be read as laments in that they both expose able-bodied people's unwillingness to hear and receive them as faithfulness and call the church back to God and toward a risky new starting place for ministry with disabled people. But this chapter reminds us to slow down, to sit at the feet of Jesus, and to listen. In our breakneck, problem-solving culture, even churches have jumped too quickly to trying to fix disabled exclusion, isolation, and ministry without really listening. We must "choose the better part," recognizing that the voices of those who cry out are the very voices of Jesus in our midst, calling us not to rush past the hurt and the pain. Going toward the pain by listening deeply may be scary, but it is a faithful form of prayer. Disabled people know that no matter the hurt or the pain, God can take it. What if the church only witnessed to that truth, as well?

4

Listening beyond Rebuke

[31]Then he began to teach them that the Son of Man must undergo great suffering, and be rejected by the elders, the chief priests, and the scribes, and be killed, and after three days rise again. [32]He said all this quite openly. And Peter took him aside and began to rebuke him. [33]But turning and looking at his disciples, he rebuked Peter and said, "Get behind me, Satan! For you are setting your mind not on divine things but on human things." [34]He called the crowd with his disciples, and said to them, "If any want to become my followers, let them deny themselves and take up their cross and follow me. [35]For those who want to save their life will lose it, and those who lose their life for my sake, and for the sake of the gospel, will save it."

—Mark 8:31–35

INTRODUCTION

A few years ago I created a Twitter account and began connecting with a new kind of community online. Because I'm an academic who studies disability, I was instantly connected with a number of my non-disabled and disabled peers. But over time, I also began to follow disabled activists, writers, and artists, like Imani Barbarin, Lydia X. Z. Brown, Talila Lewis, Mia Mingus, Andrew Pulrang, Vilissa Thompson, and Alice Wong.[1]

[1] Portions of this chapter appeared in Erin Raffety 2021a, "2nd Sunday of Lent," *Disabling Lent: An Anti-Ableist Devotional*, published online in *Unbound: An Interactive Journal on Christian Social Justice*, February 5, https://justiceunbound.org/2nd-sunday-of-lent/; and Raffety 2021b, "Listening Even

Imani Barbarin Tweet
Image description: Tweet
from Imani Barbarin, MAGC/
Crutches . . . , blue check
certification @Imani_Barbarin.
To the left, profile photo of black
woman with long hair in pink
blazer. Text reads: "Ableds:
ableism only effects disabled
people. *pandemic starts with
public told not to panic because
only disabled and elderly people
would be affected leading to mass
disablement and 400,000+ deaths.
Disabled people: how do you feel
about ableism now?" Timestamp:
6:07 pm, January 30, 2021.
351 Retweets 1 Quote Tweet
1,295 Likes.

Especially during the pandemic of 2020, these disabled activists helped me perceive and experience the world in new and important ways. Among these disabled activists on Twitter, ableism wasn't an afterthought or even a question, like it still is in the church. Instead, ableism was a fallen reality that disabled people resisted and against which they created flourishing lives of protest.

But disabled activists were also pissed off, heartbroken, frustrated, tired, and indignant at the world's obliviousness to their injustices, concerns, and suffering. They were constantly fielding threats against their livelihoods, their employment, their healthcare, their necessary accommodations, and even their dignity. Even though their lives were living proof of the injustices plaguing this country, they were still frequently questioned and scrutinized. Their angry "call outs" definitely didn't make people happy.

But they also sounded kind of like Jesus.

In the eighth chapter of the gospel of Mark, on the way to Caesarea Philippi, Peter emphatically declares that while others call him John

Alice Wong Tweet

Image Description: Andrew Pulrang retweeted Alice Wong, certification blue check mark @SFdirewolf. To the left, profile picture of Asian woman wearing respirator, drinking coffee out of cup through a straw, wearing black hooded jacket. Text reads: "Ableism in healthcare leads to rationing of treatment & discrimination in hospitals during the pandemic (and way before). Also relates directly to high risk disabled people not prioritized for vaccinations #HighRiskCA #CripTheVote #NoBodyIsDisposable #COVID19 #HighRiskCOVID19"

the Baptist or a prophet, Peter says to Jesus, "You are the Messiah." But when Jesus begins to teach about his immediate future of suffering and persecution, Peter dissents. The Message version says in Mark 8:32 that Peter "grabbed Jesus in protest." And Jesus' rebuke is sharp. In Mark 8:33, the gospel continues, "Turning and seeing his disciples wavering and wondering what to believe, Jesus confronted Peter. 'Peter, get out of my way! Satan, get lost! You have no idea how God works.'"

No idea? This is Peter, disciple extraordinaire, follower of Jesus, declarer of Jesus' Lordship! But he doesn't get it. Peter wants a gospel that avoids suffering. He wants a Messiah who avoids discomfort. He tells Jesus that he shouldn't talk about his suffering, the cross, or the Christian life in ways that are so extreme. Somehow Peter thinks he knows better than Jesus. He doesn't think Jesus' suffering is real or warranted.

Sound familiar?

In a church that fetishizes crucifixion, we have surprisingly little tolerance for the injustice, the suffering, and the humanity that come with it. How often have able-bodied people, like Peter, spoken over our disabled siblings in Christ or purported to know better than they do, even though, especially during a time of COVID-19 and police violence against Black and brown people in America in 2020, it is *their very bodies*

Vilissa Thompson Tweet
Image description: Tweet from Vilissa Thompson, blue certification check, @VilissaThompson. To the left, profile photo of black woman with black hair, wearing white short-sleeve top. Text reads: "Black Disability History IS Black History, Get into it. #BlackHistoryMonth" followed by three brown circles. Link from rampyourvoice.com shared via Tweet, black background with white text reads: "Why Black Disability History Matters During Black History Month." Timestamp: 1:11 pm, February 1, 2021.

that are on the line? In churches that emphasize truth and speaking truth to power, has it never occurred to us that we are the ones who may need to hear from Jesus?

This chapter invites congregations to listen faithfully to the laments of disabled people—not just within the walls of the church, but rather, to go where they are to be found. In foregrounding the often critical work that lament does, I help congregants recognize that lament, even though it is prayer, is also by nature unpalatable, implicating oppressors in its audacious cries for justice. I help congregants realize that the invitation to lament alongside disabled persons thus often requires the accountability, confession, and repentance of able-bodied persons and congregations. The interrogative, public nature of lament is provocative, political, and pro-phetic: to listen is not passive or unchanging. Rather, to practice listening to disabled persons, as introduced in the previous chapter, involves listening prayerfully not just to emotions but to what is actually being said, regard-ing the prophetic character of lament from seemingly unlikely sources and places. My experience listening to disabled activists has helped me to see that what the church needs is not always within its walls but is readily available if we're only able to witness God's work on the margins.

THE RISKINESS OF LAMENT

Although the lament psalms, or even the book of Lamentations, may be what first come to mind when Christians think about lament, biblical scholar Claus Westermann argues that because the reasons for the Israelites' enslavement and deliverance from Egypt are never given and God's saving acts cannot be boiled down to a single soteriology (as is often the case in the New Testament), lament functions as the language for God-talk in the Old Testament (1974). Westermann identifies three stages of lament in the Old Testament: short laments in narrative found in Genesis and Judges; rhythmic laments in the Psalms, Lamentations, and prophetic books such as Jeremiah and Isaiah; and serving as a structural element in Deutero-Isaiah and the book of Job. He concludes, "Any survey will show that laments pervade the entire Old Testament and that they are an essential part of what the Old Testament says happens between God and man" (1974, 24).

Westermann identifies a clear structure of lament in the psalms of address in introductory petition, lamentation, turning toward God/confession of trust, petition, and praise (1974, 26). Distinguishing between laments for the dead and laments of affliction, he argues that laments for the dead reach backwards, whereas laments of the afflicted reach forward (22). Westermann writes, "What the lament is concerned with is not a description of one's own sufferings or with self-pity, but with the removal of the suffering itself. The lament appeals to the one who can remove the suffering" (26). But perhaps most importantly for our purposes, Westermann identifies three constitutive subjects in lament, including God, the lamenter, and an enemy (27).

What seems clear-cut, though, for Westermann, is not necessarily the case for the three subjects in lament. In other words, we have already touched on the fact that all too often in church contexts, especially when it comes to accommodations and injustice, disabled people are received by the church not as faithful lamenters or even dynamic advocates, but as enemies. Many scholars have noted that in modernity, the church has lost its appetite for lament (Brueggemann 1986; Katongole 2017; Rah 2015; Swinton 2007). Practical theologian John Swinton points out that in our post-Enlightenment, reason-ready, problem-solving culture, we tend to equate suffering with evil, quickly glossing over or looking past the suffering to try to reconcile or remedy its cause (2007). Old Testament scholar Walter Brueggemann argues that our wealthy triumphalist church is often unwilling to acknowledge lament because it exposes real injustice in our society (1986). The very stance of inclusion and inclusive ministry, with its presumption of what effective disability ministry should look like, often fails to make space for suffering, lament, or their faithful practices and potential. But evils like racism, sexism, and ableism, and the suffering they produce, cannot simply be solved by better ministry, especially when the church is complicit in them. Rather, they call forth a lament that God longs to hear. What a shame that the church often refuses to hear it, or even silences it, in the name of ministry!

Indeed, Rebekah Eklund, in a chapter of her 2015 book entitled "Empires and Enemies: Re-Reading Lament in Politics," argues that lament is inherently political. Drawing on lament in the New Testament, and particularly Revelation 21:3–4, Eklund writes, "Lament functions as resistance and renarration: resistance to the idea that the oppressor gets the last word, and a renarration of the present injustice in light of God's inexorable promise of peace and justice for those who suffer" (2015, 19–20). It is this resistance and renarration that congregations often find so off-putting, because it draws attention to the sin of ableism, the way inclusive ministry may be complicit in that sin, and the enduring injustices for disabled people in which "the last are still last; the emperor still reigns; the faithful are dragged to trial and still killed; Christ has not yet returned and creation groans with longing for that day" (21). Eklund, like John Goldingay, reminds us that although lament is prayer and it is directed toward God, it is not penitence, but protest. As Westermann writes, it is a pleading for a removal of suffering; too often, however, that suffering exists not because of a single, named oppressor, but because of systemic injustice.

This all poses the question: Who is the oppressor in the laments of disabled persons today? For one, although there may be pain, discomfort, and disease—suffering associated with disability—disability itself should not be misinterpreted, especially by able-bodied people, as suffering. This is often a key miscommunication in lament: disabled persons come to the church lamenting injustice toward disabled persons in society and the church responds with pity for their disabilities, furthering alienating and marginalizing them. In the previous chapter, as Michelle was forced to talk about Jonah in terms of his deficiencies and Lisa was made to feel like a liability, we saw the ways in which churches can inflict further suffering on disabled people by viewing their disabilities as deficiencies or liabilities—by making the person the problem, rather than the lack of accessibility or the injustice.

Another problem with this perspective is that it insists on an able-bodied interpretation of disability rather than listening to the heart of the concern brought forth in the lament. As analyzed in the previous chapter, for instance, although disabled people may name isolation as a primary concern, it is important not to assume where that isolation comes from or to gloss over it in order to fix it, but rather to linger in the discomfort of how people who may or may not be members of a church still feel isolated, even as they are pouring their hearts out before a community of people. In the same way that the church may mistake lamenters for the enemy, the church runs the risk, if we do not listen closely to the laments of disabled people, of further alienating them by mistaking disability as the enemy of lament.

A far greater risk in lament, and perhaps the reason why churches so struggle to hear the laments of disabled people, is that the church may hear itself as the enemy, the object of complaint and protest. The power of lament lies not in its constitutive parties but in their interrogative nature: as disabled persons call out the ableism they experience in institutions such as government, education, healthcare, and religion, they implicate the church in their experience of pain and suffering. In his book *Risking Truth: Reshaping the World through Prayers of Lament*, Scott A. Ellington remarks upon the seeming absence of lament from the New Testament scriptures. The New Testament is peppered with what Ellington refers to as "lament fragments" (2008, 165), leading him to conclude that even though the content of lament doesn't loom large for Jesus and his followers, it is "embedded in the fabric of the New Testament . . . Lament . . . communicates in a type of shorthand that carries with it an excess of meaning" (167). One such shorthand that is worth digging into more deeply is Bartimaeus' seemingly simplistic and repeated invocations in Mark 10:47 and 48: "Jesus, Son of David, have mercy on me!" Although many scholars have been puzzled by this unique address to Jesus, Jack Dean Kingsbury notes that when "Son of David" is used in the Gospel of Matthew, it never comes from Jesus, his disciples, or prominent religious leaders, but from those without position or prestige, or even outsiders (Kingsbury 1976, 599–60).

For instance, in the "most structurally complete prayer of lament in the New Testament" (Ellington 2008, 177), the Canaanite woman mirrors the boldness of Israel to invoke, complain, plead, and argue about why she should be heard, all in the face of a silent God (178). As such, Ellington writes,

> The Canaanite woman holds Jesus to a higher standard of godhood than he initially wishes to meet. She demands that he respond to the prayer of lament, even though it is offered by one who is outside the covenant. The unclean outsider takes the lament of Israel on her lips to address Israel's Messiah and through it forces entrance into the community of the clean for whom God acts to save. (178)

What is powerful to note here is both the continuity of lament as biblical practice of faithfulness from Old Testament to New and the way in which lament "accompanies the proclamation of the gospel and is inseparable from it, both in the announcement of the arrival of God's kingdom and the waiting for that kingdom to fully manifest" (180). As such, Bartimaeus' appeal to Jesus as "Son of David" must be taken seriously as a cry that is particularly unpalatable and offensive to the crowds, not just because it is unruly and disruptive but because it asserts the initiative and insight of a lowly and blind beggar in calling upon the Messiah as especially accessible and attentive to the victimized. Ellington continues,

> A more basic risk run by the continuation of lament . . . is the risk of the loss of hegemony by the established church. Prayers of lament fail to observe the niceties of due process. They are jarring, even violent in their assault on decency and order. They are the language of the nobody, the outsider, and the foreigner. Rachel's cry reminds the prosperous Western church that a gospel proclaimed without tears is a distortion and a mockery. The protest of the Canaanite woman will not accept Gospel hand-me-downs, but demands a place at the table and a voice among the children of Israel. Blind Bartimaeus will not lower his voice, speak civilly, and wait his turn. The poor widow will not settle for what is legal, but demands what is just from the judge who has lost all concern for the defenseless in society. The continued presence of lament in the New Testament not only suggests that the "nobodies" of society have a place at the table, but that those who weep may take precedence over a Church that is committed to the avoidance and denial of pain. (182)

This vision for the church, with its precedence for those who weep and its council of "nobodies," is still a far cry from the meaningful listening sessions we encountered at St. John's in chapter three. In his vision of transformation, Ellington imagines a prophetic listening to the world that disrupts the hegemony of the church, a hegemony of ableism. Thus, we see that although transformation may begin with listening to those in the pews, it does not end there. The struggle is that the further divorced one becomes from suffering, as is the state of able-bodied churches, the more difficult it is to perceive and receive the prophetic cries of the nobodies. As I point out in the opening of this chapter, so many disabled people have left the church or are not even appealing to the church, because they do not trust congregations to listen truly to their laments, let alone do anything to ameliorate them. Yet churches have an opportunity to be vessels for the cries of those who are suffering, if they would only incline their ears.

RISKING EVEN GOD?

But might it also be that the church struggles to hear the laments of disabled people because their laments not only charge the church with injustice but implicate God in the hurt and the pain? In lament, can God be the enemy? And what does it mean for the church if that is the case? Should we still be listening?

As Eklund writes, "The fundamental problem of every lament—whether the symptom of the problem be sickness, slander, or exile—is a rupture in that relationship, a threat to the integrity of God's own character and promises" (2015, 29). This is why Ellington titles his book *Risking Truth* and talks so frequently about lament as a theological risk. Even biblical scholars and theologians have often struggled to know what to do with unruly figures such as Bartimaeus, the Canaanite woman, and the poor widow, precisely because their emblematic lament so clearly calls God to accountability and throws our neat theologies, theodicies, and perhaps especially Christologies into disarray. To see Jesus as outwitted, beholden, or swayed by the Canaanite woman, for instance, often invites speculation and concern about his power or lack thereof, rather than insight into not only his humanity but his emotional, relational character as God with human beings.

Throughout his book, Ellington, like Eklund, reminds the reader that at the heart of lament is a crisis of relationship rather than a theological question. He points out that traditional readings of lament often seek to downplay what's rightly at stake by trying to make sense of a crisis between belief and experience by way of doctrine, theodicy, or theology. For instance, with respect to Job, Ellington chides,

> To approach the book of Job as a detached doctrinal treatise dressed up in a colorful story is to misinterpret its core message. Job is not concerned with a doctrinal contradiction, but rather with a fundamental betrayal of trust . . . Whereas Job's friends seek to insulate their understanding of God from experience, Job is able, through the practice of lament, to re-examine his most deeply held beliefs about God in light of new

experiences of God and to explore places in his relationship with God
that his friends are unwilling and unable to enter. (2008, 110–11)

Thus, the work of lament to which many disabled people and their families call the church risks concern not merely about the church's failure,
but God's failure. What if, in the wrestling and reckoning of relationship, God shows Godself to be silent, unfeeling, callous, or even weak?

My own listening to Bartimaeus has shifted over this last year,
thanks to an interpretation by Moira Egan, a blind academic advisor at
Queens College of New York.[2] Egan's interpretation has helped me to
reconsider how even the widespread invitation that scholars have issued
for Christians to listen to lament as a force for justice often still subtly
demands that lament be made palatable to those who are listening. Egan
has helped me see how important it is that Bartimaeus' lament makes
no apologies and presses in on the hearer, Jesus, almost to rebuke. It's a
far more challenging question to wonder not what to do with a disabled
person who is unruly, but what to do with a Jesus who fails, at least at
first, to listen. Where has the church failed to listen, because we did not
want to hear what was being said?

When I have traditionally read and taught Bartimaeus (Mark
10:46–52), especially with able-bodied churches, I have emphasized the
dramatic opportunity it offers for perspective taking, inviting readers
to ask questions of themselves and the text. Will they be like the crowds,
which sternly order Bartimaeus to be quiet but then exhibit a dramatic
change of heart when Jesus calls Bartimaeus to him? Will they be like
Jesus, who invites Bartimaeus to him, stands still so he can find him,
and ultimately asks what it is he wants rather than assuming it? Or
will they be like Bartimaeus, ardently pursuing Jesus even when others
find their pursuit unruly, unpalatable, and untamed? The trouble with
these ideal roles, though, is that they ignore many of the nuances in the
text, precisely because they separate the actors from one another. In
other words, although perspective taking is a valuable exercise in biblical interpretation, much is lost if it serves to remove the relationships
invoked, created, broken, or negotiated by the interactions—the way
people hear what they hear, the reasons people do what they do, what
compels them to one another.

---

2 Egan's interpretation is featured in Erica Rasmussen's article "Inclusive Prayer Service for People with Disabilities Marks 30th Anniversary of the
ADA," *America: The Jesuit Review,* January 2021, https://www.americamagazine
.org/faith/2020/11/27/disabilities-prayer-service-god-ability-xavier-ada-239345.

In fact, the relationships in this text are far more complicated than immediately meets the eye. Understandably, first-time readers, particularly able-bodied folks, often want to focus on the surprising conversion or even "healing," of the hearts of the crowd from bigots and naysayers to open-minded followers of Jesus. But besides the note of encouragement to Bartimaeus to approach Jesus in verse 49, there's no overarching evidence for the crowd's full conversion or a real relationship with either man. Furthermore, by centering the presumably able-bodied crowd or even able-bodied Jesus as the arbiter of healing, Bartimaeus is arguably relegated yet again to the sidelines. In other words, even redemptionist readings of the text often reify implicit ableism—so what else is it the text might be saying? Are we ready to listen to where disabled readings and interpretations may lead?

Although I've long interpreted the text as pointing to Bartimaeus, not Jesus, as the protagonist (Raffety 2020b), I've also been guilty of not taking Bartimaeus' words seriously enough. As I describe earlier in this chapter, following Ellington, Bartimaeus' address "Son of David" is a type of lament "shorthand that carries with it an excess of meaning" (Ellington 165; 167). Hence, the term contains a subversive, critical edge that likely implicated Jesus in a way that made him uncomfortable. Moira Egan further claims that the term, in its invocation of David and Jesus' ancestry, "reminds Jesus that if Joseph had not believed Mary and trusted God, Jesus would still be sitting by some roadside, too" (Egan as qtd. in Rasmussen 2020, np).

Scholars have pointed to what we might broadly call Jesus' privilege (see, for instance, Johnson 2017; Monro 1994; Scott 1996) in the parallel lament in the story of the Canaanite woman (Matthew 15:12–28). Note in this passage that the Canaanite woman, a cultural outsider, invokes the same plea as Bartimaeus: "Have mercy on me, Lord, Son of David." Jesus does not initially answer the woman's plea, and here the disciples, similar to the "many" in Bartimaeus, urge Jesus to send her away due to her shouting. Jesus protests initially that he has only come for the lost sheep of Israel and demonstrates his own prejudice by arguing that it would be unfair to take children's food and throw it to the dogs. Yet, as Ellington interprets, "Taking up Israel's most powerful weapon for attacking divine silence, [the Canaanite woman] unleashes lament on a silent Christ and insists that *today* is the day when those who come from afar will no longer have to crawl under the table for scraps, but can sit down with

Abraham and Isaac and Jacob and share in the feast of the Lord's table" (Ellington 2008, 180).

My point is that to read this passage faithfully, with Bartimaeus as the protagonist to whom Jesus and the passage itself point, is to face the fact that even in the face of Bartimaeus' rebuking cries, Jesus just kept walking. Even though Jesus and the disciples can see Bartimaeus for themselves, they walk right past him. Perhaps Jesus doesn't just fail to hear Bartimaeus. Perhaps, as in the case of the Canaanite woman, Jesus doesn't *want* to hear him. Perhaps Jesus even fails to listen.

In her interpretation of the passage, Egan describes Jesus as enjoying the privilege of being able-bodied and reimagines Bartimaeus as a "minster of truth who wanted to give him an opportunity to rethink his behavior" and whom Jesus eventually comes to see as someone who may help him learn a few things (Egan as paraphrased and qtd. in Rasmussen 2020, np). A critical point when it comes to Jesus' interactions with the Canaanite woman and with Bartimaeus is that Jesus both struggles to listen and is ultimately moved by the cries of the oppressed. In both cases it appears that his privilege makes it difficult for him to receive the insights of cultural outsiders, even when they invoke honorary titles and use paradigmatic prayerful pleas.

In our case, privileging Jesus' ministry and leadership in these stories mutes the counternarrative of the marginalized ministry and leadership of the Canaanite woman and blind Bartimaeus. Yet, especially given their shouting, that's a particularly unreliable reading. Indeed, we do well to grapple with their unpalatable, uncivilized, and unruly lamenting leadership. In this passage, lament leans hard toward the particularly unpleasant form of rebuke, a genre I always assumed was reserved for Jesus and Jesus only until disabled activists and leaders helped me to begin taking stock of the jagged, jarring edges of lament. Like rebuke, the above quotation indicts a church that espouses a hatred for injustice yet deems those who protest too unruly, too uncivilized, too angry to advocate against it properly. The Spirit, however, is not a Spirit of civility (Betcher 2007), but a Spirit of truth. What do Christian congregations do with a God who is seemingly silent in the face of injustice and a Jesus who, at least at first, fails to listen? How do churches respond to lament from disabled people?

A GOD WHO LISTENS

During 2020, the year in which the world shut down in fits and starts due to the COVID-19 global pandemic, racial violence and protests raged in the United States, and churches struggled to grapple with their newfound digital ministries, my husband and I began attending a small Zoom prayer gathering at a nearby church in Trenton, New Jersey. The church posted an online litany and liturgy, prayers, videos of songs, and the sermon, which congregants could interact with on their own time, but gathered on Zoom for just thirty minutes on Sunday mornings to lift up prayers of the people. Over Zoom, we got to know people we had never met in person, especially the challenges of their lives as Black and brown people in an economically depressed city. Although no one in our household had had COVID-19, here nearly everyone was touched in some way by the virus. They continued to meet online well past the time when many churches went back to in-person meeting, so great was the devastation of the virus on their community. Praying weekly with people who were suffering was important and meaningful. We shared our struggles, too, as parents caring for a child who was immunosuppressed and could not yet be vaccinated, but we also listened to the many stories and got to know the many faces of suffering. And God knit us together in the prayer. We felt known by this community, even though we had never met. We were so grateful for the companionship.

In 2021, as churches began to reopen their doors, began meeting in person, or even removed their masks, perceiving that the threat was abating, our family realized something strange. When we came for an outdoor Sunday gathering on Pentecost, we realized that this church that had ministered to us so poignantly during the pandemic was fundamentally inaccessible to our daughter, who is in a wheelchair. Not only could she not scale the steep stairs up to the sanctuary, but once she was in the sanctuary, there would be more stairs to access the bathrooms or other parts of the building. The pastor and a church elder reached out to our family and spoke lucidly about the physical challenges of the building, but it was shocking to think that had it not been for COVID-19, we never would have gone anywhere near this church. We couldn't even have gotten in the building.

Meanwhile, as congregations around us permitted vaccinated adults to remove their masks, it was too great a danger to our unvaccinated, immunocompromised daughter to return to church in person and indoors. For children and immunocompromised people in general, churches became inhospitable places, because, especially in areas with high infection rates, vaccinated people could still contract or transmit the virus. The Zoom services that sought to keep everyone together, to protect everyone, were abandoned for the appeal of "getting back to normal," being able to sing and be together. But meanwhile, our family was still left at home. It was as if we were on an island by ourselves.

I was consumed with anger, especially anger against the church, which had an opportunity to put vulnerable people first and yet refused to do so. I wondered how someone could live with so much anger every day. I advocated, I spoke up, I did what I could, but in the end, I felt alone and angry at the beginning and end of every day. Gradually, though, I started to remember what I used to tell my students—that whatever it is, God can take it. I dumped all my emotions, my pain, my rage onto God, directed it to God, channeled it toward God, because raging at the church felt impotent: it felt like that rage went into a deep, cavernous void.

Yet, in my prayer life God did not abandon me. I found comfort in the fact that my anger was okay, it was acceptable, it was meaningful in the eyes of God, because God, too, hates injustice. I told the pastor of the church we were attending how angry I was, but I also invited her to rage alongside me. I told her I couldn't see a way forward just yet myself, and it seemed the only faithful thing to do. She didn't try to prod or correct or channel my anger in a productive direction, but rather, she validated it. Anger is not only faithful in the face of injustice, it is also necessary, because it points us toward the truth, and, as such, back toward God.

I would like to be able to say that all that raging has led to radical change, but it hasn't just yet. Still, perhaps equally importantly, it has led me not away from, but in fact closer to God. It sounds bizarre to say that what the church can offer to disabled people who are lamenting injustice is a God who wants to hear their pain, but that, for me, has certainly made all the difference. A robust theology of lament invites pain, sadness, and anger at injustice into the church, because God wants to hear it, even if it seems like that has not been or is not the case.

But before that can happen, able-bodied people often need to grapple with our own reactions to lament that may impinge on those giving testimony, much as Job's well-meaning friends did. It is hard for human beings to let pain just hang out there, in the balance, as it is hard for us to let God in, even in prayer. Job's friends' first mistake was in trying to fill the silence. Their effort in trying to fill the silence expressed their own anxieties about where God was, how a good God could let this happen, and whether God would even show up for Job. But the reason lament is such a meaningful discipline for both those who are lamenting and those who are listening is that it invites God, not us, to action.

As Emmanuel Katongole writes in *Born from Lament: The Theology and Politics of Hope in Africa*, pain has the ability to render a victim silent and powerless. But in lament, speaking the unspeakable pain actually serves as "a form of resistance against the paralyzing silence" (2017, 56). In the Old Testament, the book of Lamentations and the Psalms of lament demonstrate how lament doesn't just further complaint but also furthers relationship by bearing authentic pain and perseverance on the part of the protestor. The laments are directed in dynamic relationship to the God of the covenant: as such, God can receive them, and we can receive them as a sign of faithfulness in relationship. Rather, the repetitive, even complaining nature of these laments is not a sign of faithlessness or stagnation, but a sign of engagement with the God of the covenant who is faithful in listening (Katongole 2017, 110). When it comes to Job, Ellen Davis writes, "Job rails against God, not as a skeptic, not as a stranger to God's justice, but precisely as a believer. It is the very depth of Job's commitment to God's ethical vision that makes his rage so fierce, and that will finally compel answer from God" (Davis 2001, 133).

Hence, even when God appears to be silent, or those who lament and protest rage against a God whose silence stings, the scriptures and the shape of Christian salvation reveal that God may not be unresponsive in silence, but attentive, actively listening, crying, grieving, and being with us in our pain (Katongole 2017, 112). The Pentateuch features a God who is pained to see Israel suffer; the prophets speak of a God who is not unfeeling but feeling-full for his people when they are in pain and suffering; and the New Testament shows us a Jesus who not only suffers but fears and weeps and cares, suffering with us. As Katongole and others have argued, the church has mistaken God's silence for our moment to speak, but if we are to stand with those who suffer, who find themselves in pain and alone, churches must be willing to listen.

As the church listens to lament, though, our own discomfort often sets in. In order to resolve that discomfort, we often stop listening. If we don't have to hear the cries of lament, we don't have to consider how they may implicate us in their charges and accusations. Alternatively, if we seek to resolve the lament, we assume a powerful, stable role. We get to stand outside the hurt, we get to act, and we get to take control back from those who are pleading their cases. In his reflections on Luke 18 and chapter 6 of Revelation, John Goldingay, Professor Emeritus of Old Testament at Fuller Seminary, reminds us that laments are not just protests but prayers for justice. Goldingay reminds us that psalms of protest call on God "not to stay aloof but to act" (2020, np). Importantly, though, it is God, not we, who are called to action in prayer. Although Goldingay is quick to state that prayer is not subordinate to action, he maintains that our action means nothing without God's action. As he puts it,

> Prayer is not enough without action, but our danger is the opposite one. It's that we think that our action is crucial. In being concerned

for justice remember that justice requires the activity of God and its achievement belongs to the end with a big E. Our action will achieve little if it's not accompanied by as much energy given to the kind of prayer the widow prayed and the kind of prayer the martyrs prayed and the kind of prayer the Israelites prayed. . . . (2020)

One crucial distinction here is that the "we" Goldingay is talking about is not the widow, the lamenter, or, as such, disabled people who are lamenting. Their desperation, their suffering at the hands of injustice, has moved them to cry out. Rather, the "we" he implicates are the hearers of the prayers of lament, those who can choose whether to hear the prayers, join in, or dismiss them, because it is not their suffering we are talking about.

I have already shown how lament radically engages disabled people with God in that cries express a faithfulness to be heard, a conviction that things are not as they should be, and an invocation that injustice still reigns yet justice must be done. But for the hearers of such lament, there is also an invitation to prayer as an "unselfing," as Eugene Peterson calls it (1993). Yet, "unselfing" is neither subtle nor stabilizing. As Goldingay analyzes, prayers of lament over injustice, prayers for justice and for Jesus to come, are prayers that indict those in power, because in order for justice to be done, not only must the valleys be lifted up but the mountains must be made low. Hence, Goldingay points out that when prayers for justice are uttered, and we find ourselves on the side of the Empire, the superpower, the oppressor, prayers for judgment really only offer us one faithful way out. And it is to pray for repentance. As Goldingay convincingly quips, "We can't help being members of the superpower, so we better plead for mercy." (2020)

This is a fitting depiction of what it means to be able-bodied in a world that confers and configures able-bodied privilege without ever asking anything of able-bodied people. But thankfully, there is also an invitation for able-bodied people in receiving disabled laments to turn to God in repentance. As Goldingay argues,

> Our prayer needs . . . to take up the prayer of the widow and the prayer of the martyrs not because we're in their position but because we commit ourselves to identifying with them. It might even lead to a difference in our action, though it's important that we don't think of prayer in utilitarian or instrumental fashion as if prayer is designed to change us. [Rather], prayer is designed to change God and it needs to change God for only God can bring in the reign of justice. (2020)

To think that we the church (especially if we the church are oppressor and not God or lamenter) do not need God to change the world is a dangerous precedent. Yet the paradigm of inclusion has often bidden us to think it is we the church who do the including, rather than we the church who rely on prayer, especially the prayers of those in need, to perceive and receive God's action in the world. Therefore, lament ultimately offers an invitation, not just to God to respond to the cries of those suffering injustice and to act in justice but also to those who hear themselves as enemies, to repent of their sins and join in prayer to God.

And in being faithful in listening, God deepens the understanding of the church. In the book of Lamentations, for instance, in the first poem, a detached narrator blames Daughter Zion for her ill fate and her suffering (Katongole 2017, 51). But, as Katongole notes,

> In the second poem, something has happened to the narrator. He no longer speaks as a distant observer but as an overwrought participant in Zion's unbearable suffering. He stands with her and speaks on her behalf. He no longer blames her; instead he accuses God of the violent abuse of daughter Zion . . . Zion's pain affects him so deeply that it becomes his as well. (51)

This is the risky element of lamenting with, standing with disabled persons and families who are isolated: we may not totally understand what it is they are asking, let alone what they are feeling. We may not understand how God is implicated or what God is to do. But "in refusing to accept things as they are, in protesting the conventional, stable, and safe forms of addressing God, the one who laments abandons the known world and any vestiges of order and refuge that it provides" (Ellington 2008, 111). This is the risk that we who are not weeping must assume in weeping with those who are weeping: we must be willing to trust God enough to compel God to be there in deep injustice and suffering, and to forego this world and its injustice for something new. It is one thing for clergy and church leaders to know and hear about the isolation of disabled people and their families, but it's another thing for them to be willing to feel it. It is another thing for them to sit at the feet of disabled people and truly listen. If the church cannot be the place disabled people can openly express their hurts and frustrations, then the church cannot be a place for disabled people.

However, even as beginning with lament offers churches a shift from a paradigm of inclusion toward a paradigm of justice in ministry with disabled people, able-bodied people must not, as Goldingay warns, instrumentalize prayer or lament as a mere vehicle for reconciliation (2020, np). Rather, repentance and confession as prerequisites to joining with disabled people in lament are an internal shift that must not masquerade as performance or action but be true penitence and turning toward God. One way that churches, clergy, and able-bodied leaders maintain a subtle stranglehold on disabled persons and power over them is by policing their laments, trying to shoehorn them into palatable, civilized prayers.

Yet lament is by nature unpalatable and off-putting to its oppressors. And this is why, even as the book of Job, Lamentations, the Psalms, Bartimaeus, the Canaanite woman, the pleading widow, and even Jesus offer a rich tradition and theology of lament, churches must not use their testimonies to silence other unruly protest in our midst. Reading Bartimaeus through the lens of Egan reminds us that even Jesus was conditioned to turn away from suffering and injustice because of his own able-bodied privilege. I suspect many of us will want to save both Jesus and the church from the likes of Egan's reading, but I can't help but think of my own daughter, of Bartimaeus, of the Canaanite woman, and how important it is that no one, not Jesus, not the church, not the disciples, not the crowds, speak for them. Able-bodied folks in their midst must be humbled to listen if they really want to hear what it is disabled people have to say.

Thus, the listening groups in the previous chapter may be a starting point for many churches doing ministry with disabled people, but most churches will also need to turn a listening ear to communities they haven't even known exist, to people like Bartimaeus, who are outside the church walls. Here I suggest that Twitter and its robust disabled people's activism may be offering new litanies and liturgies for the church to witness and embrace as calls to prayer and justice. Instead of just taking up praying the psalms, as Goldingay does, on behalf of those who are suffering, able-bodied people, apart from disabled people, can pray Twitter liturgies and read disabled authors, grappling with the call to repentance in their own circles, so that when they are in the presence of hurting disabled people who are lamenting, they will truly have not just ears but hearts to listen, even unto rebuke.

CONCLUSION

A few months after Pentecost, I was distraught by the increased risk of going into stores and establishments where people were no longer masking in accordance with the CDC's new provision that vaccinated people no longer needed to wear their masks. In desperation, I called up the owner of our local grocery store and told him how worried I was about bringing COVID-19 back to my daughter, who is immunocompromised. "What would help you and your family to feel safe?" he gently asked. Over the phone that evening, we conjured up the idea of offering special shopping hours for folks who were immunosuppressed, during which all shoppers would be urged to wear masks and all employees of the store would wear masks in solidarity with their customers. "I know this is something our employees would absolutely be willing to do," the store manager said confidently, and just a week later, he sent me the imagery for the announcement for my approval and launched the shopping hours. They've continued ever since.

During the pandemic, when classes were not meeting in person, a former kindergarten classmate of Lucia's, whom she had invited to her birthday party, began to send her handwritten letters and gifts in the mail. She called to Facetime with Lucia, which got our families talking to one another. The girls coordinated "couples costumes" at Halloween two years in a row: one year her friend dreamed up the idea that she'd be a farmer and Lucia in her wheelchair would be a pumpkin in a pumpkin patch. This year they were mice, and Lucia's wheelchair was the mousetrap, too! That these now second-graders developed an intimate friendship in the midst of a global pandemic seemed a sheer impossibility. Watching them just go and do it, while the rest of us wring our hands, has been a thing of beauty.

As children went back to school this fall, their mask-wearing sodden with political controversy, my daughter was advised by her neurologist to stay home due to her high-risk status. But the school district arranged for her therapists and teachers to come offer her lessons on our patio. The first day her new teacher arrived, she spent nearly an hour of the first lesson reminding Lucia how much everyone at the school loves and cares about her—though, mind you, this teacher had never met Lucia herself in person. "They all love you so much, Lucia, so I know I'm going to love you." She played videos from friends and teachers at school for Lucia to listen to to reinforce the point, and Lucia giggled with delight.

I was nearly brought to tears. Here was this schoolteacher using the language of love when that was not what the school was being required to provide. Here was this grocery store owner, offering me the most profound experience of pastoral care I'd had in the pandemic, and he was just a secular clerk. Here were these seven-year-olds finding no barriers toward just showing love to one another, when all the while adult friendships were disintegrating around them. When I spoke with my secular friends about the way that churches in our area had moved on from the pandemic, allowing vaccinated adults to remove their masks at the expense of danger to immunocompromised people, they instantly railed with frustration on our family's behalf. When I emphasized the collective grief that all families are experiencing amid the pandemic, a secular friend stopped me and clarified that my grief was not hers. Her family, with typical adults and children, had merely been inconvenienced by all this, while my daughter's very life was in danger.

On the one hand, it gave me such help and hope and solace to note that even when the church was failing our family, God had not abandoned us. God was working through secular people and institutions to support our family. God had heard our cry. But I wondered why God could not use the church, especially when we needed the church most, to minister to us, to remind us that we weren't alone—and, perhaps most importantly, to be changed and called to prayer, solidarity, and action by our pleas and our cries. I rejoice that on Twitter, in the grocery store, on our patio, even the stones are crying out (Luke 19:40), and yet the church itself could be filled with these lamenting, praying voices, a vessel for justice in a hurting world. What a beacon it is that God is not silent, even when we are. What an invitation it is to listen to the cries of those who suffer, for the church to be a space for discontent and protest, especially in a world of injustice.

5

Following Jesus toward Justice

[17]He came down with them and stood on a level place, with a great crowd of his disciples and a great multitude of people from all Judea, Jerusalem, and the coast of Tyre and Sidon. [18]They had come to hear him and to be healed of their diseases; and those who were troubled with unclean spirits were cured. [19]And all in the crowd were trying to touch him, for power came out from him and healed all of them.

[20]Then he looked up at his disciples and said:

> "Blessed are you who are poor,
>> for yours is the kingdom of God.
> [21]"Blessed are you who are hungry now,
>> for you will be filled.
> "Blessed are you who weep now,
>> for you will laugh.

[22]"Blessed are you when people hate you, and when they exclude you, revile you, and defame you on account of the Son of Man. [23]Rejoice on that day and leap for joy, for surely your reward is great in heaven; for that is what their ancestors did to the prophets.

> [24]"But woe to you who are rich,
>> for you have received your consolation.
> [25]"Woe to you who are full now,
>> for you will be hungry.
> "Woe to you who are laughing now,
>> for you will mourn and weep.

[26]"Woe to you when all speak well of you, for that is what their ancestors did to the false prophets.

[27]"But I say to you that listen, Love your enemies, do good to those who hate you, [28]bless those who curse you, pray for those who abuse you. [29]If anyone strikes you on the cheek, offer the other also; and from anyone who takes away your coat do not withhold even your shirt. [30]Give to everyone who begs from you; and if anyone takes away your goods, do not ask for them again. [31]Do to others as you would have them do to you."

—Luke 6:17–26

INTRODUCTION

"But what do we do with a Jesus who heals disabled people?" It's the question many students and people in the pews utter when they begin to read Bartimaeus and other disabled persons as the protagonists in scripture, when they begin to notice able-bodied people as obstacles to Jesus' ministry, when they begin to wonder if we have to throw even "Jesus out with the ableist bathwater" (Fox 2019, 2). Regrettably, immense damage has been done by Christians in ministry to disabled persons by creating a "cult of healing" (Block 2002) that equates their bodies with sinfulness, accuses them of faithlessness, and objectifies them (Betcher 2007; Fox 2019; Swinton and Raffety 2021, among others). These are certainly readings the church needs to avoid when we take up the healing narratives of Jesus and disabled people.

While the problem of what to do with a Jesus who heals often comes from a place of genuine concern on the part of non-disabled folks, it may still be a problem nonetheless. For one, it assumes that Jesus is "one of us," an able-bodied "healer-hero" (Betcher, 2006, np) when Jesus does not belong to any of us or to this world, for that matter. For Sharon V. Betcher, theologizing Jesus not as an insider to humanity, pain, injustice, alienation, and ostracization but as a "healer-hero" theologizes a "Jesus who seems not to have been counted among his lists of outcasts" (2006, np). Our tendency in our readings to try to possess Jesus because we want to be on the right side of power is the ultimate colonialist move. In such readings, Jesus becomes the ultimate configuration of pastoral, colonial power, objectifying bodies that simply will not do because they are grotesque, impure, and deficient. But when we look more closely into the scriptures, we are confronted with a Jesus whose allegiance is neither to this kind of power nor to a "nominally 'multicultural' community as a dominant base within which the different are paternalistically accommodated" (Betcher 2006, np). Rather, the Jesus of the Beatitudes, the Jesus of the kingdom, proclaims a dismantling love as one who has come to align himself with those who suffer, and who will suffer himself from pastoral power.

Second, an able-bodied concern with healing often forgets that Jesus asks Bartimaeus what he needs and Bartimaeus responds by asking to regain his sight. Bartimaeus participates in healing in a way that simply looking to Jesus in the text roundly disregards. When we look closer, we see a Jesus whose definition of justice takes seriously disabled people's own, contextualized experiences of injustice. We see a Jesus who decenters himself by calling Bartimaeus to him, dialoguing with him, and extoling his faith. We see a Jesus who understands disabled ministry as a ministry of justice in which disabled people play a central role.

Finally, all too often our analyses of the healing narratives in the Bible are read as isolated, individual stories of miraculous cure or ableist polemic rather than as integral to Jesus' political campaign to usher in the kingdom of God. As Bethany McKinney Fox argues, Jesus' miracles, especially healings, were clear signs to both insiders and outsiders that Jesus was the Messiah, a formidable force challenging the powerful Roman Empire (2019, 39–47). Betcher help us see that although it is Jesus' healing that appears to be the problem in these Christologies, the far greater problem is our unwillingness to regard injustice for what it is, despite Jesus proclaiming a kingdom in which his very body is crucified and the able-bodied no longer reign. The passage with which this chapter begins, the Lukan version of the Beatitudes, shows that healing is intricately linked with Jesus' work for justice in the world, but when we insist that Jesus stands apart from the crowd as a healer-hero, we forget the context of his day: that he came to be "God with all of us." Likewise, when we, his community, "the body of Christ," become so concerned with *our* action, *our* ministry, *our* justice, we threaten to colonize the very body of Christ, withholding it from the work of justice in the world by reproducing it rather than allowing it to be crucified and resurrected. Simply put, when Jesus is constantly pointing us to rampant injustice in the world and uplifting disabled ministers, why is it that we, especially able-bodied people, are so fixated on healing? Is Jesus not clearly calling us toward a ministry of confessing and healing (our) injustice?

In this chapter, I reexamine how Bartimaeus' healing illustrates a context of injustice in Jericho that many of us are unable or unwilling to see. However, this injustice is the crucial context in which Jesus dialogues with Bartimaeus, heals him, and extols his faith, and Bartimaeus then follows him on the way. Therefore, the text offers a clear invitation to churches to recognize disability ministry as justice ministry, in which disabled persons are listened to as authorities with respect to their own experiences, desires, needs, and gifts. Jesus shows us that true justice does not solve problems for people but rather demonstrates that he is with people, as he draws near to them, seeking to understand their circumstances. The church has the opportunity to affirm justice for disabled people by amplifying their voices and gifts for ministry. Finally, Jesus shows himself throughout his ministry to be concerned with a bold redistribution and reinvention of power in the world. In our efforts to do justice, we must not try to possess Jesus or his justice but must let him lead us, sometimes uncomfortably, toward the reality of God's work in the world. In other words, picturing ourselves as "on the way" with Jesus and Bartimaeus reminds us that as the church, the work of justice is not ours to do or possess, but ours to behold and receive.

NAMING INJUSTICE

In 2018, I led a team of researchers conducting ethnographic fieldwork with families with nonspeaking disabled children. Although the focus of the research was to try to describe joy and learn more about joy through immersion in these families' contexts, understandably, much of the research focused on communication. All too often, because our society so elevates speech and language, these disabled, nonspeaking children were instantly perceived by non-disabled people as lacking communication. Both because their communication looks different from established disabled forms of communication such as braille or ASL, and because they have been labeled as intellectually and developmentally disabled, their communication was literally imperceptible to many individuals outside their family and family culture.

Yet we discovered that within the environment of the home, communication between disabled, nonspeaking children and their mostly typical family members was decidedly fluid and unstrained. Parents, siblings, trusted babysitters, and therapists did not struggle to know what children were saying or trying to say, even if much of that communication happened through sounds, body language, or walking, rather than words. Of course, these families had had time to practice and learn one another's modes of communication, therefore becoming attuned to one another, often working in concert together. But if we know that so much of communication is nonverbal in the first place, and human beings have the capacity to adapt to communication in different modes, why was nonverbal communication so frequently misunderstood?

In their work studying autism and communication, psychologists Nameera Akhtar and Vikram K. Jaswal suggest that it is able-bodied people, in their misperception of disabled people, who often unwittingly shut down communication (2019; 2020). For example, because things like lack of eye contact, pointing, the presence of echolalia (repeated speech), and hand flapping are behaviors that are often misinterpreted by non-autistic people as representing an autistic person's lack of social interest, non-autistic recipients of such communication often assume the person is uninterested in connection, so they shut down their own efforts to communicate—they may literally turn away from the person in avoidance. Jaswal and Akthar point out that the reinforced social isolation of autistic people can cause them, too, to abandon their efforts, because it's so exhausting and ineffective to try to communicate in the first place. As one autistic informant commented in another study, "I have been endlessly criticized about how different I looked, criticized about all kinds of tiny differences in my behavior. There's a point where you say to hell with it, it's impossible to please you people" (qtd. in Jaswal and Akhtar 2019).

Therapy for autistic people often includes requiring them to mimic socially acceptable behaviors; but why should they be forced to abandon their bids for social connection, for instance, avoiding eye contact precisely in order to maintain conversation, or repeating phrases in order to foster deep connection, simply because they are deemed unacceptable by an able-bodied majority? Might the more fruitful way of expanding communication be for able-bodied people to be trained to recognize and interrogate their own behavioral norms in order to appreciate and wonder about different ways of connecting? Might we instead long for a world in which collaborative communication offers dignity to different ways of being, so that justice emerges as a shared, creative new possibility for all?[1]

In Bartimaeus' story, Jesus and his disciples are on the way out of town when they encounter Bartimaeus. It is no accident that Bartimaeus is pictured begging on the very fringes of society, removed from social life. These Roman cultural norms presumed persons with bodily differences deficient and even sinful, ostracized them from society and religious communities as a result of being blind or "lame," and forced them to beg without dignity for their livelihood. These are realities that the text introduces us to, but because they were considered "normal," they made Bartimaeus' circumstances as a presentation of injustice largely

[1] There is so much to be said about the neurodiversity movement and neurodivergence, especially with respect to Christian ministry, but for starters, see, for example, Daniel Bowman Jr., *On the Spectrum: Autism, Faith, and the Gifts of Neurodiversity* (Grand Rapids: Brazos, 2021).

imperceptible to those around him. As Betcher furthers, slaves of the Empire were also maimed by their owners as a sign of conquest (2006, np). Therefore, the connotations of notable physical or mental impairment in such a world signaled not just incapacity but injustice. Of course, we cannot know how or why Bartimaeus lost his sight, but in a world in which impairment was not just inconvenient but reprehensible, it is highly significant that this text comments otherwise.

Furthermore, Bartimaeus' shouting is not perceived as a bold act of faith, but as a wild, transgressive imposition. He is rebuked, ordered to be quiet, even though he calls on Jesus through the recognizable structure of prayer, lament. To interpret the miracle in the text, then, as the restoration of Bartimaeus' sight is to miss the profound impact of his social exclusion, or the way the two are bound up in one another. Rather, Jesus' communication with Bartimaeus, as Jesus is literally stopped in his tracks by Bartimaeus' words, then calls Bartimaeus to him, just as he has called disciples and dignitaries and religious leaders and prophets, is also boundary-breaking and miraculous. As described in the previous chapter, we cannot know what happens in Jesus' mind or Jesus' heart as he shifts from walking to standing still, to calling Bartimaeus to him, but this radical recognition of Bartimaeus in a society that chooses to look past him is Jesus' first acknowledgment of injustice.

We who enjoy able-bodied privilege are not ignored, discriminated against, or struggling to access what we need on a daily basis. We can also remain out of earshot or eyeshot of those realities if we choose to, as disabled people are infrequently positioned at the literal roadsides, and systematic ableism, in the form of access denied to disabled folks with respect to education, employment, healthcare, and citizenship is often subtle, nearly invisible. But Jesus clearly wants us to see injustice for what it is. Jesus wants us to stop and regard people's humanity when it is being undermined. Because Jesus concerns himself with this work not just here in this passage but throughout his ministry, it is ours, too, even when it is difficult, costly, and inconvenient.

This is where the language of welcome and inclusion fails to respond to Jesus' radical call to perceive injustice or to help others perceive it. In fact, ministry is often "all about us" in the church, rather than about disabled people who experience injustice. "We welcome all people regardless of sex, gender, or disability," church welcome statements will articulate. And this is good. But how does the church stand with and alongside disabled people by welcoming them? Doesn't the church need to stand against the injustice of ableism in order to stand with disabled people? Doesn't the church need to renounce the evils of ableism in order to fulfill its baptismal vows? We cannot affirm disabled people without condemning ableism in all its insidious, worldly forms.

This is the critical, prophetic part of Jesus' ministry with which we are often uncomfortable, because it also radically implicates us where we have been bystanders to injustice or when we have sought to possess the things of this world rather than stand with those in need. That prophetic ministry that culminates in Jesus, as Walter Brueggemann has noted, holds together a dialectic of criticism and energizing (2018, 3–4). Brueggemann chides that liberals have often majored in the criticism, forsaking social action for the gospel, while conservatives willfully imagine a new world apart from criticism—but is not the common denominator that Christians who are in power will always hear Jesus' criticism as meant for another? After all, it is the crowds who not only ignore Bartimaeus but actively work to silence him, rebuking him as he is pursuing Jesus. A church that wants to welcome must become critically aware and vocal regarding the injustices disabled people face not just in this world but in our churches, our theologies, our worship, and our ministry.

Of course, renouncing injustice also calls the church to accountability. In the previous chapter we talked about how lament offers a space for disabled people to grieve injustice and long for a more just world, for God to be called upon to act, and for able-bodied people to attune their hearts to suffering. But the Bartimaeus text and Jesus' radical openness to Bartimaeus' experiences and desires remind us that it is not for able-bodied people to articulate, determine, or undermine what suffering may look like or feel like for disabled people. Indeed, the thing the church often gets wrong about healing is that we use it to reify our worldly categories of difference rather than let Jesus throw them into disarray. As Fox has argued, Jesus is not a Western physician, who seeks to make those who are languishing healthy or whose "healing powers are . . . a perfected, idealized form of biomedicine" (Fox 2019, 29–32; 53). Rather, Jesus' healings are miracles precisely because they do not conform to the problem-solving logic of biomedicine, nor do they ignore the experiences of the persons in front of them.

In the next part of the passage, Jesus crucially teaches us that justice cannot be done without partnership with disabled persons in ministry, recognizing and nurturing their faith and their calls to ministry. This is critical, because if churches work to rewrite their mission statements and reform their ministries apart from disabled persons, they will be like noisy gongs and clanging symbols. Their statements will dispossess disabled persons of their dignity, all the while possessing Jesus in the process. After all, it is one thing to ask humbly, as Jesus does, "What do you want me to do for you?" but quite another to issue that question as an exasperated, indignant defense of the church's more pressing missions. In his prophetic critique of the powers that be, Jesus identifies injustice, stands with those who experience it, and invites the church to do the same. But this affirmation of injustice will require a radical openness toward ministry with Jesus. We will need to let Jesus be Jesus, calling down not just the blessings but the woes. We will need to remember that at the heart of the church is not a valiant savior but a crucified God who dies for our sins.

ASKING THE QUESTIONS

From the time my daughter, Lucia, was little, we have been sharing things about her and our lives on social media. I don't always love making our lives so public, but I don't feel like we ever had much of a choice. When people ask me what the most helpful thing has been in supporting our family, I always respond by telling them about Medicaid. At the age of one and half, we were able to complete the proper paperwork for Lucia to qualify for Medicaid based on her disability and her medical needs, and since that time, Medicaid has stepped into pay for vital supports like equipment, medication, private insurance copays, and private duty nursing, all benefits that our private insurance, despite coming through one of the best universities in the world, has denied. People don't know what they don't know, so I try to show them that all sorts of families benefit from Medicaid; I try to help them understand that it doesn't matter how hard you work or what job you have in the United States—private insurance rarely covers what disabled people need.

And I have had to speak out because even though Lucia is only eight, we have gone through numerous private and public battles that have threatened her Medicaid coverage, her healthcare, and her life. This is the reality of living with a disability in America: even if you can find a respite from physical pain, medical challenges, or mental fatigue, you are always faced with threats to the very supports that make your life possible. You are tasked with doctor's visits to prove your disability, paperwork to prove your disability, phone calls to insurance companies, and advocacy to prove to the state, private companies, doctors, employers, and the public that your disability is real, your supports are necessary, and your life matters. This so called "health tax" is just one of the ways ableism is embedded in our systems that purport to care but often serve to keep disabled people poor. In order to qualify for disability, disabled people face income restrictions, keeping them from working even though most disabled people really want to work. And during the COVID-19 pandemic many states and countries issued guidelines that rendered people with disabilities ineligible for receiving lifesaving care.

Although my daughter's experience certainly differs from Bartimaeus' experience, so often my family's struggle and advocacy are dismissed as too political for congregational ministry. Instead of being consulted, our experience is rebuked, undermined, or ignored. But Jesus is clearly affected by Bartimaeus' advocacy, so much so that he extols him for his faith. In fact, without Jesus, not just Bartimaeus' struggle but his faith and ministry would have surely been invisible to those around him. When I think about the question Jesus asks of Bartimaeus in this passage, "What do you want me to do for you?" it brings tears to my eyes. What a difference it would have made if Pastor Brad had asked this question of Jonah and Michelle! What a difference it made when Father Ed Hallinan, pastor, made listening the heart of his ministry at St. John's! What a difference it makes when the church, like Jesus, recognizes that to be in ministry with disabled people we have to take seriously what ministry and justice look like to them!

There is a radical openness in Jesus' heart for justice in listening to those who have been most affected by injustice and striving to understand what it is they truly need. As this book has criticized, too often the church has warm-heartedly moved toward trying to create better ministries for disabled people, without stopping to consider that their perspectives are integral to it. By taking on ministry as its own work, the church forgets that we are on a mission of following Jesus toward justice for disabled people, and Jesus makes clear that disabled people's concerns, dignity, and faith are at the heart of that ministry. But Jesus stops to ask the question. This is a radical reorientation in ministry, because it makes clear that disabled people and disabled knowledge are critical to disability ministry. It makes clear that at the heart of justice, and ministry for justice, is Jesus' incarnation, his radical willingness to be with people, and his desire to understand them. Otherwise, ministry becomes mere transaction or service.

Therefore, the work of justice comes in seeking Jesus by seeking understanding of disabled people's experiences and seeking to understand and value what it is they want and need. This offers distinct challenges to the way churches often do and have been doing ministry. For instance, in her qualitative research with disabled Christians, Naomi

Lawson Jacobs talks about how Anthony, a churchgoer with Asperger's syndrome, felt that the pressure to join in social activities at church often came off as the church oddly "refusing to take no for an answer" (Jacobs 2019, 136). Describing the perils of friendship in neurotypical spaces, Anthony thoughtfully articulates,

> I think like with anything else, when people think of friendship, they think of perhaps what *their* idea of friendship is. And if they are . . . a non-disabled person, who is active in the church and has a lot of friends who are likewise, as far as they're concerned that's what friendship is . . . But it's sort of a question again of them having to learn about us, and us having to learn about them. (136–37).

Even though friendship may be a well-meaning tool of churches for including persons with disabilities, it may not do them justice if it loses sight of what disabled people want and need. As Jacobs points out, friendship has been described as a particularly meaningful mode of inclusion for mentally disabled folks, who have often been excluded from the disabled persons' movement or for whom the movement is arguably irrelevant (Swinton 2011). However, "the lack of a voice for those with intellectual impairments—often literally—may make them an expedient group for theologians to claim solidarity with, with the potential for their exploitation for legitimation of theologies" (Jacobs 2019, 96). In other words, friendship without justice may not be friendship at all. As Jacobs points out, friendship can become an individual versus a corporate solution to the injustice that disabled persons face (96). In this way, friendship can even reinforce an individual versus a social model of disability, further disenfranchising disabled persons from one another. Jacobs' research and Anthony's testimony remind us that friendship must not become a site for churches to displace and ignore the more critical exclusion disabled persons face in society.

In his article "From Inclusion to Belonging," John Swinton contrasts the idea of inclusion, regulated by the law, with the experience of belonging that only Jesus can offer (2012, 182). He presents the example of Elaine, an elderly woman with intellectual disabilities, who is included in her church fellowship on Sunday mornings for ninety minutes, but beyond that, no one really reaches out to her, visits her, or knows her (181). Therefore, one of the critical differences in belonging for Swinton is that it does not just acknowledge everyone's presence; rather, with belonging there is a shift in relationship with one another. He writes,

Only when your absence stimulates feelings of emptiness will you know that you belong. Only when your gifts are longed for can community truly be community. When we belong people long for our presence in the same way as the prodigal son's father longed for the presence of his wayward son (Luke 15:11–32) and in the same way that God longs or us to be present with God. (2012, 183)

Belonging, according to Swinton, begins with looking not toward others or to ourselves but to Jesus for the "beginning point of dealing lovingly with difference" (185). When we belong to one another through Jesus alone, Swinton concludes, "Within that space disability might continue to exist, but it will not be negativized. The love of Jesus overcomes all difference" (188).

Swinton, drawing on Jean Vanier and Dietrich Bonhoeffer, offers a compelling interpretation of belonging in the body of Christ. Especially poignant is the description of Elaine's cursory inclusion: no one can argue that she does not belong and the vision Swinton presents of Christian community longing for her presence is powerful. However, because Swinton argues that the solution is in Christ and not legislation, society, or modernity, he swiftly moves away from the roots of Elaine's exclusion and isolation and toward the solution for helping her to belong. Although he points to Jesus as the source of all belonging, the implication is that Christian community, despites failing Elaine, can still muster such belonging because of Jesus, and even overcome difference in the process. Swinton argues that Jesus "offers us a thick description of who God is and what it means to be a human being . . . a thick description of what it means to sit with the marginalized, to befriend the stranger, to offer hospitality to those who are radically difference from one's self" (185).

Yet, for Swinton, Jesus is he who ministers, Christian community is that which follows Jesus, while Elaine is still positioned outside, on the margins, the recipient of ministry, even in this renewed vision of belonging. But with Bartimaeus and with justice, we see a transformation in Christian community, because as Jesus receives Bartimaeus' faith and Bartimaeus follows him on the way, Jesus shows that Bartimaeus was never really on the outside. The fact that the same Jesus who beholds the blind man's injustice is on a trajectory toward disability himself makes Jesus' incarnation both miraculous and perilous. These miracles will be the stuff that bring about Jesus' crucifixion. Jesus' disorderly conduct, Jesus' upside-down, flies-in-the-face-of-the-authorities' ministry will be his downfall. Jesus will trade places with this Bartimaeus, who has been so belittled, ignored, devalued. And because Jesus' humanity is all about a kingdom, an incarnation that trades places, he listens rather than assumes. He does well to come in close to Bartimaeus' experiences when the rest of the world has left him to shout on the roadside.

Belonging cannot reinforce disabled persons as a ministry of non-disabled persons in the church: as such, it will not be an instrument of injustice. In an article entitled "From Belonging as Supercrip to Misfitting as Crip: Journeying through Seminary," Miriam Spies, an ordained pastor with cerebral palsy, talks about how she worked to fit in all her life, to prove her capacity, against that of her intellectually disabled peers, for instance, in school settings, or socially in church settings, in order to be accepted and understood as fitting in. However, in her final year of seminary, something shifted:

> In my quest to be an experienced "traditional leader" who loved designing liturgies, preached the Word, and extended pastoral care . . . I was and I am shaped by the compulsory . . . able-bodied culture that insists it is incumbent upon me to prove my abilities, to demonstrate that I can fit in and undertake this vocation like my able-bodied peers. Of course, I had conversations with my candidacy and internship committees as they discerned with me my suitability for ministry, but this experience was not unfamiliar for me. I believed I could change people's perception of me through being in relationship with them. It wasn't until my final year in seminary that I began to consider the ways in which my disability impacts my ministry and education. (2021, 299)

Spies' testimony reminds us that belonging may not be the sign of Christian community that we imagine it to be in that it often demands much more of disabled people than able-bodied people to fit and conform to a norm and standard that is not Jesus. Drawing on Robert McRuer's concept of "compulsory able-bodiedness," Spies argues that even at the heart of Christian ministry there can be a tacit assumption that able-bodied ways of being in the world are not just the norm but the preference, demanding, as McRuer writes, that "people with disabilities embody the affirmative answer to the unspoken question, 'Yes, but in the end, wouldn't you rather be more like me?'" (2006, 9). Even as belonging purports to reorient our relationships to Christ and one another, it cannot do that if it also demands compulsory able-bodiedness from people like Miriam and Elaine. Jesus cannot be Jesus if he is asking disabled people to shed their disabilities in order to be of service to him.

CENTERING DISABLED MINISTRY

This is why Nancy Eiesland's image of the scarred body of Jesus, *The Disabled God*, remains so powerful in that it radically refigures what has too often come to be at the heart of the gospel—a sense that those who are able-bodied are the insiders, while those who disabled are always on the outside trying to get in. In her 1998 book *Claiming Disability*, Simi Linton wrote that although they have been hidden from the public, things are changing as disabled people "come out not with brown woolen lap robes over our withered legs or dark glasses but in shorts and sandals, in overalls and business suits, dressed for play and work—straightforward, unmasked, unapologetic" (3). Linton continues,

> We are everywhere these days, wheeling and loping down the street, tapping our canes, sucking on our breathing tubes, following our guide dogs, puffing and sipping on the mouth sticks that propel our motorized chairs. We may drool, hear voices, speak in staccato syllables, wear catheters to collect our urine, or live a compromised immune system. (4)

In these poetic passages, Linton offers images of disabled bodies encroaching on institutions that clearly do not want them. "We further confound expectations," she writes, "when we have the temerity to emerge as forthright and resourceful people, nothing like the self-loathing, docile, bitter, or insentient fictional versions of ourselves that the public is most used to" (3). The disabled people's movement, with its emphasis on disability pride, rights, and acceptance, may seem to be in direct conflict with Bartimaeus' request to be cured of his blindness, and yet the movement's mantra of "Nothing about us without us" also makes space for justice to look different, depending on the person, their experience of disability, and their needs. In striving to understand Bartimaeus' particular situation, we must not discount the diversity of experiences of disability or the relationships among bodily autonomy, integrity, and justice.

But what the disabled people's movement has done so radically, that Jesus also does, is to center disabled people as insiders to ministry and justice. It seems rather obvious to remark that disabled people should be consulted when it comes to disability ministry, but their gifts, their insights, their faith are too often an afterthought rather than integral to how things are done. In fact, it is important to note that without disabled ministry, justice decidedly cannot be done. This is why it is so significant that Jesus recognizes Bartimaeus' faith, that Bartimaeus moves from the roadside to following Jesus on the way. The climax of this story is not

Bartimaeus being cured of his blindness but Bartimaeus finding his place as a minister in Jesus' kingdom.

DECOLONIZING JUSTICE

As an ethnographer, I am always asking questions, but it is not always easy for me to remain really open to the answers. After all, in remaining open to the answers, even someone else's answers about what justice looks like, I am in some sense yielding my experience to theirs. I am trying to see that the vision of justice that I held dear, for instance, for my daughter and disabled persons in America may actually foreclose justice for others. I am trying to remain open to the fact that Jesus' vision for justice may be more radical than I had previously imagined and that to try to articulate justice on my own will always be my downfall. Rather, as Jesus teaches, we need other voices to understand the complexity of the human experience. As Jesus teaches, justice does not belong to any of us if it does not belong to all of us.

The movement for disability rights did not end in 1990 with the Americans with Disabilities Act or the Individuals with Disabilities Education Act, but few of us tell the rest of the story. That story admits that legislation, inclusion, and accommodations have not brought the access disability activists were fighting for. The work is far from over. However, I think another reason that we don't tell the full history is that it makes white people in this country uncomfortable. For one, the vision for disability justice that emerged in the early 2000s in the United States identifies and critiques prejudice within the movement that undermines access for Black, brown, queer, and trans people. Therefore, disability justice advocates present a vision that does not just build rights and accommodations into an existing system but targets the system itself.

The original Disability Justice Collective was founded by Patty Berne, Mia Mingus, Leroy Moore, Eli Clare, and Sebastian Margaret in 2005. The movement can also be traced to Sins Invalid, the Disability Justice Performing Collective founded by Patty Berne and Leroy Moore, as well as the explosion of disability justice art and activism over the last decade, including the Disability Visibility Project, the Spoonie Collective, Deaf Poets Society, and Krip-Hop Nation, to name just a few. Many of the activists on Twitter whom I name in chapter 4 are also critical to the disability justice movement that Leah Lakshmi Piepzna-Samarasinha notes "did not happen because the able-bodied people decided to be nice to the cripples" (2018, 19). Poignantly, she continues,

[The movement for disability justice] happened because disabled queer and trans people of color started organizing, often with femme disabled Black and brown people in the lead. Much of that work has been done through writing, storytelling, and art as activism. Much of our coming together has been through zines, online disabled QT/POC communities, Tumblr and blog and social media posts, or through three people getting together at a kitchen table or a group Skype call to hesitantly talk about our lives, organize a meal train, share pills and trips, or post the thoughts we have about activism and survival at two in the morning. It is underdocumented, private work—work often not seen as "real activism." But it is the realest activism there is. This is how disability justice art and activism change the world and save lives. (2018, 19)

What gave birth in many ways to disability justice advocacy was the exclusion of Black, brown, queer, and trans activists from white disabled spaces, the recognition that the focus and the fruits of white disabled activism did not extend to Black, brown, queer, and trans people. Justice, or what looked like justice but was only for white people, had to be decolonized if it were truly to do justice in the world. What emerged was an unabashed yet expansive movement from inclusion toward justice anchored in particular stories and grounded on the margins. Black, brown, queer, and trans disabled people organized in free spaces online, around kitchen tables, and on Skype, because they would not settle for what white activists told them justice should look like.

This is why the ten principles of disability justice outlined by Patty Berne, and edited by Aurora Levins Morales and David Langstaff, on behalf of Sins Invalid begin with intersectionality—recognizing the varied shapes of disability experience as grounded in "race, gender, class, gender expression, historical moment, relationship to colonization, and so much more" (reprinted in Piepzna-Samarasinha 2018, 26). The next two highlight the importance of the leadership of the most impacted and the anti-capitalist politic, given how capitalism reinforces normalcy through productivity and labor. Principles four through seven, cross-movement solidarity, recognizing wholeness, sustainability, and commitment to cross-disability solidarity, express the sophisticated yet slow networked and wholistic work of disability justice that recognizes the integral yet embedded nature of disabled lives and concerns. As Piepzna-Samarasinha puts it,

When we do disability justice work, it becomes impossible to look at disability and not examine how colonialism created it. It becomes a priority to look at Indigenous ways of perceiving and understanding disability, for example. It becomes a space where we see that disability is all up in Black and brown/queer and trans communities—from Henrietta Lacks to Harriet Tubman, from the Black Panther Party's active support for disabled organizers' two-month occupation of the Department of Vocational Rehabilitation to force the passage of Section 504, the law mandating disabled access to public spaces and transportation, to the chronic illness and disability stories of second-wave queer feminists of color like Sylvia Rivera, June Jordan, Gloria Anzaldua, Audre Lorde, Marsha P. Johnson, and Barbara Cameron, whose lives are marked by bodily difference, trauma-surviving brilliance, and chronic illness but who mostly never used the term "disabled" to refer to themselves . . . (2018, 22–23)

Thus, the decolonizing work of disability justice distinguishes it from accommodations, inclusion, or diversity recognition. Disability justice advocates actively confront colonialism and its systems, often betraying the very institutions, nationalities, and politics to which they seem to belong in search of a broader, wholistic identity. The last three prongs of disability justice, interdependence, collective access, and collective liberation, seek to free one another in a collaborative move toward justice in which we take responsibility for one another and in which, as Sins Invalid proclaimed, "we move together, with no body left behind."

Although it would be imprecise to presume that the movement for disability justice speaks for the sixty-one million adults living with disabilities in the United States today, what emerges in the movement is an expansive vision for justice that does not solve problems for disabled people but recognizes that greater coalitional conversation is critical in collectively figuring out how to deconstruct systems of complex oppression. The movement also locates resources within the disability community, not just in terms of leadership and insight but in experiences of suffering that pinpoint care as a relational, collaborative strategy rather than a colonizing force. Justice cannot be imposed but must be relationally negotiated, worked out by disabled people and for disabled people so that it is sustainable, liberating, and meaningful.

CONCLUSION

Jesus does not use disabled people as object lessons; rather, Jesus' ministry with disabled people centers disabled people, their lives, their experiences, their suffering, and their injustice as critical to enacting the kingdom of God. This means that churches must receive the gift of disabled ministry and nurture the calls of disabled ministers and leaders in order to receive Jesus' vision for justice. Justice does not problem-solve for people; rather, it seeks Jesus with them. In Jesus' openness toward Bartimaeus, he reminds able-bodied people that they must not move on to their own visions for justice but rather appreciate the wisdom and insights of disabled persons when it comes to seeking Jesus' justice on the Earth. In becoming recipients of a vision for justice, the church celebrates the ministry and leadership of disabled people, making way for the Spirit to shake up the church and lead us toward renewed faithfulness.

6

Ministers Each and Every One

[1]I appeal to you therefore, brothers and sisters, by the mercies of God, to present your bodies as a living sacrifice, holy and acceptable to God, which is your spiritual worship. [2]Do not be conformed to this world, but be transformed by the renewing of your minds, so that you may discern what is the will of God—what is good and acceptable and perfect.

[3]For by the grace given to me I say to everyone among you not to think of yourself more highly than you ought to think, but to think with sober judgement, each according to the measure of faith that God has assigned. [4]For as in one body we have many members, and not all the members have the same function, [5]so we, who are many, are one body in Christ, and individually we are members one of another. [6]We have gifts that differ according to the grace given to us: prophecy, in proportion to faith; [7]ministry, in ministering; the teacher, in teaching; [8]the exhorter, in exhortation; the giver, in generosity; the leader, in diligence; the compassionate, in cheerfulness.

—Romans 12:1–8

INTRODUCTION

Each month at St. John Chrysostom in Wallingford, Pennsylvania, a sign language interpreter and a shortened liturgy, as well as disabled lectors, altar servers, and cantors, mark the "mass of inclusion." A few minutes down the road on Friday nights in Springfield, Pennsylvania, Tree of Life Presbyterian Church hosts Our Community Cup, a meal, coffeehouse, and karaoke session open to disabled and non-disabled folks who mill about, eating, drinking, chatting, and playing cards. On a Sunday afternoon in a noisy sanctuary in Hamilton, New Jersey, children and adults alike clamor to take hold of the "prayer rope" that comes down the aisle as they recite the Lord's Prayer together during a Joyful Noise service of worship for families with disabled children at Resurrection Lutheran Church.

These scenes are significant because we don't always see disabled people visible in worship. Instead, when it comes to worship, disabled people often present problems for congregations. Like Bartimaeus, shouting by the roadside, their bodies frequently do not conform to pews, altars, or pulpits, their voices may disrupt the solitude and reverence of sacred spaces, and their actions are often deemed inappropriate within a service of prescribed calls and responses. Indeed, throughout the scriptures it is notable that when disabled people are described, they often sit on the roadsides, on the outskirts of the temple, rather than inside the temple, so threatening were their bodies and their presence to the sanctity of the religious and social order.

When disabled people do show up to worship, sometimes they are included; they are welcomed into the sanctuary, they are handed bulletins, they may even be given directions as to where to sit and how to participate—but is this enough? What do we mean when we talk about something like "inclusive worship?" It may surprise readers to find that the churches described above in which disabled people were visible, present, and active in worship weren't necessarily ones with fully accessible buildings or perfect ministries. These churches, denominationally, demographically, aesthetically, and architecturally, had little in common. Rather, their worship looked consistent and characteristic of the creeds and traditions they claimed, but it was clear, as argued in chapters 2 and 3, that inclusion was not the end of worship but a mere beginning in ministry with disabled people. For each of these churches, although inclusive worship served as a signal to the community of their theology and welcome to ministry with disabled people, such worship was, in fact, part of a significant theological and cultural shift in the relationship between congregational worship and ministry.

Yet the services and ministries described at St. John's and Resurrection Lutheran happened but once a month, and the Our Community Cup night hosted weekly by Tree of Life was a fellowship night. Although they welcomed non-disabled and disabled people alike, some people might characterize them as segregated rather than integrated ministries, worship spaces set apart for disabled people from the normal, routinized worship of the church. Could they be separate, yet equal? And if they weren't divisive or dismissive, what purpose did they serve?

Many churches we talked with were quick to point out that they don't do segregated ministries for disabled people; rather, they heralded the moral and theological superiority of ministries and worship services of inclusion. Many congregational leaders and congregants were vehement that segregated ministry was exclusionary and discriminatory: disabled and non-disabled people should worship together. But this opposition between segregated and inclusive worship and ministry often proved to be a false and surprisingly flimsy construction. Although it was easy to demonize segregated ministry for its abuse of able-bodied power in relegating disabled people to a secondary and subservient role of recipients of ministry in the church, it was all too often the case that inclusive ministry did not actually resolve these power differentials but rather thrust them further underground. Indeed, in the typical space of the church, disabled people were not often prominent in using their gifts for ministry and leadership in worship. We did not meet many disabled council members, session members, deacons, or pastors.

Yet time and time again disabled people themselves defended the value of "separate" spaces. As nine-year-old Morrigan told me on the very first visit I made to her family's apartment, "I like Joyful Noise, because it's a place where my family can be together and worship." Morrigan seemed to be indicating that regular worship was not so much a space for *her* family, whereas Joyful Noise, a once-a-month separate service developed by Lutheran churches in New Jersey especially for families with disabled children, made her feel more connected to her family and comfortable in worship. Bailie, a twentysomething seminarian in the Presbyterian ordination process, fantasized about a church for mentally ill persons, where they could be free to express themselves. And Noah Buchholz, a Deaf pastor and scholar, stressed the need for Deaf Christians to have opportunities to worship God in their native language, American Sign Language (ASL), to say nothing of asserting leadership and autonomy over worship.

Building on the arguments of the previous chapters that identify ableism as the greatest barrier in congregational ministry with disabled people, in this chapter I draw attention to the way ableism often undermines "inclusive worship" by subtly demanding conformity from disabled people while maintaining power hierarchies between able-bodied and disabled leaders. Ultimately our research finds that separate spaces, elsewhere known in the literature as free spaces (Evans 1979; Evans and Boyte 1986; Polletta 1999) or user-led spaces (Barnes, Mercer, and Shakespeare 1999; Jacobs 2019), can offer important solidarity, creativity, critique, and resistance from outside that cannot often be cultivated inside traditional spaces. Indeed, in this chapter I demonstrate how separate worship and ministry spaces for disabled people intervened to challenge and transform general practices of congregational worship. These interventions did not just make congregational worship safer or more inclusive for disabled people but actually made worship more faithful and meaningful for the entire congregation.

In receiving critical perspectives from disabled people's experiences in worship, churches were invited into practices of worship that offered greater participation and freedom to all congregants. We see these churches being transformed by disabled practices of worship leadership in ways that inform contemporary understandings and practices of worship and human relationship with God. Disabled leadership in worship stands to invite broader participation, increased freedom, and interdependent leadership that unites the congregation in renewed, embodied sanctification of humanity and glorification of God (Saliers 1998, 22). Furthermore, enhanced participation in worship leads to renewed and refreshed faith formation for the congregation. Therefore, throughout our study, disabled people were helping our research team and their churches ask the far more important question: what is worship?

Ironically, in an environment where churches have been overly cerebral in their approach to belief and its subsequent practices (in varied traditions) of baptism, communion, confirmation, affirmation of faith, and membership (Swinton 2016), the different ways in which disabled people worship and learn often invite more participatory practices for others in worship and practice. Drawing on pedagogy scholar Paulo Freire's critique of education as oppressive and his case for the liberatory practice of teaching and learning, I argue that disabled people are transforming our congregants from passive recipients of worship to active participants in worship. In the Reformed tradition, the oft-repeated phrases "the priesthood of all believers" and "ministers, each and every one of us" hold little meaning in worship spaces where leadership and ministry are clustered in the pulpit, clergy, and able-bodied leadership. However, what we have seen among the churches with which we have studied is that God is working through disabled people to bring something new, something freer, and something more interdependent to contemporary worship, if congregations will be willing to receive it. This is part of a larger shift toward leadership that is more diffuse, egalitarian, and interdependent, a topic the next few chapters take up as well.

PRAYERS OF THE PEOPLE

It happened gradually, I think, although as with anything that happens gradually, I'm rather powerless to describe it. Over the several years I pastored a church in Central Jersey, the prayer requests, especially the requests of intellectually and developmentally disabled adults, began to punctuate, flood, and inflect our weekly services with the neediness and the messiness of human life, alongside the often-uncomfortable conviction that worship involved laying these prayers bare before God and one another. I used to find it incongruous and unsettling, especially that a prayer for healing, for instance, would butt up directly against praise for a new job or a birth. But gradually, I also started to see my own faithlessness in my eagerness to mediate and control these requests, to order them in such a way as would be truly pleasing to God. Could they not be pleasing as the people uttered them? Could they not be signs of active faith? After each, I would proclaim, "Lord, in your mercy," or "Lord, in thanksgiving," and the congregation would reply together, "Hear our prayer."

Many disabled people waited impatiently for the time for prayer to come in the service, shooting their hands up the second I invited the prayers to come. And many of the prayers were ruddy, rugged, unpolished, and lilting; "God's gotta do something about my back," one woman chided, "I'm really uncomfortable." Another woman living with depression and borderline personality disorder prayed every week for her depression to get better. Another young autistic man made periodic announcements about when he would be absent from church during the upcoming holidays due to his warehouse job.

After the worship service, some people would complain that their prayers were dominated by "the disabled people." Some people complained that each person should be given time for only one request: getting two wasn't fair. Rhonda, an older, intellectually disabled woman, often complained that she wanted to know more about God and she wanted to learn how to pray. Ironically, she was one of the most vocal during prayer time in the service, so my pastor colleague and I wrestled earnestly with how we could support her desire to know God more and to have a more active prayer life—we worried that she had begun to equate prayer with this specific time in the service. On communion Sundays, for instance, when we skipped this extemporaneous prayer time in exchange for a more efficient, written liturgy of prayer, Rhonda complained, "We didn't have prayer today. I didn't get to pray." Reminding her that prayer could take place in myriad ways provided little solace. She wanted to see and experience that God and others had heard her prayer.

Perhaps the most striking part of these prayers of the people at this otherwise rather unremarkable, small Presbyterian church was that they took something people could have actually done alone or clergy could have done with efficiency and expertise and made it deliberately collective, corporate, and participatory. Of course, that was not the intent—there was little intent behind how this prayer time came to be. Instead it was made what it was by the people who chose to pray and share their prayers together on any given Sunday. That is what made the prayers so powerful—they intruded, they demanded, they impinged upon each person at that service. You couldn't *not* hear them, you couldn't *not* respond to them; by participating in worship, suddenly you were implicated in a reality of your neighbor's that you hadn't chosen to receive, let alone bear.

In an interview with Jan Ammon, Princeton Theological Seminary's Dean of the Chapel, and Noah Buchholz, Deaf pastor and PhD student, Noah told a story about attending a hearing church and watching an older man who was struggling to walk come to the pulpit to read scripture:

> [H]e was trying to put the paper on the podium, and the papers crashed all over the floor, absolutely everywhere, and you could see his embarrassment. He turned red in the face, and everyone sat there in stoic silence. And [there were] maybe 10 people in the choir, sitting right next to that man, and easily any one of them could have gone helped him pick up the papers, but instead, they all sat like statues. And the man, you could see he was very embarrassed, was picking up his papers, and then he began to speak.
>
> And I thought, "Something like that would never happen in a Deaf church." Maybe five or six people would scramble to come and help him pick up those papers with him. I thought, it's so important that worship give a lot of room for flexibility. Because that leads to inviting grace into worship.[1]

As Noah named those gifts of flexibility and grace that he has experienced in Deaf worship, I pressed him and Jan with the question that came up over and over in our research: "But what is worship after all?"

Notably, even those who lead worship for a living struggled a bit with the question. Jan began to talk about the way students leave their school bags at the doors of the Seminary Chapel for worship, so if you come late, you can see that visible symbol that people have left these things at the door and have come to engage with one another in

---

[1] Fieldnotes, October 29, 2019.

a different way. Noah began to talk about how traditional worship has often been harmful to Deaf people, how Deaf people were once not permitted to be priests because they were not able to physically say aloud, "This is my body, this is my blood." Deaf people were not allowed to sign in church, so they would huddle outside the sanctuary together and try to understand what was going on (see Lewis 2007 and Portolano 2020). All of this prompted Noah to reply that whatever worship is, it has to be relational, an idea with which he credits Jan, and one that came up over and over in the interview when Jan talked about planning services that are neither soliloquy nor performance but create space for God to move.

I believe Noah and Jan are right, but in order to really comprehend the meaning of something like relational worship, we also have to grapple with "un-relational" worship—Deaf people standing outside the sanctuary because they were not allowed to sign inside, no one picking up the papers for this older man in worship, or the protests from my congregation that disabled prayers were taking up too much time or that no one should be allowed more than one request. The implication in these accusations, complaints, and omissions is that people should not make demands on God and one another in worship. But how can one have relationship without obligation? How can one have intimacy, fellowship, and communion without mutual formation? And how can we be mutually formed without being implicated, inconvenienced, involved in God's and one another's lives?

Although Rhonda came to her pastors wanting to grow closer to Jesus and learn how to pray, I think her own presumed intrusion into the space of worship brought valuable theological insight into how it is we are formed in Christ and how it is we pray. Rhonda knew that we are shaped by how we pray—that it wasn't that God didn't hear our prayers on those communion Sundays, but that when we didn't hear one another's prayers, this presented a problem for our community of faith. If we were being shaped by praying together, not hearing one another's prayers one Sunday a month still caused us to forget both the beauty and the imposition that it is to pray together. Especially on the Sunday we gathered to commune with Jesus, how could we forget one another and ourselves before God? She detected a withholding in our worship, due to demands of time and order, that ironically kept us at a distance from one another on the very Sunday we sought to commune with Jesus.

On the other hand, Joanne Van Sant, pastor at Friends to Friends, a Reformed congregation in North Jersey comprised almost entirely of people with intellectual and developmental disabilities, tells us that on communion Sunday, worship pretty much consists of communion and, of necessity, little else:

> For us, communion is our own design. So you come forward and you get a piece of bread but you drink your juice out of the cup and you take your cup put it in the basket and walk around church back to your seat. But when we do communion with 70 or 80 people, our whole worship time is communion. We have announcements and prayers and then we're into communion liturgy because for us to do that takes a while. I never liked that people who couldn't come forward had to wait until the end.[2]

Joanne continues, "For us, communion is not always quick, because for some people it takes time to chew, they may not have teeth, they may drink with a straw." In talking with Joanne, the abundant space made for everyone to take communion in worship was striking, especially given the failure of my own worshipping community to take seriously the demands of its disabled congregants on communion Sunday.

Across our multidenominational study, communion frequently appeared (as it does in chapter 3) as a gatekeeping activity for churches with respect to disabled people. On the one hand, we might say that churches struggled to accommodate the needs of disabled people at communion, but that retelling profoundly eclipses and minimizes the agency of disabled people in the act of worship. Rather, across contexts, we should be clear that we also witnessed disabled people crying out to partake of communion. We witnessed the active role of disabled people in worship.

For instance, one night when Arundel Clarke was putting his autistic son, J'den, to bed, J'den asked him, "Dad, does Jesus love me?" "Yeah, of course Jesus loves you, buddy," Arundel remembers responding. And then, directly after, J'den replied, "Well, then I want the body and blood of Jesus." Arundel says he walked out of the room and called to his wife, Jessica, bewildered, and said, "Jess, I think J'den just asked me for communion."

Jess and Arundel, who are Lutheran church leaders, said they were reticent to push J'den's first communion, but when he asked and kept asking, they made arrangements for him to study with the pastor so that he could understand what it meant, and he made his first communion six months or so later. "And it explained a lot," they ruminated, "because he would have these huge breakdowns as we were going up for communion

---

    [2] Fieldnotes, November 5, 2019.

at the altar, and we couldn't figure out what was going on. Eventually we could tell that he wanted it, and of course everyone just wanted to give it to him, but we wanted him to take his time to understand what he was doing."[3]

There is no mistaking in J'den's insistent words that he wants to be included in and receive the sacrament: indeed, he demands to receive Jesus. Yet, even his parents, who encourage him to make his first communion, are understandably eager to quell his outbursts, which pose a seeming disruption to worship. There's a perception on the part of the congregation, even on the part of J'den's parents, that his breakdowns are out of place.

Meanwhile for Jeb, who is a nonverbal adult with intellectual and developmental disabilities, researcher Lottie finds that his attendance and participation at a large evangelical church goes swimmingly, except on the Sundays on which they take communion. When Lottie accompanies him to church one Sunday, she notes that Jeb stands and vocalizes with songs he knows during the opening worship at an evangelical church, his caregiver, Jamal, at his side. During intermission, church members mill around and greet Jeb, whose mother attended the church up until her death. Jeb and his caregiver Jamal communicate mostly through touch and sound. When the pastor begins to show a video about Pharaoh that portrays him as a monster, Jeb vocalizes distressed noises, and Jamal guides him out to the narthex.

When they return, it is time for communion, and Jamal whispers to Lottie, "Oh, this is awkward. This happened once before, Jeb doesn't eat solids and one time the minister came up . . . we usually just stay in our seats." Everyone files forward to receive the elements then returns to their seats, while Jeb and Jamal stay seated. At the moment at which the pastor proclaims, "This is my body broken for you," Jeb lurches into Jamal's arms and flings his arms around his neck. The room is filled with a soft crunch, crunch, as the congregation chews the crackers. Lottie keeps her eyes on Jeb and Jamal—denied the eucharist, they nonetheless find communion with each other in this clumsy embrace, Jamal trying to keep himself upright under the weight of Jeb's arms, and Jeb with no intention of letting go.[4]

Disabled people help identify some of the problems and biases in contemporary worship by calling churches to new forms of relational worship that demonstrate an active, disruptive, unbridled pursuit of

---

[3] Fieldnotes, May 29, 2019.

[4] Fieldnotes, Nov 2, 2019.

Jesus. However, as we have seen above, these critical insights are often happening in the shadows—for instance, Jeb's embrace of Jamal—or off to the sides, like Joyful Noise's separate worship service on Sunday afternoons. How do we make sense of this separation and the role it plays in congregational life today? How do we distinguish between separated and segregated spaces? And if inclusion is not the answer, what is it that we are after?

SEPARATE NOT SEGREGATED

By the time Pastor Maggi was called to Resurrection Lutheran Church, they had been running a Joyful Noise service once a month for about two years, modeled after another Lutheran Church in the area. The previous pastor at Resurrection and the Clarke family, Arundel, Jess, J'den, and Morrigan, had helped start up Joyful Noise as a place for disabled persons and their families to worship. Once a month, between ten and twenty disabled people and their families gathered for worship in their sanctuary. Jess told me they had families come from all over New Jersey: for some, this was their only church community, the only place they felt they could bring their kids and their families and be themselves. Jess and Arundel talked about how they had canceled the once-a-month service when it fell on Easter Sunday the previous year. "Boy, did we learn a big lesson," they said. "Consistency is key. The families were very upset. We assumed that they wouldn't want Joyful Noise because it was Easter, and it was just the opposite. From that point on, no matter what, we never canceled," they chuckled.

At a glance, Joyful Noise functions somewhat like a mission to disabled people. Although it was started through a generous donation by one of its congregants and made possible by volunteers, it's not highly attended by families at Resurrection Lutheran. Rather, it is more of an outward-facing ministry of the church to which others are invited. It's also seemingly segregated: few non-disabled people or people who are not connected to disabled people by family or close relationship participate in the service. So what role does something like Joyful Noise play in disability ministry and the church? Is it progressive? Is it faithful? What does it do?

In an early conversation with Pastor Maggi, it was clear that because she was so new to the church and Joyful Noise was relatively new to it, it was difficult to ascertain what the service was doing theologically and where the ministry was headed. When I asked her about the purpose and theology behind Joyful Noise, she originally expressed that she thought it was making a space for parents to be freed of some of the guilt and self-judgment they often felt when their children did not conform to typical worship services. "You know, like fulfilling Jesus' command to care for the least of these," she gestured to Matthew 25. "You can't care for every least of these, of course," she reflected, but she anchored Joyful Noise as a particular ministry to families in need that Resurrection could and did offer.

And yet, when asked to reflect on the particularities of Joyful Noise, Pastor Maggi mused thoughtfully, "The Spirit, I look at this right now and I see the Spirit moving, but I can't define it. With our Joyful Noise ministry, I don't see us growing us this ministry like you would want to grow your church, I see this as a deepening." She went on to share that one afternoon at Joyful Noise she didn't have anyone to help her serve communion. "[It just kind of] happened out of nowhere," she explains.

> I looked up and I said who's my communion assistant and nobody came forward, and I said, okay, who wants to be my communion assistant and this little boy went I'll do it, and I said, okay, come on, and you know what? He knew what to say, I didn't even have to tell him to say, This is the blood of Christ shed for you. He knew it. The only thing I maybe had to do was from the pulpit, get him to hold the chalice with more reverence, maybe then like this (she gestures and laughs), but he was so happy, so happy.[5]

Pastor Maggi goes onto say that because this boy served communion in Joyful Noise, other kids wanted to do so, not just in Joyful Noise, but in the typical service.

> [So] the giving of communion seems to be of interest to typical kids, and I thought okay, not only can they do it in the Joyful Noise service, they can do it in the typical service as well. So things that start over there [in Joyful Noise] can transfer to the typical service, whereas I would have expected that things in the regular service would have transferred to the Joyful Noise service, but it seems the other way around.[6]

The contrast Pastor Maggi identified between growing the church and deepening life in the Spirit is clear in the example she shares above of what Joyful Noise offers. Within the ecosystem of the church, Pastor Maggi nurtures Joyful Noise as a creative, celebratory space, where not only is there potential to try new things in worship, but people within

---

[5]   Fieldnotes, June 11, 2019.
[6]   Fieldnotes, June 11, 2019.

that space, namely children and disabled children, experience value and opportunity in their own leadership. Relatedly, that space has value for the congregation as a whole. The perception may have been that Joyful Noise would fulfill Jesus' command to care for the least of these, yet Pastor Maggi notes that the lessons from Joyful Noise filter into regular worship, offering greater active participation and leadership opportunities for laypeople.

Since the publication of Sara Evans' *Personal Politics* in 1979, the terminology of free spaces and their analogues, such as "protected spaces," "safe spaces," "spatial preserves," "havens," and "spheres of cultural autonomy" (to name just a few), have abounded in sociological and political science scholarship. Twenty years after Evans, Francisca Polletta summarized the term as identifying three main attributes: these are small-scale settings that are, first, removed from the direct control of dominant groups; second, participation is voluntary; and third, they "generate cultural challenges that precedes or accompanies [sic] political mobilization" (1999, 1). Although we have already begun to see and will see further evidence of the cultural challenges that stimulate theological dynamism (the third point), the first two are equally important. For spaces to offer freedom, they must offer enough autonomy that not only is participation voluntary, but they are primarily controlled by disabled people. "User-led," "disabled-led" groups, or Disabled People's Organizations (DPOs), are a critical pillar of the disabled people's movement in that they seek to criticize, change, or influence society, rather than offer therapeutic supports, which has been the function of many non-user-led groups for disabled people (Barnes, Mercer, and Shakespeare 1999).

In some cases, like the Deaf church or even the Black church, this question of control requires little explanation. But with respect to, for instance, adults with I/DD, or with a space like Joyful Noise that involves many children with I/DD but is primarily led by non-disabled adults, who is in control may be questionable. This is where considering definitions of freedom and autonomy with respect to the disabled people's movement and the independent living movement is insightful. For instance, Simon Brisenden, in his early writing on independent living (1986), reclaims—much as disabled people have reclaimed the term disability—the term independence. Brisenden writes, for instance, "We do not use the word 'independent' to mean someone who can do everything for themself, but to indicate someone who is taking control of their life and is choosing how that life is led" (1998, 26–27). Brisenden goes on to explain that communities and societies need to be restructured so that independence is not a gift or a privilege, but a right for all people (27). Since Brisenden, many disability justice advocates have criticized the goal of independence itself, arguing for the pursuit of something more like interdependent living, which confronts neoliberal capitalist modes of being more broadly (Fineman 2005, 2008; Piepzna-Samarasinha 2008).

This, in fact, raises the question and the implicit critique as to why the church itself is not and cannot be a "free space" within society. Ostensibly what disabled people call attention to when they insist on and participate in free spaces set apart from dominant groups is that the church remains a place controlled by dominant groups in which they do not have freedom of expression and, therefore, they need separate space. In her thesis work, Naomi Lawson Jacobs notes that in the UK, for instance, informal activists and user-led church groups are emerging, but they still tend to operate on the edges of established churches and online, because it has been difficult to gain traction or recognition from mainstream groups (2019, 34–35). Jacobs argues that this is because a pastoral model of power continues to operate in the church, addressing disability primarily through individualism, charity, and care, rather than a paradigm of advocacy and justice (2019, 3).

Indeed, disabled-led groups emerged in the disabled people's movement because of segregation, enforced and patrolled by dominant groups, intending to keep disabled people out of spaces that did not belong to them. Thus, user-led free spaces necessarily have a critical edge to them: the formation of Joyful Noise, however structured by parents and families who are not necessarily disabled people themselves, nevertheless functions as a critique of the able-bodied prejudice that underlies traditional worship. Thus only because it stands in tension with the traditional service can it help illuminate what is lacking, what needs reform about the way worship has traditionally been done.

It stands to be pointed out, then, that if it is not primarily disabled people, families of disabled people, or lay people advocating for that separate space, but rather those in dominant groups, that separate space runs the risk of reinforcing segregation rather than nurturing gifts and stoking resistance. This is because the space is then never truly separate, nor does it provide freedom from dominant modes of power and being. By contrast, disabled people and their families can invite established, non-disabled leaders, like Pastor Maggi, into their spaces, and they can still serve as places of freedom and resistance as long as such a group maintains its own rituals, practices, and culture. Meanwhile, by playing host to disabled-led groups, mainstream congregations demonstrate their support for disabled ministry rather than their need to control it. But congregations tamp down the goodness of freedom and the creative potential for the movement of the Spirit if they either overtly or subtly demand conformity from free spaces. Indeed, the congregation is all too often invested in being in charge of its own transformation rather than trusting that God, Jesus, and the Spirit will bring transformation in wild, surprising, and uncontrollable ways.

Likewise, my interview with Pastor Maggi presented two competing theologies of ministry and worship with disabled people: on the one hand, she had seen and experienced firsthand this strange movement of the Spirit over at Joyful Noise and witnessed to the way in which folks at Joyful Noise were living out their passions faithfully in a way that was deepening their faith and worship as a congregation. On the other hand, she felt a need to capitalize on it—for instance, talking about the twenty families with children who came on a Sunday to Joyful Noise, she lamented a bit that their congregation did not even have twenty families with children; they could hardly get twenty families to come to anything. "So maybe we do a service for families, maybe they separate for the Bible part and they come back together and eat and play games once or twice a month?" she tossed out casually.

There is absolutely nothing wrong with Pastor Maggi's eagerness to support and provide a place for families, but Joyful Noise's liminal agitation, its boundary-challenging ministry, demonstrates the pastoral challenge of separate spaces. Able-bodied leaders often have an anxiety and an urgency to bring people together. However, we need to stop and explore how much of that anxiety reflects a real need from people in our pews or society—or, rather, reflects our own discomfort with the failure of the church to receive not just the gifts but the prophetic criticism of the people it has snubbed and harmed. In my eyes, Pastor Maggi was right where she needed to be in her ministry, but it is important to point out that it was anything but easy or comfortable for her. It was hard for her to be on the receiving side of change rather than the creating side—on the receiving side, she and Resurrection Lutheran had to grapple with the injustices that made Joyful Noise both necessary and a force for change in the first place. On the receiving side, she had to relinquish control, even over worship, the very thing over which pastors preside! On the receiving side, she had to do this dance of welcoming critique in order to welcome transformation and the Spirit. The Spirit, it turned out, needed its own space to flourish and do this work of deepening. There was no guidebook or five-year plan for that.

CULTIVATING CRITICAL RESISTANCE

"At Our Community Cup," Pastor Pam McShane had said, "people don't have to be anything for anybody else. They can just be themselves." Pam went onto say that in nearly every other space for disabled adults, whether it be their day programs, their therapy programs, or even their own group homes, something was always required of them to prove themselves or conform to what programs or people wanted of them. In hosting Our Community Cup, Pastor Pam and Tree of Life Presbyterian Church had intentionally sought to create a space for fellowship and leisure, and people clearly felt that they belonged there.

Spencer and Sam, a father-daughter pair, came every Friday night and called it their "Friday date night." After the meal, they usually set up shop at a table near the front where they got an Uno game going for anyone who wanted to play. Mike, who is autistic, talked a lot about the dangers in his neighborhood and told us that a bullet just went through his window last month. He wants to move. But in contrast to the other autism support groups he goes to, "where everyone sits in a circle and shares," he said emphatically that "OCC is the best social thing in my life right now." On December 13, up on stage, several folks crooned Christmas carols in the background, while others sipped on coffee around the room or busied themselves coloring a large mural at the back of the room. "This is going to take us forever," one woman observed while looking at the mural, and we all laughed together.

OCC had the distinct feel of a free social space in that although activities would be provided on occasion—for instance karaoke, and even, on one night, a visit from yoga goats—there was no pressure to do these activities or all be together doing the same thing. After Pastor Pam would make some brief announcements and say a blessing, a meal would be served, but people would go up casually, at their leisure, watching for the line to die down, not everyone ate, and no one seemed anxious for people to get up in an orderly fashion. Activities were presented but not pushed—the point, it seemed, was for people to have an opportunity to socialize in whatever way they saw fit, but nothing was required.

OCC also rather bewildered our researchers, especially on the first few outings, because it was not readily apparent who had disabilities and who did not. People at OCC shared generously and effortlessly about their lives with our researchers; some mentioned disability, some did not, but in this free social space, it just did not really seem to matter. There were often aides who sat at the edges of the room, chatting with one another, but even this did not bother Pastor Pam. "I want them [the aides] to know that they're welcome to take part in whatever they want, but if this is social space for them, where they feel like they're not on duty for once, that also seems great." Pam names some of the flexibility that OCC had cultivated, not just for disabled people but for many people; there was a contentedness, a suspension of time, an air of celebration at OCC that felt novel, comforting, even worshipful.

One Friday night, Pam walked us down the hall and showed us some of the bulletins from their Sunday worship service. She talked about how they'd added these icons next to the order of worship to help everyone follow along, even folks who don't read. They'd adapted the music to be more repetitive and meditative, singing the same songs over and over so everyone could learn them. They'd begun to use drama to tell the stories of scripture, and Pam noted that these adaptations made worship better for everyone, not just disabled people. "It's hard for Presbyterians to worship with fewer words," Pam chuckled, "but we're trying!" They didn't necessarily make these adaptations for folks from OCC—there were only a few who came to Sunday worship, because many couldn't get transportation or had to work—but they made these adaptations because of what they'd learned, felt, and experienced at OCC. Here was another way in which a seemingly frivolous free social space intervened in Christian worship in instrumental ways.

At OCC, disabled people are free to mill about, engage in activities, and explore their desires freely. At Joyful Noise and in the prayers of people at my congregation, disabled people demand participation in the elements of worship—they are actors in the worship service. By contrast, however, traditional worship, with the clergy at the helm and congregants in the pews, has widely "passified" congregants, placing them in a mere receiving mode. Thus, because disabled people faithfully demand and seek out participation, they critically call attention to ways in which worship is lacking, inviting congregations to the active pursuit of Jesus, participatory practices, and greater freedom in worship.

In 1968, Brazilian education theorist Paulo Freire published *Pedagogy of the Oppressed*, in which he argued that education had become yet another instrument of oppression. According to Freire, in typical classrooms all around the world, teachers objectified students by enlisting them to conform to immovable relationships of oppression with those in power. Freire famously contrasted the banking model of education with the problem-posing model. In the banking model, students become receptacles or containers of knowledge that are filled by the teacher (1993, 71–72). The teacher possesses the knowledge and the students are mere depositories (72). The teacher is the Subject, the students the Object, and as the students are educated, they become further entrenched in the oppressive relations of power that drain them of their very humanity.

But for Freire, humanness lies in freedom and critical consciousness: therefore, in the problem-posing model of education, students confront and collapse the vertical mode of education by asking questions that make reality and the world around them the classroom, rather than focusing on the matters imposed by the teacher. "The students—no longer docile learners—are now critical co-investigators in dialogue with the teacher," Freire writes. As he summarizes,

> Whereas banking education anesthetizes and inhibits creative power, problem-posing education involves a constant unveiling of reality. The former attempts to maintain the *submersion* of consciousness; the latter strives for the emergence of consciousness and the critical intervention in reality. (1993, 81)

As worship scholar Don Saliers has written, "What is done in our public worship of God rehearses who we are to be in our life relationships. Issues of justice and power are symbolized in worship services, whether we are aware of this or not" (1998, 30). Clearly, the church cannot be a free space if the same politics of oppression that operate in the world play out in our sanctuaries, not just alienating clergy from congregants but anesthetizing creative power, sublimating consciousness, and failing to interrogate the oppressive nature of reality. Of course, historical innovations in the life of the church, like the Protestant Reformation and, more recently, Vatican II, have worked to identify such tensions within congregational life and propose the way forward for needed reform. The Reformation emphasized the agency of everyday congregants by recognizing their direct access to God and their common yet distinct vocation of discipleship as "the priesthood of all believers." In Vatican II, not only did the mass enter the language of the common people but the Constitution of the Sacred Liturgy spends nearly five paragraphs emphasizing the importance of the "full, conscious, and active participation" of the congregation in worship (Pope John Paul VI 1963).

But how can individuals become "conscious" if the very institutions in which they worship have not only taught them how to worship but, in the process, "passified" their ways of knowing about God? Freire writes,

> The more students work at storing the deposits entrusted to them, the less they develop the critical consciousness which would result from their interventions in the world as transformers of that world. The

more completely they accept the passive role imposed on them, the more they tend to adapt to the world as it as and the fragmented view of reality deposited in them. (1993, 73)

Freire is writing about education, not worship, and he is using the concept of consciousness to refer to critical engagement with the world and one's relationship to it, rather than to one's relationship with God. However, if we return to the hypothesis that worship is relational, then, as Noah said, if that critical dialogue between ourselves and God is constrained by the very structures or order of worship, we certainly lack both consciousness and freedom.

The trouble is that in eagerness to free people and to solve the problem of the lack of consciousness, freedom, and relationship in worship, reform has tended to come from the top down. Even in the Reformation or Vatican II, to a certain extent, the way of reform was to simply give more power to the people—but as Freire has pointed out, the bonds of oppression are not easily loosed by the oppressor. Freire himself has become something of a household name in Western education programs, but as Natalie Wigg-Stevenson points out (2018), reading Freire in an elite, dominant group should provoke a different response than reading Freire from the underside of empire. As Freire himself writes,

> The truth is that the oppressed are not "marginals," are not people living "outside" society. They have always been "inside"—inside the structure which made them "beings for others." The solution is not to "integrate" them into the structure of oppression, but to transform that structure so that they can become "beings for themselves." Such transformation, of course, would undermine the oppressors' purposes; hence, their utilization of the banking concept of education to avoid the threat of student *conscientizacao*. (1993, 74)

Thus, approaches to ministry, like inclusion, that focus on integration but maintain the structures of power will always maintain the conditions for oppression. Yet transformation of the structure of oppression also serves to undermine and disrupt the oppressors' purposes. Like Pastor Maggi, clergy have tended to dream of and envision pastoral solutions to perceived ecclesial problems. But letting the congregation itself pose the very problems to address starts to move transformation out of the hands of those in power and create opportunities for transformation.

CONCLUSION

If able-bodied people in congregations create separate spaces for disabled people, they will be hard pressed to transcend the confines and routines of congregational worship and practice and will easily tend toward segregated spaces. But if able-bodied congregations invest in and nurture free spaces where disabled people are experiencing freedom, as this chapter shows, they are then doing work that ministers not just to disabled people but to the whole church. Rather than require that disabled people come to worship in places and spaces that may not work for them, congregations can put their resources into disabled ministry and worship, trusting God to bear fruit in that ministry, because disabled people are being dignified and equipped through disabled ministry and leadership. This is a hard sell—ultimately the church often wants to have something to show for its efforts, something tangible to display to the community. And the critiques of separate ministries are widespread and loud. "Why do you need to have a separate service for people with disabilities?" people will ask. "Shouldn't you all be together?" many will chide. As Pastor Maggi lamented, although many people participated in supporting the Joyful Noise service, few people from Resurrection Lutheran participated in worship—it was mostly people from the outside.

But that was certainly demonstrative of the problem. The regular worship service wasn't ready to receive the ministry and leadership of people with disabilities, except by proxy—except when that transformative work of the Spirit was so dynamic and didactic that it simply could not be ignored. Therefore, the challenges for congregations that are hosting or supporting separate ministries and relinquishing control for the Spirit to move are both to witness to the goodness and freedom of those Spirit-led spaces and to be willing to receive their critical feedback as a way of always reforming. It is clear from our research that people with disabilities and their families knew what they needed and recognized it when they saw it. "I like Joyful Noise, because it is a place where my family can be together and worship," nine-year-old Morrigan articulated. One father compared the atmosphere at Joyful Noise at St. Thomas Lutheran in Brick, New Jersey, to being at a Yankee game with other Yankees fans, knowing that you're all on the same team together, and everyone can let themselves go, be comfortable and spontaneous. As Mike at OCC said, "This is the best thing in my life right now." This kind of freedom, spontaneity, and participation in worship needs to be celebrated where it is found, but too often churches are worried that because it's happening outside of the regular or traditional space of worship, it is somehow not good enough, remedial, or minor. Instead, by investing in and celebrating these ministries, congregations can help nurture gifts for ministry and leadership among people who would not have encountered them in typical church spaces.

Furthermore, by receiving the critical value of lessons from these separate worship spaces, congregations recognize their prophetic value in ministry and leadership and amplify their gifts. The challenge with such Spirit-led transformation is that it cannot be staged or forced but must happen organically. It also cannot happen if the congregation loses touch with the separate ministry, takes control over the separate ministry, or refuses to receive from the separate ministry. This confessional orientation to ministry must be evident in relationships between congregations and disabled free spaces in order that these spaces not be overrun with ableism and ableist leadership and that congregations not shield themselves with their ableism. This is a messy, uncomfortable process—indeed, Pastor Maggi often found herself wanting to make Joyful Noise into something that served or reflected the wider church. But her faithfulness in respecting the integrity and space of Joyful Noise allowed its critical tension to flourish and to encroach upon worship practices at Resurrection. Too often, of course, congregations do not really want to change—they do not really want to receive ministry and leadership from elsewhere—but if this critical openness cannot be cultivated, God cannot do anything new in our midst.

Finally, the point of this chapter has not been to lay groundwork for integration of congregational worship between non-disabled and disabled people. Rather, the point of this chapter has been to show how so many disabled people are in radical pursuit of Jesus in worship in ways that Christian worship desperately needs. J'den and his family, Jeb, Rhonda, Sam, Spencer, and Mike all remind us that when disabled people show up with expectations to meet God in worship, that is a good and right and prophetic thing. Their expectations create space for disabled people to be themselves and for God to be God, and we may be the ones who need to move aside if that ministry is to happen.

It can be easy to see this as purely a mainline Protestant problem, as Protestant churches often emphasize intellectual preaching or long, responsive liturgies than can be prohibitive to people with I/DD. But in the evangelical world, a professionalism and production value in worship has become prohibitive to people with disabilities as well. Steeped in ableism, congregations and their worship are often spaces that do not feel comfortable or welcoming to many people with disabilities and their families, and this is a problem that able-bodied people cannot solve with new paraments or better liturgies. Indeed, the point of this chapter has been to show that these problems in worship are not just cultural but ecclesial and theological problems. They demonstrate our contemporary passivity as Christians in worship, which shows that we neither believe nor experience God as active in our lives. We imagine and extol ourselves as independent, but in our independence, we have no need or desire for God or one another.

But disabled people invite us to worship God with that desire and obligation as central and vital to faith. Prayers that intercede with God and others remind us that we are instruments of faith in one another's lives. A desire not just to receive but to serve communion reminds us that we are all both guests and hosts at the table of Jesus. One of the biggest effects of the sin of ableism is the way it alienates us from one another and from God. That sin cannot be ameliorated through mere integration or inclusion, especially if it is driven by able-bodied clergy and congregations—but receiving the Spirit's radical call to freedom and participation in worship may awaken us to listen and behold our neighbors afresh.

7

A Disabled Critique of Christian Leadership

[11]We set sail from Troas and took a straight course to Samothrace, the following day to Neapolis, [12]and from there to Philippi, which is a leading city of the district of Macedonia and a Roman colony. We remained in this city for some days. [13]On the sabbath day we went outside the gate by the river, where we supposed there was a place of prayer; and we sat down and spoke to the women who had gathered there. [14]A certain woman named Lydia, a worshipper of God, was listening to us; she was from the city of Thyatira and a dealer in purple cloth. The Lord opened her heart to listen eagerly to what was said by Paul. [15]When she and her household were baptized, she urged us, saying, "If you have judged me to be faithful to the Lord, come and stay at my home." And she prevailed upon us.

[16]One day, as we were going to the place of prayer, we met a slave-girl who had a spirit of divination and brought her owners a great deal of money by fortune-telling. [17]While she followed Paul and us, she would cry out, "These men are slaves of the Most High God, who proclaim to you a way of salvation." [18]She kept doing this for many days. But Paul, very much annoyed, turned and said to the spirit, "I order you in the name of Jesus Christ to come out of her." And it came out that very hour.

[19]But when her owners saw that their hope of making money was gone, they seized Paul and Silas and dragged them into the market-place before the authorities. [20]When they had brought them before the magistrates, they said, "These men are disturbing our city; they are Jews [21]and are advocating customs that are not lawful for us as Romans to adopt or observe." [22]The crowd joined in attacking them, and the magistrates had them stripped of their clothing and ordered them to be beaten with rods. [23]After they had given them a severe flogging, they threw them into prison and ordered the

jailer to keep them securely. [24]Following these instructions, he put them in the innermost cell and fastened their feet in the stocks.

[25]About midnight Paul and Silas were praying and singing hymns to God, and the prisoners were listening to them. [26]Suddenly there was an earthquake, so violent that the foundations of the prison were shaken; and immediately all the doors were opened and everyone's chains were unfastened. [27]When the jailer woke up and saw the prison doors wide open, he drew his sword and was about to kill himself, since he supposed that the prisoners had escaped. [28]But Paul shouted in a loud voice, "Do not harm yourself, for we are all here." [29]The jailer called for lights, and rushing in, he fell down trembling before Paul and Silas. [30]Then he brought them outside and said, "Sirs, what must I do to be saved?" [31]They answered, "Believe on the Lord Jesus, and you will be saved, you and your household." [32]They spoke the word of the Lord to him and to all who were in his house. [33]At the same hour of the night he took them and washed their wounds; then he and his entire family were baptized without delay. [34]He brought them up into the house and set food before them; and he and his entire household rejoiced that he had become a believer in God.

—Acts 16:11–25

INTRODUCTION

In the sixteenth chapter of Acts, Paul and Timothy are on the move, flummoxed by a mysterious obstinance of the Holy Spirit (see verses 6–8). When Paul finally has a vision from God in a dream that the Macedonians need help (9–10), they set sail for Macedonia. It is there that they find the mesmerizing Lydia, a receptive merchant of purple cloth, who, after being baptized, "prevails upon" Paul and Timothy to stay as guests in her home (14–15).[1]

By contrast, the next day, they meet an enslaved girl who has the spirit of divination and keeps following Paul and Silas, crying out that, "These men are slaves of the Most High God, who proclaim to you a way of salvation" (16–17). Annoyed after several days and eager to silence her, Paul orders the spirit out of her in the name of Jesus Christ and it immediately flees.

We hear nothing more of the girl, but this spontaneous "healing" sets in motion a chain of events that ends with a miraculous unleashing of the Spirit. The girl's owners have Paul and Silas dragged into the marketplace and flogged for disrupting their livelihood (19–23). Then Paul and

---

[1] Portions of this chapter were previously published in my guest editorial, Raffety 2020a, "From Depression and Decline to Repentance and Transformation: Receiving Disabled Leadership and Its Gifts for the Church," *Theology Today* 77, no. 2: 117–23.

Silas are thrown into jail for their crimes—but deep in the night, on the heels of their prayers and hymns, a great earthquake loosens their shackles, resulting in the spontaneous conversion of the jailer and his family, apologies from the magistrates, release from prison, and a triumphant return to Lydia's abode.

I am drawn to this girl, though, and her misfitting in this story. I'm drawn to the way in which the spirit of divination that possesses her is not the "correct spirit" and yet it is the one proclaiming God's ministry, with the same words Mary uses in the Magnificat, no less, for all to see. It's an intrusive spirit, for sure. The crying out reminds me of blind Bartimaeus. There is nothing mild here, and in fact, the girl's boisterous, annoying proclamations make the perfect foil to Lydia's receptive and respectable nature.

Lydia is so often extolled for her hospitality, the jailer praised for his change of heart—but what was it about the enslaved girl's proclamations that Paul and Silas found so inhospitable? Was it her invocation of their parallel servitude that irked Paul so much? Was it the imposition that an alternate spirit found reverence for the foreign God they sought to proclaim? Or was it simply that she was proclaiming that which they thought was *their* lot and *their* ministry and *their* role? And not at all in the way they had envisioned!

Whatever the case, it is undeniable that the unleashing of the Spirit on the prison that night is tied to the unleashing of the spirit from this humble girl. There is at once an enticing decolonizing of the Spirit in Acts 16 with the release of the enslaved girl, the fall of the prison, the conversion of the jailer, and Lydia's hospitality. But there is also the problem of virtually reading her out of the story, dealing with her, taking care of her, as Paul does, by silencing her, doing away with her, and refusing to look with more care or caution or nuance at her state, her following, her proclamations. It strikes me that the very actions for which the enslaved girl is rebuffed are the same actions for which Bartimaeus is reproved, and that at the close of Acts chapter 16, it is far too easy to run away with Paul and Silas and Lydia from the ambiguity of Christian ministry and leadership, from the mysterious ways of the Spirit, and from the radical unleashing of the Spirit from an enslaved girl on the way.

Simply put, I want to ask what's stopping Paul from receiving this enslaved girl as a minister. Where might and should and could the boundary lines be drawn? And if we bring the Spirit back into it, what is it that this passage is saying, especially about leadership?

WHOSE LEADERSHIP?

There is, understandably, much handwringing in American theological institutions today about the demographic decline in Christian congregational affiliation, which has triggered a passionate and sometimes desperate call not only for new models of ministry but for new models of Christian leadership. Many pastors and Christian leaders are searching for flexible and adaptable paradigms of leadership that can accept, embrace, and, most especially, anticipate change in congregational ministry contexts. This reveals not only a willingness to adapt on the part of church leaders but a conviction that prior paradigms of leadership and training were molded and wedded to a concept of congregational ministry that is now outdated and obsolete. "What do pastoral leaders look like in a post-Christendom world?" many of us are asking; and theological educators especially are asking, "How can we train them up?"

There are at least two problems, however, with not just the makeup but the object of these conversations. First, conversations about religious decline tend to ask existing leaders to reinvent the molds for leadership and ministry. In so doing, they fail to recognize that the most-needed conversation partners for such transformation may not even be at the table. However, as this book argues, mere inclusion fails to undo or expose the reliance of Christian leadership on a theology of ability. As argued in chapter 2, for instance, it is not enough for the church to invite disabled people to an existing table; rather, they must be willing to let go of the table, repenting of and lamenting the sins of ableism in the church in order to listen to disabled people (chapters 3–4) and nurture and receive their ministry (chapters 5–6) and leadership.

Yet, in conversation after conversation, we also tend to presume that the term leadership is a given—that we all agree upon some standards or qualities for leadership that can be assumed, or that Christian leadership is necessarily the business of theological institutions, congregations, and the salvation of the church. It is pretty clear that Christian leadership casts a wider circle than just pastoral leadership, while still including pastoral leadership. Mainline denominations and their pastors also bemoan the lack of lay leadership in the church today and decreasing involvement of the laity, but what is the role of the laity in defining or even reshaping Christian leadership? Perhaps most importantly, how is Christian leadership defined theologically? In other words, how does not just who we are, but who the Triune God is, bear upon who we are called to be in the church? Thus, before we can appreciate what disabled leaders may offer to the contemporary church, we must examine what is at the heart of our definitions of Christian leadership and how it impacts our theology and ecclesiology.

Throughout this book I have talked about a necessary shift from focusing on ministry programs that solve problems to focusing on participating with people in the ministry of God. But in our conceptions of Christian leadership and our leadership training at theological institutions, I argue, we have trained future pastors to major in solving problems. In so doing we have equipped pastors to navigate complex systems, demonstrate proficiency of skills, and even do so with a "non-anxious presence." However, we have thus unwittingly reinforced the very conception this book seeks to confront: the idea that people in the pews are problems to be solved, obstacles to ministry rather than partners in ministry and leaders themselves. This poses a severe crisis of leadership, not simply because it undermines the dignity and humanity of the congregation, or because it objectifies the ability of the pastor to solve problems, but rather because it domesticates Spiritual leadership as technical ability (Betcher 2006, np). It is first and foremost a theological or an ecclesial problem—a Spiritual problem with a capital S.

In other words, God does not look at God's church or God's people as problems to be solved. Jesus does not come into human form with an ulterior motive: rather, Jesus' very vocation is simply Emmanuel, "God with us." By the same token, as Sharon V. Betcher observes, the Spirit of God is not an instrument of neoliberalism, reputedly redemptive but effectively colonizing, in the way it pushes people on the margins back toward politics, habits, and practices of normalcy, propriety, respectability, and civility. As Betcher writes, "Rather than 'saving' or 'healing' the other, our 'love' may then actually end up insisting upon its own way, insisting upon our own psychopathological orientation to normalcy, that is" (2006). Here Betcher is making reference to the way in which the countercultural, otherworldly work of Jesus' healing ministry has been narrowly interpreted as the redemptive colonizing of discordant bodies and social ways of being. Instead she calls for a "transvaluing Spirit from guarantor of miraculous remediation towards the recognition of persons living the variability and vulnerabilities of bodies with real presence to life" (2006).

Indeed, ministries of welcome and inclusion in the church, or efforts to expand theological education's notions of diversity and inclusion, simply have not led to the embrace of disabled callings to ministry and leadership. And this problem cannot be solved by non-disabled leaders. Yet I also cannot in good conscience write a book about disabled leadership apart from able-bodied leadership, when able-bodied leadership has been squelching disabled leadership in the church for centuries. Rather, as with previous chapters, this one stakes any hope for disabled leadership on the relinquishing of power and control of non-disabled leaders over not just positions but paradigms of power. I argue that the "hegemony of normalcy" found in ministries of inclusion in previous chapters is extended through paradigms of Christian leadership, subtly preventing not only disabled people from pursuing leadership in the church but also able-bodied gatekeepers from perceiving or receiving their leadership as such.

This chapter deconstructs contemporary literature for pastors in pews and teachings (my own) on Christian leadership in the academy, arguing that a theology of ability masquerades at the center of systems theory and adaptive leadership, two popular paradigms for contemporary ministry. In other words, this chapter identifies the ways in which we have a built up an industry of Christian leadership around Paul, Silas, and Lydia, obscuring the ministry and leadership of those who have been enslaved and dismissed under the guise of propriety and normalcy. Although I name this theology of ability and recognize this threat as a Spiritual one to congregational leadership, this chapter, with its emphasis on able-bodied leadership, concentrates on analyzing such paradigms, whereas the following chapter draws on examples of disabled leadership to offer some constructive examples of the Spirit in action.

It is not my intention to suggest that simply replacing Christian leadership with disabled leadership will usher in the kingdom of God. Rather, I believe that the critiques disabled readings of Christian leadership offer call into question the notion of leadership itself and suggest something far more radical when it comes to justice—not just for disabled people but for all people. However, the problem is not so much that God is not using folks like the enslaved girl or disabled folks in ministry: it's that we have found all sorts of reasons not to affirm, consider, or behold their leadership. Hence, I see disabled leadership as a step toward restorative justice, because it's already an anti-leadership of sorts, with its networking, plural, interdependent, and creative characteristics. It exposes our cathecting to normalcy and points to a more expansive vision for the kingdom of God. But more on that in chapters 8 and 9. For now, what do we do with the mainstream literature on Christian leadership, the terrifying problem of church decline, theological education, and congregational ministry in the twenty-first century?

ADAPTATIVE LEADERSHIP AND ITS PROBLEMS

Although it is beyond the scope of this book to trace the history of the field of Christian leadership, it is fairly easy to assess the critical concepts around which contemporary discussions of Christian leadership have crystallized. In a scoping article that takes into account transnational approaches to leadership and Christian leadership, Volker Kessler and Louise Kretzschmar posit a provisional definition of a leader as someone whom others follow and a Christian leader as someone who follows Christ and whom other persons follow (2015, 2). They also helpfully locate the study of Christian leadership within the disciplines of Practical Theology and Theological Ethics.

However, Christian leadership also stands at a crossroads in that biblical insights for leadership are anchored in antiquated and outdated contexts, yet today's congregations are significant organizations that require managerial and financial skills for leadership and growth, just to name a few. Within the United States, especially with the advent of evangelical megachurches in the 1980s, Christian leadership has also become a multimillion-dollar industry, borrowing heavily from business and managerial science to inform its practices. Indeed, despite the fact that neither the Old Testament nor the New Testament uses the term "leaders," most major seminaries and divinity schools in the United States, from conservative to liberal, have doubled down on leadership as a critical capacity, furthering courses or centers in Christian leadership that aim to provide comprehensive training to future clergy. From the Bill Hendricks Center of Christian Leadership at Dallas Theological Seminary to Southeastern Baptist Seminary's M.A., DMin, and PhD programs in Christian leadership, to McCormick and Yale's focus on prophetic leadership and transformative leadership and Fuller Theological Seminary's Master of Arts in Global Leadership or Lifelong Leadership cohort, everyone is drinking the leadership Kool-Aid.

Although the concept of Christian leadership includes a broader audience than ordained leaders or clergy, it often fixates on clergy as potential changemakers in dysfunctional congregational systems. Beyond the clerical specialties of teaching, preaching, worship, and pastoral care, Christian leaders must possess relational, managerial, financial, and visionary expertise in order to guide congregations not just in maintenance of the status quo but in growth and change. Indeed, the latter two foci represent contemporary shifts in the landscape of Christian leadership over the last several decades, because in both mainline and evangelical circles, experts recognize that exponential church growth is no longer possible due to demographic and value shifts that make congregational context impossible to ignore (see, for example, Bendroth 2015; Branson and Martinez 2011).

Simply put, in an age of uncertainty, adaptive leadership is all the rage. Contrasting technical problem-solving with adaptive problem-solving, pastors and theologians like Gil Rendle pull from business leadership strategies, especially those developed by Harvard business scholars Ronald Heifetz and Marty Linsky (2002), to inform Christian ministry and leadership. Whereas a technical problem is one that has a clear solution to its puzzle, an adaptive problem represents unknown, uncharted territory. Rendle compares the current landscape of congregational ministry to the biblical paradigm of the wilderness (2010); in *Canoeing the Mountains*, pastor Tod Bolsinger compares contemporary pastoral leadership to the adventures of Lewis and Clark (2015).[2] When it comes to adaptive problems, leaders must first recognize that they do not possess the tools or capacities to solve such problems. They then must lead their congregations in learning about the problem, experimenting with various ways to confront the problem, and taking risks that threaten the very heart of the institution. Finally, the solution to an adaptive problem often involves multipronged change that can threaten even the best leader's leadership.

In a class that I taught on mainline decline and the major demographic transitions facing churches today, students practiced identifying technical versus adaptive problems and developing multipronged approaches to solving these problems. There were some clear benefits to this approach: students took time to try to understand the complexity of the problems they faced, they understood that good solutions would take time and cooperation, and they expressed humility in recognizing that they themselves were not necessarily the solution to such problems. I do think that these moves are quite beneficial in building flexible, self-aware leadership capacity.

Yet about halfway through the semester I also realized that I had inadvertently reoriented students to see their congregations as problems themselves rather than as partners in their work of seeking God in the world. Indeed, one might argue that the course itself was an adaptive problem-solving enterprise, and it is tempting to hope that the decline of the church, especially the mainline church in America, can be solved by

[2] I do not address the problematic notions of comparing twenty-first-century ministry to a colonialist, anti-indigenous mission in this chapter, but this is certainly worthy of much concern and scrutiny.

something as strategic and concrete as adaptive leadership. But despite its liberatory roots (see chapter 6), this problem-posing orientation invited students first to identify problems within society or congregations and then necessarily to turn away from those people as they worked to solve those problems they had identified on their own.

Students began to see congregations not as a subject or an agent but as an object in their ministry: if they could just solve the problems facing congregations, their savvy leadership could usher in better ministry and better futures. Indeed, even as contemporary leadership literature rejects the "lone ranger" approach (see Rendle 2010, 85, for instance), many of the practical instructions to pastoral leaders—"be self-differentiated," "provide a nonanxious presence," or "get out on the balcony"—emphasize the necessity and wisdom of leaders doing enlightened, separated work from their congregations in order to see them or themselves more clearly. Again, with these movements, it becomes very difficult for leaders not to objectify the congregation, to see it as a problem in the world, rather than a person or a group of persons with whom they are in relationship. The folly of this perspective is not only that the congregation ceases to be a partner in ministry but that they are misperceived as passive and cohesive, when they are truly active, dynamic, and multifaceted.

One might argue that this is not adaptive leadership, but adaptive leadership gone bad, because at its heart adaptive leadership, in its disciplined learning, is slow, humble, and cooperative. Yet as long as adaptive leadership remains a tool of the privileged and an instrument of expertise, it remains hard-pressed to break out of the problems of the problem-posing paradigm. In the previous chapter, Paulo Freire's problem-posing paradigm of learning was presented as a liberating instrument of change for congregations, especially congregations with disabled people. But Freire's own context, as a teacher of the illiterate poor in 1970s Brazil, is also paramount. Indeed, when educators in Western privileged contexts try to poach Freire's lessons for liberation into their classrooms, they may merely supplement and stoke the tools of the oppressor rather than participate in liberation. In his critique of educators' misuse of Freire in Western collegiate education, Peter Elbow argues that professors are "bamboozling" their students in that they may say they are using Freire in their classrooms but few are actually letting their students pose problems (1973).

To be fair, the entire pursuit of Freire with privileged students in privileged institutions is fraught, and faculty rarely have much control over their curriculum, their classrooms, or even their methods. But I was one of those educators. On both occasions that I taught Ministry with People with Disabilities at Princeton Theological Seminary, I carefully selected texts for the course that emphasized ministry *with* disabled people rather than ministry *for* or *to* disabled people (hence the rather awkwardly worded course title), arranging them alongside critical weekly questions and multimodal learning frameworks. In my ivory tower, I prepared the course as consciously and equitably as possible.

And then the students arrived. A student in a wheelchair could not get into the building without assistance, because one of the heavy doors in the circuitous path he needed to take from the accessible parking spot up an elevator several floors was closed to him. A few weeks in, several students pointed out that despite how much they were enjoying the course, the attendance policy, which I had pasted straight out of the faculty handbook, was menacing and prohibitive to disabled and chronically ill folks—certainly not in line with the things I was teaching in the course itself. And although I did much to get out of that inaccessible, normative space of the classroom, either bringing in panels of disabled leaders who could speak beyond my own experiences or visiting a local Citizens for Independent Living home, students rightly criticized that those experiences came off as supplementary rather than central to course learning. There was no opportunity to develop relationships with disabled people, beyond the students who were willing to share their experiences in the course, and so many of these opportunities felt like appendages, trite and performative, rather than integral to course learning.

The experience made me stop in my tracks and wonder: Why is it that we presume students do ministry or are equipped for leadership *after* they graduate, when we have the opportunity to dialogue with them as they practice now and to help them see themselves as ministers and leaders as they learn? Clearly, my students were ministering to me, teaching me, within the space of the classroom, but why was it that practical theology courses were confined to these classroom models in the first place? If I was trying to teach students about congregational ministry, why were we so far afield from congregations themselves? Finally, if we were truly to learn from disabled people and disabled perspectives, it would not do to ignore the inaccessibility inherent not just in the structure of buildings but in the nature of theological education and its coursework.

When I looked around the academy and our congregations, I saw a paucity of disabled leaders and disabled perspectives. That could not be ignored in teaching, but it was also I who had subtly reinforced those barriers with my classroom, my syllabus, and my learning strategies. The very structure of the academy, with its individualization of expertise and its ideology of ability, was antithetical to approaches that would value disabled methods, insights, and perspectives—and yet, despite my training as an ethnographer, my own approach to learning from congregations, I had fallen into the trap of making learning with disabled people performative versus central to the course: there really was no opportunity to be in "ministry with people with disabilities," as the course itself so boldly advertised.

In her critique of the use of ethnographic methods in theological education, Natalie Wigg-Stevenson identifies how easily professors can fall into simply teaching to different modes of expertise, rather than truly working with students to dismantle the edifices that laud expertise in the first place (2018). Wigg-Stevenson's point is that ethnographic methods become yet another skill and discipline for students to master—another tool of the oppressor, embedded in capitalist, elitist educational culture—rather than avenues to liberation. This leads her to remind educators that "Western pedagogy is designed largely to conform to and reproduce Western culture, not to decolonize (i.e. dismantle) that culture" (2018, 110). Therefore, to be better educators, as well as better ethnographers and theologians, we must "[imagine] the alternate reality in which the last shall be first, and the first shall be last, every valley shall be filled in and every mountain made low," heeding the woes and not just the blessings of the Beatitudes (Luke 6:24–25) (110). "That means that in the largely privileged context in which I teach," Wigg-Stevenson writes, "my students and I need to partner in self-sabotaging acts of justice-making; we need to work together to pursue our own woe" (111). Wigg-Stevenson concludes that teaching ethnographically, then, is less about helping students hone the methods of ethnography than about incorporating "values like reflexivity, curiosity, and participation into assignments" and pressing them "to practice patience, empathic listening, and attentiveness in ways that open them up to the people they encounter rather than allow them to instrumentalize those people toward their assignments' ends" (113).

Why digress into this critical treatise on theological education when it's congregations and congregational leadership we are talking about? Because if congregations are seeking to move away from paradigms of inclusion in ministry with disabled people toward paradigms of justice, we must be concerned that theological classrooms, even those with the best intentions, are not necessarily instruments of justice but subtle instruments of oppression. Not only might lessons from the academy need to be unlearned in ministry but the students we need in ministry, particularly those with disabilities, are not necessarily being formed in academies. As such, they do not conform to the modes of Christian leadership our academies and congregations have extolled. But if we heed Wigg-Stevenson's call to "work together to pursue our own woe," we would also do well to critique the terms of Christian leadership itself in order to open theological classrooms and congregations up to new modes of Spirit-led leadership.

Current paradigms of Christian leadership do not exist in a vacuum but instead provide distinct service to institutional inequity and power in both seminaries and congregations. My argument in the next section is that adaptive leadership presents as a similarly bamboozling pursuit in theological education and budding congregational ministers: it purports to offer change, even as it restricts and consolidates power among able-bodied people. In what follows, I analyze the ways in which techniques of Christian leadership continue to pathologize and problematize disabled ways of being and doing, suggesting that this much sought-after change in the church is not so much a mission of Spirit-led transvaluation, making space for multiple modes of flourishing, as it is a transformation that demands that the health of the system manifest in ability and normalcy.

WHY SELF-DIFFERENTIATION, NONANXIOUS PRESENCE, AND GETTING OUT ON THE BALCONY ARE ABLEIST

In chapter 5, we discussed some of the ways contemporary worship dismisses our embodied selves and demands discipline over the disabled body as a prerequisite to full participation. Hence, the barriers to disabled ministry are structural and physical as well as social and relational: they inhabit the ways we relate to one another, especially the behaviors and disciplines we expect of Christian leaders. In this section, I draw on the heralded practices of self-differentiation, nonanxious presence, and getting out on the balcony as exemplary disciplines of Christian leaders. However, at the heart of each, I argue that there is an ideology of ability that undermines the ministry of disabled leaders. Not only does such analysis reveal the persistent, often cloaked biases toward disabled people in Christian leadership but it also begs for a theological revision of practices of leadership themselves.

In the 1950s, observing families with "dysfunctional offspring," Dr. Murray Bowen developed his psychotherapeutic approach to family therapy, which attempted to remove the pathology from an individual and focus instead on the interdependence of how individuals behave in a system. Thus, family systems theory was born. Bowen's theory is notable for making clear that individuals cannot be understood in isolation from one another, as well as for its theories of relationship triangles, self-differentiation, intergenerational transmission, and emotional cutoff, among others.

Over thirty years after Bowen's work, Edwin H. Friedman, a family therapist and rabbi, sought to apply family systems theory to congregations in the comprehensive volume *Generation to Generation: Family Process in Church and Synagogue* (1985). Coining the term "self-differentiating leader," Friedman argued that rather than pathologizing weakness or pathology within the system, leaders should focus on developing their own relational strengths, balancing separateness and closeness within the system. Friedman's book has become a kind of bible for congregational family systems theory and has led numerous Christian authors to attempt to integrate lessons from family systems theory into congregational and pastoral ministry (see, for instance, Ronald W. Richardson and Peter L. Steinke). This novel approach to viewing congregations as systems, rather than pathologizing individuals, has merit and function and has helped leaders identify ways in which they themselves are subconsciously influenced and pulled by the system.

However, family systems theory has been patterned on white, heteronormative, nuclear families, as well as adapted to suit white-dominant, Protestant, relatively affluent congregations, ironically divorcing the systemic operations of families and congregations from the larger societal forces and prejudices infused within them and acting upon them. For these reasons, family systems theory quickly came under fire from queer, feminist, and multicultural perspectives, and significant efforts have been made to critique and refine its use and application in diverse and differentiated contexts (Brown and Gilligan 1992; Knudson-Martin 1994, 1996; Lerner 1983, 1988; Luepnitz 1988; McGoldrick 1998).

Still, family systems theory also works closely with the analogy of the integration of bodily systems, the threat of disease, even likening the self-differentiated leader to a "broad-based antibiotic" capable of ameliorating "infected" congregations (see the foreword by Gary Emanuel and Mickie Crimone in Friedman 2011, x). In a chapter on "Body and Soul in Family Process," Friedman attempts to introduce pastoral leaders to a new medical model that focuses on interconnections between the body and soul, analogizing threats of disease to the various anatomical systems of the body through the multifarious functions of emotional family and congregational systems. With respect to genetics, for instance, Friedman opines,

> Understanding of this dynamic quality in the gene pool is crucial to fostering responsible attitudes rather than victim attitudes for physical disease; it is as vital for survival in the context of physical illness as it is in the context of any other hostile challenge. The analogue to family systems thinking is that what counts is not thinking about our symptoms but thinking about our thinking, in particular the extent to which such thinking falls into category 1 (victimization) or category 2 (responsibility). (2011, 129)

Although Bowen and Friedman rarely mention the term disability, the fact that threats to family and congregational systems are distinctly analogized to medical abnormalities, deficiencies, or pathologies undermines the reliability of the systems-based approach for disabled individuals. In the passage above, Friedman also echoes an antiquated model of disease and disability, arguing for something like a "mind over matter" mentality for overcoming illness. Furthermore, even if systems theorists are able to avoid pathologizing disabled individuals or disability as threats to the system itself (which seems unlikely given the preponderance of medicalized language throughout Friedman's influential volume), a disability justice perspective raises the question as to whether systems theory is in and of itself ableist (as well as sexist, heteronormative, and racist) in that it idealizes a system in which proscribed, normative roles filled by able-bodied individuals achieve balance, harmony, and, for our purposes, ideal leadership. The norms inherent in demanding the ideal, self-differentiated functioning of each individual in order to balance the system expose the narrow-minded avenues for success and human flourishing inherent in the theory, not to mention the extent to which Friedman's theory at best dismisses the necessity of a transformative God, let alone makes that God into another cathected normalizing force within the system.

Even if we bracket these concerns, the further development and application of Bowen family systems theory within the field of congregational leadership studies over the following decades suggests a much more troubling reality, as authors such as Peter L. Steinke take up anxiety as the premier analogy and pathology for congregational leaders and systems (2006). In Steinke's application of self-differentiated leadership within congregational systems, he pathologizes congregational and personal anxiety as misfunction, urging leaders to practice self-control and self-regulation as antidotes to anxiety in the congregational system. Although Steinke seems to be referencing generalized versus clinical anxiety, he never makes that clear, as he also wields neuroscience to parse the deficits of "chronically anxious persons" (2006, 55, 61). In chapter 6, he compares anxiety in the system to a virus that infects a cell, yet even the analogy slips to fault anxious persons for disease: "Anxious, reactive people function in similar ways to a virus attacking a cell. As pathogenic forces invade the body, anxious, reactive people likewise violate the boundaries of others, manipulating them to the reactor's advantage" (85). Bowen and Friedman's resolve to not pathologize individuals but rather think systematically (despite the aforementioned problems with that) has gone out the window: Steinke's fixation on anxiety literally pathologizes anxious individuals and makes Christian leadership the antidote to anxiety: "leaders supply for the community what is the immune system for the body" (89). Taken to its logical conclusions, people with anxiety not only make poor leaders, they must also be reformed, treated—or, even worse, euthanized.

Now perhaps I am being too hard on Bowen, Friedman, and Steinke. Perhaps their theories and especially their metaphors have just aged poorly. Who could have predicted that anxiety disorders would become the most common forms of mental illness in the United States, affecting forty million people a year? Yet the point is not so much that Bowen, Friedman, and Steinke were out of step as that they were *in* step with the cultural scripts surrounding mental illness, disability, and disease. Indeed, by pathologizing disease-related insults to wholistic congregational systems, whose norm it is to self-regulate, they demonstrate that the medical model of disability is very much operative, even as it often slides by, undetected, under the radar. Even if one disputes the point that systems are all about enforcing normalcy and thus remain hostile to disabled people and disabled modes of ministry and leadership, Steinke's adaptation of Friedman's congregational systems approach demonstrates how difficult it is for such systems to avoid enforcing normalcy with respect to their disabled congregants and leaders. The open pathologizing of individuals, particularly those with anxiety, as unfit to be leaders demonstrates how rampant an ideology of ability is throughout the current paradigm of Christian pastoral leadership. Even if disabled people with bodies that have been impacted by genetics or disease or mentally ill people somehow find their way into positions of church leadership (which, of course, they will and do, given the ubiquity of disability in the human population), approaches like Steinke's will uncritically undermine not just their leadership but their very ways of being and doing as unfit, improper, and defective.

Although adaptive leadership approaches avoid pathologizing disabled bodies and minds, the trusted strategy of getting up on the balcony—despite its thoughtful, shared approach to leadership—still fails, like systems theory, to situate leadership within a critical context of injustice and inequality. Gil Rendle helpfully distinguishes that getting out on the balcony is a strategy to avoid the reactive space of pathologizing people and problem-solving. Instead, in the strategy of moving to the balcony, leaders invite others in the system to go with them to a space other than the boardroom, where decisions are made, relying on the shift in space to prompt conversation and creative discernment (2010, 96). It may seem trite to note that the analogy of the balcony space itself, though not steeped in metaphors of disease, is literally inaccessible to paradigmatic representatives of disability, wheelchair users. Of course, balcony-style conversation can happen anywhere—in a parking lot or a diner—rather than a lofted vantage. But the presumption that boardrooms include only people who can make it onto balconies should not be lost on us either. Getting out on the balcony involves inviting a subset of church leaders to create and converse with the pastor, yet if the balcony is fundamentally inaccessible to disabled leaders, shouldn't we be worried that the heart of adaptive leadership has in mind an able body and a fit mind as precursors to the type of change they want to see in the church, let alone the world?

CONCLUSION

The point is that in the syntax, the metaphors, and the theories of power in the church, disabled people misfit (Garland-Thomson 2011). That misfitting is almost always perceived as discussed, as a threat to the system or to leadership paradigms, and therefore, disabled people conform to fit as best they can the demands of Christian leadership. But this chapter points to some of the ways in which the effect of misfitting may be so subtle that it glides almost undetected under the surface for most of us but is nevertheless present for disabled minds and bodies. It makes me wary as I examine my own participation in training up the next generation of leaders: surely, I, like Paul, would have silenced the enslaved girl. Surely I, like Jesus and the disciples, would have walked right past Bartimaeus' cries. And then I realize how easily I've still read myself into the story as the able-bodied Christian leader, even in the very profession of my sins.

It is precisely because of this subtle yet reinforcing move that I make in my classrooms, my ministry, my writing, and precisely because I embody the paradigm of Christian leadership—or because I am not even conscious of my compulsion to embody it continually—that I fail to view the world from the vantage point of those like the enslaved girl or blind Bartimaeus who openly misfit. The trouble, as I have tried to show, is not so much that I do not perceive them as leaders but that even in my effort to pursue, as Wigg-Stevenson so aptly writes, "my woe," I simply *cannot* perceive it, because I live within a world that constantly affirms my ability to walk, to see, to be disease-free, nonanxious, and stair-climbing as the opposite of woe, as the very prerequisite for Christian leadership.

If the entire industry of Christian leadership is cloaked in power, yet drenched in woe, is Christian leadership even faithful? Insofar as it continually draws us toward pathologizing, treating people as problems, propping up the same people, paradigms, and privilege, merely clothed in new theories, it does nothing but adapt itself to circumstances rather than draw itself closer to God, Christ, and the Spirit. A disabled perspective on leadership may be just what is needed not to fight church decline but to appreciate it, to appreciate what it is about the church that has to die if it is to be resurrected, and Christian leadership may be part and parcel of that necessary decline. Indeed, we need to really listen in and hear the enslaved girl's story, her prophecy, her history, her experiences. Not as Paul is telling it, but as she would tell it—the good, the bad, and the ugly.

One of the reasons disabled leadership must be heeded is that it will not do for those in power simply to imagine the church differently. Rather, disabled leaders must be listened to, believed, trusted, and allowed to be who they are and follow the Spirit, whether that leadership is immediately recognizable to others or not. "The wind blows where it chooses, and you hear the sound of it, but you do not know where it comes from or where it goes. So it is with everyone who is born of the Spirit" (John 3:8). The next chapter provides some glimpses of the Spirit in disabled leadership, which have blown in despite the stranglehold of inclusive ministry and Christian leadership. The church does not need saving; God has already done that. But the church does need leaders born of the Spirit, a decolonized Spirit, breathed out, lifted up for its disruptive creativity. For such a time as this.

8

New Modes of Disabled Leadership

For now we see in a mirror, dimly, but then we will see face to face. Now I know only in part; then I will know fully, even as I have been fully known.

—1 Corinthians 13:12

INTRODUCTION

Bailie, a disabled seminary student, talked wistfully about keeping many of the details of her bipolar, anxiety, and PTSD diagnoses and her life from those in her church, only giving people "the mental illness they want." Growing up in a conservative denomination in Oklahoma, her late father had lived covertly with schizoaffective disorder. A dynamic leader in the church, people loved him when he was charismatic and musical, but they didn't see or preferred not to see the mania that came in between.

Because I knew Bailie was in the ordination process in the Presbyterian Church, I pushed her to talk about it, but I could tell she was wary of how much she shared. She talked about how the pastor at the church at which she was doing an internship that summer had made a crack about bipolar illness during a session meeting one evening. She pulled him aside later to say that she really is bipolar; they never spoke about it again. As Bailie spoke, she was lavishly transparent with us, but I could hear the cost of such vulnerability in her voice: she laughed garishly at herself; she dropped her voice at times. She had a dynamism, a largeness of personality that was contagious, and yet the stigma that has followed her around has caused her to hold back, to check herself, to look around corners before she steps plainly into the light.

For Bailie, the ordination process was a misfit, not because she did not have the skills or aptitude to be ordained, but because the process idolized and projected certain typical abilities, like being a nonanxious presence and timed test taking, and so she got the message that her mental illness was something that needed to stay hidden in order for her to fit into the church as a future pastor. Furthermore, Bailie told us that she lacked "mirrors," as she would call them—other leaders and mentors living with mental illness who could show her the way in ministry and in life. Bailie's dad, exuberant and talented as he was, had passed away many years before, and he had always kept his mental illness hidden from the church.

Meanwhile, Jess struck me as someone who just makes things happen. A special education teacher by training, she was also on the council, the leadership body of her church; her husband, Arundel, served on the regional leadership body, and together they ran a service called Joyful Noise. They were in their second year of running their Bible School for disabled children, Jess led the youth group, her son, J'den, was involved in Special Olympics, her daughter, Morrigan, spoke about disability rights to the school board and anyone who would listen, and the kids attended inclusion camps! One afternoon as we spoke, Jess told me how they kind of "take people along with them," like J'den's former special education teacher, who now regularly helped them out as a babysitter, or her pastor friend from Pennsylvania who had filled in at their church when they had a lapse in pastoral leadership and whom the kids affectionately called "Titi"—"Auntie" in Spanish.

But as Jess spoke about the transition in leadership at their church and especially how it had affected the Joyful Noise service, she remarked how firmly the kids had initially bonded with the head pastor, who had now been gone for over a year and a half. For any kid, but especially for kids like J'den, who are on the autism spectrum and rely on routine, as well as on knowledgeable and consistent adults, this was a blow. Jess was able to arrange for the denomination to approve Titi to come in to run the service for several months while they waited to call another pastor, and so the service went on, uninterrupted. In fact, Titi was so unflappable that Jess giddily tells a story about how, during a particularly lively Christmas service, she continued to preach as children rolled toys up to the chancel: she rolled them back, unfazed!

Bailie's experience navigating the ordination process as a person with a disability and Jess's comments about transitions in pastoral leadership are instructive to all of us in the church, particularly when it comes to disabled children and adults. I have rarely heard anyone talk as Jess does about how these transitions affect children; perhaps we take for granted that they bounce back, perhaps we think they simply don't notice. But she pointed out how markedly her autistic son was affected by the transition, how he had a hard time at worship when their pastor left. As both leaders spoke so pointedly about these administrative challenges in leadership, however, I felt a little wistful: I mean, what, really, could the church do about that? Pastors were always going to come and go, and if that is so, how can we do better by disabled people?

And then I realized that the answers had been sitting right in front of me. The Clarke family had made a radical departure from the transactional ministry mentality, a service-giving and consuming exchange that cheapens and sidelines Jesus' ministry. As discussed in chapter 3, this kind of ministry puts the onus on persons with disabilities to advocate for what they need, relegating disabled people to recipients of the church's services. But this type of ministry also threatens or fortifies the church's leadership and authority through the primary provision of adequate services. The church's ministry and leadership are relative to their ability to provide robust services.

Yet the Clarkes don't simply expect the church to minister to them or the pastor to do all the work; they expect to be part of a church that ministers to others. In fact, are they not ministers themselves? As Christians, do we not believe the Holy Spirit is alive and active in each person's ministry? That which has obstructed the church from receiving the ministry and leadership of disabled people is not just administrative or structural. Rather, this chapter argues that when it comes to disabled people's leadership, the church has a Spiritual problem (again with a capital S).

The Clarkes, likely out of both survival and resourcefulness, have formed a network of people who understand, care, and support their family, both at church and in their community. In fact, they have integrated the two networks: for two summers now Jess has employed special education colleagues at her Bible School for disabled children. This integration between contexts, this sewing of a network between the church and other aspects of disabled people's lives, is something able-bodied clergy often struggle to understand, support, or strengthen. If they were a typical family, their devotion to the church and their hustling would be celebrated, but because they "misfit," their ways of being are materially and socially misaligned with the world (Garland-Thomson 2011, 592). "You have Joyful Noise," naysayers complain, "why do you now need Bible School for disabled kids?" The notion that disabled people's needs are cumbersome, whereas able-bodied people's needs are typical and self-evident, threatens to undermine the dynamism of the Clarkes' ministry. For the most part, misfitting is resolved through disabled conformity, but this tends to resolve tension only superficially and is costly to disabled people.

This chapter identifies how the misfitting of disabled leaders, like Bailie, the Clarke family, and Lisa, a blind Catholic lector, both exposes and impinges on ableist practices of leadership, thoughtfully carving out space for new modes of leadership in the church. The point of this chapter is not to reformulate the qualifications and tasks for ordained ministry and leadership or dispense with ordained leadership altogether. Indeed, the ecumenical nature of our study would make it difficult to make broad claims about ordained versus lay leadership or the office of ordained ministry given the diversity of structures, traditions, and practices of American congregations.

Rather, the point of this chapter is to draw on ethnographic data to shape and reshape who we know pastors to be, rather than use standard qualifications, which necessarily present ableist biases, to do that work. This changes the role of the church in the nurturing of leadership and ordination from a primary posture of authority to a primary posture of listening to the Spirit. By listening well and perceiving new modes of leadership from disabled people, I invite congregations to reflect critically on the ways in which integrative, collaborative, and creative leadership may provide fresh insight for our standards, processes, and most important, our ministry.

Yet in identifying these features of Spirit leadership, I also compel congregations to reflect on ways in which their nurturing and equipping of leaders may be domesticating or distorting the Spirit among them. By introducing the Spiritual characteristics of misfitting and transvaluing and telling stories of unlikely leadership modes, I provide glimmers of the kingdom as the Spirit disrupts convention, propriety, and conformity. In drawing on these examples of disabled leadership, I show how the Spirit is ushering in a more varied and robust concept of human flourishing that pushes against the confines of normalcy and inclusion, making way not just for disabled leadership but for new instantiations of church as we know it.

MISFITTING IN MINISTRY

In her article "Misfits: A Feminist Materialist Disability Concept," disability theorist Rosemarie Garland-Thomson attempts to shift the concept of disability off and out of the bodies of disabled persons and onto the lived environment that they experience and which is shaped by them. Like so many theorists before her, Garland-Thomson is trying to account for both the social-political experience of disability and its embodied reality: neither can be left behind if we are to appreciate the lived, particular experiences of disabled people fully. Waxing poignant and philosophical about not just the verb *fit*, but the adjective *fitting*, Garland-Thomson contrasts the positivity of *fit* and *fitting* ("proper," "well-adapted," in "good form" or "condition") with the "jarring juxtaposition" of *misfit* and *misfitting* ("unsuitable," "inappropriate," "inconspicuously odd, unusual or antisocial behavior") (2011, 593). Her point is that however crudely those who fit are rendered proper while those who misfit are rendered unsuitable, misfitting is always dynamic, material, and relational. "The problem with a misfit, then, inheres not in either of the two things but in their juxtaposition, the awkward attempt to fit them together." You know the saying: square peg, round hole (592–93).

Garland-Thomson goes on to show that this materialist concept of disability is an important shift because it helps narrate the particularity of the politics of oppression, expose differential vulnerability, and emphasize the agency, value, and creativity of disabled persons. All too often the politics of inclusion invite us to generalize rather than hear and receive particular experiences of disability. But as Garland-Thomson writes,

> When we fit harmoniously and properly into the world, we forget the truth of contingency because the world sustains us. When we experience misfitting and recognize the disjuncture for its political potential, we expose the relational component and the fragility of fitting. Any of us can fit here today and misfit here tomorrow. (2011, 597)

Given this relational nature of fitting, Garland-Thomson theorizes vulnerability as owing to the fit versus the body of the one who misfits (600).

Finally, and perhaps most importantly for our purposes in this chapter, Garland-Thomson argues that misfitting can produce subjugated knowledges that lend value in the form of innovation, resourcefulness, and adaptability to humanity (604). The Deaf community has long spoken of this added value in using the phrase "Deaf gain" to confront both the misnomer of "hearing loss" and characterize the myriad ways in which Deaf ways of being in a hearing world have added not just rich language and culture but communication modes and mobility tools that are important and useful (Bauman and Murray 2014). Indeed, the misfit of "hearing loss" becomes meaningful within a hearing world; out of such a misfit, Deaf culture, American Sign Language, and other adaptations illuminate Deaf gain that is too often invisible or misconstrued as mere loss to those who are hearing.

In Christian communities, particularly Reformed congregations, we have a saying about leadership that leaves competence to mysterious wisdom and true capabilities for leadership to the Holy Spirit. We often say, "God equips those whom God calls," and not the other way around. Hearkening to a myriad of biblical figures like Moses, Rahab, David, Mary Magdalene, and Peter, none of whom came forward with perfect gifts, track records, or character for leadership but who were called by God into ministry, we seek to recognize that at every turn, Christian leadership is not about us but about God. Yet the radical openness to the Spirit's leadership in the church is often eclipsed by our own perceptions of "equipping." In Sharon V. Betcher's analysis of biblical interpretation, she finds that we often close in on certain forms of fixing and healing in Jesus' ministry, especially when it comes to disabled people (2006, np). The presumably liberating, redeeming, and life-giving work of the Spirit forces certain individuals to conform to the standards of modernity, in order to make them suitable for ministry, service, and leadership.

Indeed, Betcher's reading of not just the healing narratives but the domesticating work of the Spirit presents distinct challenges to our interpretation of Bartimaeus' call to ministry and leadership. Did the Spirit heal Bartimaeus? Did Bartimaeus need to be healed? In chapters 4 and 5, I argue that Bartimaeus is a protagonist in the narrative, that Jesus draws attention to Bartimaeus' agency, extolling his faith and his gifts for ministry, and the climax of the story is not Bartimaeus' healing but his following Jesus on the way. Yet questions remain for many readers, disabled and non-disabled, about whether Bartimaeus' healing is necessary or redemptive. As Betcher warns, "Spirit, in this vein, generates a zone of respectability, propriety, and civility. While such a subjective technology appears to be, perhaps intends to be, life-giving, it coincidentally serves as a mechanism of containment against its own fears" (2006, np).

The previous chapter presented a litany of critiques about the ideology of ability and normalcy at the heart of Christian leadership. Drawing on the metaphor of misfitting, this chapter expands our notions of Christian leadership by drawing attention to the stories and modes of disabled leadership. In so doing, I work against the narrow notion of the Spirit's action as "equipping" or "fitting" those who are called for ministry into some preconceived box. Instead, I offer Betcher's interpretation of "promot[ing] Spirit not as the power to rescue and repair according to some predisposed original state or ideal form, but as the energy for unleashing multiple forms of corporeal flourishing," thus directing our attention to the dynamism and diversity of the Spirit's work through disabled persons (Betcher 2007, 52).

Betcher talks about the transvaluing work of the Spirit, a leadership through which liberation is offered not just to disabled people but to all people as it turns systems and sins, such as ableism, sexism, and racism, on their heads. She argues that this comes through a *consciencization*, the Spirit bringing us face to face with the chains we have put on others and on ourselves and through a variety of ways of human flourishing, offering us a vision of the fullness of who God truly is (2006, np). Rather than a spirit of fear, timidity, or normalcy, misfitting is a helpful metaphor for Spirit-led leadership and particularly for able-bodied congregants who struggle to imagine it. Rather than looking to discipline or domesticate the Spirit, congregations are invited to behold how the Spirit may be working its wisdom of transvaluation through the misfitting of disabled leaders.

NETWORKED, NORM-BREAKING MISFITTING

The Clarkes' apartment was small and cramped, but their eagerness to share and their ease and pride with their kids made us feel warm and easy. Jessica's mother greeted us at the door and J'den was playing video games on the couch when we came in. Jess, Arundel, and Morrigan also joined researcher Gail and me on the sofa, Morrigan moving back and forth between her homework at the table and us as she talked. "Do they know he has autism?" she whispered to her mother anxiously as Gail and I tried to engage with J'den. "Yeah, they know," Jess giggled warmly, "that's why they're here." "Oh," Morrigan said, and scampered off.

I felt dizzy as we ran through the breadth of the things the family is involved in, but each activity seemed meaningful to Jess and Arundel, a natural extension of J'den and Morrigan and who they believe their family to be. They helped start the Joyful Noise service about a year ago at their church with the support of the previous chapter in a nearby town and are running their second summer of a Vacation Bible School for children with special needs. When I ask Morrigan what she likes about church, she asks, "Regular church or Joyful Noise?" "You pick," I reply. "I like Joyful Noise because it's where my family can be together," she says.[1]

What's remarkable about the Clarkes is that they are their own over-lapping network of support: Jess is a special educator who has helped J'den connect with Special Olympics and advocated for his inclusion at camps, church, and other activities; Arundel is the Vice President of the Lutheran Synod of New Jersey, preaching at various churches throughout the state and thus extending the awareness and work of their Joyful Noise service; J'den has fostered relationships with teachers and aides whom the family regularly connects with VBS and service work at their church; and Morrigan has begun to do public speaking in disability advocacy and awareness.

But it strikes me that it's not really *what* they do that's so remarkable. After all, lots of families are involved in similar activities. Rather, it's *how* they do what they do—they do it *together*. As Morrigan said, church is meaningful, Joyful Noise is meaningful, because it's a place "where my family can be together." What this implies, of course, is that there are many spaces where that isn't so possible—and the Clarkes' togetherness, which is at a glance so commonplace as to be unremarkable, is thus actually quite astounding. In his article on "Autism Parents and Neurodiversity," sociologist Brendan Hart notices that it is parents who often invert the process of normalization, the notion that everyone should have access to an ordinary life with independence, choices, and social experiences (Hart 2014, 293). Instead, when parents take their disabled children into public spaces and implicitly or explicitly ask others to tolerate their differences, they engage in a process of reverse normalization, subtly stretching and testing the boundaries of what people perceive as "normal."

This is a form of misfitting, but for the Clarkes, it is purposeful, supported, and collaborative. This does not mean that it is without rejection or stigma, but that this misfitting ultimately imagines itself as an instrument of disruption and social change. For instance, when Morrigan speaks to the school board, she advocates for a support group for siblings of disabled children, both affirming J'den's autistic identity and broadening the network of support and understanding for people in relationship with siblings like J'den. In her advocacy, she offers a critique of the school in its leaving behind of siblings of disabled kids but also imagines a fuller and broader support system for families with disabled children.

---

[1] Fieldnotes, May 29, 2019.

Although the Clarkes are committed lay leaders, we have seen how their networked leadership offers gifts to Pastor Maggi for Resurrection Lutheran's congregation. In chapter 6, we saw how Joyful Noise at Resurrection Lutheran became a free, social space where disabled persons were able to develop their gifts for ministry and leadership. Indeed, out of Joyful Noise, children began leading in congregational ministry and leadership in ways that were previously unimagined at Resurrection. This smacks of the transvaluing work of the Spirit that Betcher talks about: instead of infantilizing disabled children by trying to put them in age-appropriate Sunday school, for instance, they are invited to hone their gifts and lead as ushers, communion servers, and greeters in roles that not only offer them dignity but showcase their ministry to others in the congregation (Raffety 2020b, 207). Here the work of the Spirit in reconfiguring leadership in a free social space has to be let lie. Pastor Maggi often struggled to contain it, but for transvaluation to run its course, able-bodied pastors can and need to play the role of nurturer, witness, and recipient, not arbiter of equipping or visioning.

On a subsequent visit to the Clarkes', Morrigan answers the door when I arrive, but we have to wait for J'den to get off the school bus. Jess tells me that Morrigan stayed home today because she wasn't feeling well. I'm a little puzzled, because she seems perfectly spunky and happy as she peppers me with questions. Later, when she steps out of the room, Jess and Arundel tell me in hushed voices that the reason Morrigan stayed home from school that day is that she was sent home when the school said she had been threatening another child with scissors a few days before. "She would never do something like that," Jess protests, but she and Arundel note that Morrigan has now been hospitalized a few times with erratic, emotional behavior. She's been diagnosed with a mood disorder and she takes medication. They tell me it will likely be diagnosed as bipolar when she grows up.

Jess laughs nervously and suddenly the two of them seem to be shrinking before my eyes. "We know what to do with autism, autism we're okay with, but we have no idea what to do with mental illness. It's scary," she says. The stigma of mental illness has rendered even the boldest and most Spirit-led networked leaders stunned and fearful.

COMING OUT AS DISABLED IN THE CHURCH

Researcher Maci's time with Bailie took on a bifurcated quality: on Sundays, Maci visited Bailie presiding over worship and preaching authoritatively, albeit with her jocular, self-deprecating style from the pulpit. Bailie was doing clergy supply for a small Presbyterian church in New Jersey. But during the week, the two would meet in coffee shops or bars and Bailie would open up about her mental illness, clearly struggling to integrate the two personas herself. "I rarely have people over to my home, for instance," Bailie commented. "Because I can be messy, like really messy, and I don't want most people to see that. That's only when I can let a few people in."[2] Rather frequently Bailie would distinguish between what her brain was doing and her true self. "I try not to use this as an excuse, like to make excuses for my behavior," she commented, "but I know that living with mental illness means my brain is going to lie to me."[3]

Bailie shared with us that she has diagnoses of bipolar 2, anxiety, and PTSD. She doesn't see a lot of leaders in the church who look like her, and she says that has been difficult. She talked about how her efforts to organize an event geared around mental health at the seminary had not panned out. I remember running into her in the seminary café one day and she was devastated that the seminary had organized an alumni panel with non-disabled pastors who work exclusively with institutionalized patients with mental illness. The event she had been trying to organize was meant to showcase how people live fully and faithfully in community and lead with mental illness. She felt frustrated and betrayed that the seminary's vision for ministry with people with mental illnesses was so limited.

Yet this frustration became a catalyst for her sharing more of her personal experience online—one evening over dinner, Bailie showed Maci her Instagram posts with the hashtag #ifyouneedthemtakethem and photos of her medications and her taking them. She'd heard from many people over social media who found her messages not only affirming and encouraging but unique and necessary. "People are literally dying of mental illness, and yet we're not talking about it in the church," Bailie bemoaned. One sunny afternoon at a coffee shop, Bailie had mused that she did not agree with all of Kanye West's approaches, but his church work had prompted her to think about what a church for people with mental illnesses could really look like. On another occasion she described how people with mental illnesses could help the church "think ahead" by helping the church understand where liturgy can slow down and where church can help provide quiet spaces.

2 Fieldnotes, May 5, 2019.
3 Fieldnotes, June 12, 2019.

Poignantly, she talked about her intention to reform the church from within as a pastor living with mental illness. She talked about creating an authoritative voice for people with mental illnesses within the space of the church: too often they are not believed, they are not listened to, or they edit themselves (Swinton 2020b). Bailie mentioned again how even with her own friends she finds herself using more acceptable language like "anxiety" or "depression" rather than "manic" or "bipolar." Her visions for the church were bold, prophetic, unique.

But how could Bailie cultivate this authority if she was constantly forced to censor herself in order to be believed? How could the church care for people with mental illnesses if this culture of stigma and silence undermined their voices in the first place? Bailie's leadership demanded the ultimate, risky misfit: if she were to help build an authoritative voice for people with mental illness in the church, she would need to narrate her own call story transparently, without leaving her own mental illness out. However, if she were to do that, she could never outrun or turn away from her mental illness either. The price of Bailie's leadership would be higher than that demanded of most people, most pastors. But the Spirit was nudging her, she'd already begun to tell her story—perhaps this was only the beginning.

MAKING DISABLED LEADERSHIP VISIBLE

We didn't go looking for disabled leadership in our study. Rather, in congregations where disabled people were being listened to, where confessional modes of ministry made it possible for disabled gifts for ministry to be nurtured, disabled leadership bubbled up, evidence of the Spirit's transformative creativity and power. That evening at St. John's, when Mary had turned to Lisa, a blind lector, to ask her both what they were doing well and what they were still doing wrong, had continued to puzzle me (see chapter 4). How was it that Lisa could feel so empowered at St. John's when she had tripped over her feet her first time up to the altar? How could Lisa "do it all," as she wanted to do in leadership, if she relied on another's elbow to guide her through not just worship spaces, but life? What kind of a leader was Lisa?

One evening, researcher Maci made her way out to Lisa's friend Rod's apartment in an assisted-living home outside Philadelphia to meet up and then join Rod and Lisa for a Monday night worship service hosted there. When she met Rod and Lisa outside, they were both smiling. Rod led the way with his cane, and Lisa took Maci's arm to guide her as they walked. Maci remembers feeling a little shocked, embarrassed even, that after meeting Maci only once before, Lisa would trust her to guide her and would grasp her elbow so intimately. Once inside the apartment, Maci realized that she could not see—it was pitch black. She thought of asking Rod to turn on the lights and then realized this darkness was meaningless to Lisa and Rod. It was only she who could not see.

At the kitchen table, Lisa and Rod carried on a joking banter as they told Maci about their friendship and their faith backgrounds. Rod belonged to a Baptist church and was preaching at the Missionaries gathering that evening. When we had first told Lisa about our study, she was eager to introduce us to Rod. Rod and Lisa met at a life skills class for blind people. They quickly became friends, going to each other's churches and Bible studies, memorizing each other's schedules, and getting to know each other's friends and families. In many ways, they depended on each other. This seemed to be especially true for Rod, who Lisa mentioned had short-term memory issues. During the conversation, Lisa often prompted Rod or reminded him about certain details he seemed to forget.

Before they headed upstairs for worship that evening, Rod and Lisa marveled at how uncomfortable some people seemed even using the terms "blind" or a "blind person." They lingered on this point much more than on the grievances they mentioned about the lack of braille resources or broken links for televised worship at their churches. People don't know what they don't know, Rob and Lisa seemed to believe, and they are doing their best. But they wished people wouldn't use fear as an excuse not to engage or approach them, they said.

Upstairs in the community room, where folks gathered for worship, Maci noticed that she and Lisa were the only non-Black persons gathered for worship. She instinctively became a bit uncomfortable in the space, but Lisa called out to folks she knew as she recognized their voices in the crowd, greeting each person they passed as they entered worship with knowing warmth. Rod preached a soulful message entitled "All Are Welcome," based on Mark 10:13–16. As he began to preach, Lisa asked Maci to help her Facetime Rod's brother so he could hear the sermon.

When Maci arrived at St. John's Parish House a few weeks later for a community meal with a group of blind friends, it was Lisa who recognized her voice even before she'd had a chance to cross the room to greet her. Lisa called her over to the group with which she sat, introducing her to everyone who was gathered for the dinner by name.

In her lecture, "God on Wheels: Disability Liberation and Spiritual Leadership," Rabbi Julia Watts Belser argues that most of the world doesn't want to talk about disability and disabled people are therefore taught that they should take up as little space as possible and "pass" in all situations where that might be possible (Belser 2019, 7:20). Although passing can be advantageous, and there are costs to disclosing one's disability, Belser asserts that there are also many costs to being closeted about one's disability. Toward the very end of the lecture, in the question and answer session, Belser talks about how becoming a wheelchair user helped her to "claim the integrity of [her] own self" in necessitating that she take up space to be in and go through the world (2019, 67).

Contrasting two postures in her wheelchair use in the world, Belser paints a vision for disabled leadership:

> When I move through a crowd I have this posture; I call it elbows out. This is elbows tucked [she demonstrates keeping her arms close to her chest]. This is elbows out [demonstrates pushing her elbows away from her body]. Elbows tucked and elbows out, the motion that I'm making here with my elbows, is actually only about two inches different max in terms of the actual physical space that I take up, right? So we're not talking a major change.
>
> Here's the thing, though—elbows out reminds me that I don't give way, other people move. So when I move through crowds with a person who's not a wheelchair user, with a walker . . . a person who's a strider I like to say, they don't go first. They don't move with enough—they don't move, they're always worried to make sure that I'm going to keep up. I'm like, no, no. Get out of my way. I'm going first and you follow after. They're always trying to, like, clear a little path. I'm like, no, no, we're going, we are moving, and space will get made. (Belser 2019, 67–70)

With "the elbows out" wheelchair user at the helm, the "strider" encounters space in the crowd, space that is opened up in a new way. Belser illustratively decenters able-bodied paradigms at the center of leadership, offering new modes for encounter in the world. Earlier in the interview Belser remarks that "my disabled experience might actually tell me something extraordinary about the nature of God . . . this disabled body knows something about God, not in spite of it but because of it," so her question becomes "Not what does the tradition say about disability experience, but what does disability experience know that the tradition doesn't yet understand and needs to be tapped into?" (2019, 25:00)

Belser illustrates the capacious nature of misfitting, but how does her "elbows out" stance compare to Lisa taking Maci by the elbow? Is not one active while the other remains passive? How can Lisa's leadership take on the "all or nothing" quality she demands of the church? At first Maci felt slightly uncomfortable that Lisa instinctively took her arm and trusted her to lead Lisa through spaces, but from another vantage point, Lisa's seeming reliance is actually a profound way of taking up space, of misfitting. Perhaps more so than the perceived trust, this misfitting made Maci uncomfortable: Lisa refused to pass as just another person in the crowd, not just in her taking of Maci's arm but in her eagerness to play host as she greeted everyone at the gathering, her resourcefulness in supplementing Rod's memory, and her attention in picking Maci's voice out of the crowd. When Maci found herself the only one who was inconvenienced by the darkness, she realized that it was the material environment that had made her feel as though she were leading Lisa. It is in the darkness that Maci began to see the transvaluative qualities of Lisa's leadership to faith communities.

Lisa's arm-in-arm, collaborative leadership, like the Clarkes' networked leadership, Belser's "elbows out" leadership, or Bailie's narrative, authoritative voice, is a gift to the church because it reminds us of our shared yet differential experiences of vulnerability. The double-edged sword of misfitting that both Garland-Thomson and Belser theorize is one in which not only do disabled people incur dramatic costs and generate valuable insights due to misfitting but able-bodied people incur dramatic advantages that often come at the expense of anonymity. Able-bodied people are presumed to fit, they are presumed "equipped" simply because their leadership makes sense in an able-bodied world. But their advantages often compel them to eschew the unnecessary disruption, creativity, and wisdom of the Spirit. Like Maci, they presume the darkness is mere darkness, so they go ahead and turn on lights, rather than leaning into the Spirit and other Spirit-led leaders, and learning to see differently.

The point, though, is that it cost Maci very little to enter into the darkness, let Lisa lead her, and behold her ministry and leadership. Meanwhile, for the Clarkes, Belser, Lisa, and Bailie, the costs of misfitting leadership are always high. The Clarkes are perceived as burdensome, Belser's and Lisa's leadership is undermined by ableist prejudices, and when Bailie's leadership seeks authority it must do so by putting her own privacy and identity at stake. Despite our common need as Christians to collaborate with the Spirit in new modes of leadership, we must keep in view that the experiences of vulnerability among able-bodied people and disabled people are not equal. Indeed, this is why Lisa and Rod's partnership and the Clarkes' togetherness are so, so important: they create coalitions of disabled leaders whose collaboration is far more instructive and way-making than able-bodied paradigms can be. The notion that the Spirit lifts up not just individuals but a body of flourishing disabled leaders provides the ultimate paradigm shift for churches that have individualized leadership in a way that falls away from the very heart of the gospel. The church cannot receive and sustain disabled leadership if disabled leaders remain isolated: as Bailie cried out for, they need mirrors on the journey.

CONCLUSION: MAKING MIRRORS

Midway through spring 2020 in my Ministry with People with Disabilities class, I called upon local disabled leaders to host a panel discussion on ministry for my students at Princeton Seminary. The panel included two former students—Bailie, and another who is an ordained pastor and college chaplain who has cerebral palsy; a hospital chaplain who taught me clinical pastoral education back in the day and who also has CP; Noah, the Deaf PhD student, pastor, and teaching assistant for the course; and Morrigan Clarke, the nine-year old older sister and disability advocate, who has a mood disorder and whose brother, J'den, has autism. Because of the COVID-19 pandemic, the panel took place on Zoom.

I remember Morrigan being scheduled to speak third and nervously poking at her mother, bouncing up and down on the couch when it was time for her to share. Although Morrigan's voice shook a bit as she spoke, her body and her words displayed confidence as she talked about her family's advocacy for disabled people, her brother's place in the church and the world, and her vision for ministry with disabled people. Although all the speakers were insightful and dynamic, my students were particularly drawn to Morrigan, even though she didn't share about her own mood disorder that day. Students responded to Morrigan with encouragement and questions: the chat feature even scrolled by with affirmations of "Morrigan for President 2020!"

Morrigan, in turn, was not only a dynamic speaker but an attentive participant in our master's-level course. Jess, Morrigan's mother, later told me that as Morrigan listened to Bailie, who lives with bipolar disorder, teaches special education, and is navigating the ordination process in the Presbyterian Church, Morrigan whispered to Jess, "Mama, she's just like me. I'm just like her. Maybe I can go to seminary someday?"

In her comments on the panel, Bailie talked about struggling in her vocational trajectory because she couldn't find what she called "mirrors"—people like her, living with mental illness and leading in service to the church. After the panel Bailie emailed me to thank me for the experience, spontaneously adding, "Also, Morrigan was delightful and I'm so thankful that you're the kind of leader who tries to include all voices in class (quite literally)—what a great way to ground all of us in the work of the kingdom."[4] I wrote back, "I'm not sure you'll ever know the impact you had on Morrigan—without overstepping my bounds, I will say that God used you as a mirror yesterday, in a way that can only be God and no one else!!! I have goosebumps."[5]

There was a small risk for me as an educator in ceding the floor to the voices of disabled leaders that day, but there was a profound risk for Bailie as she shared, in front of her peers and other leaders in the church, the challenges of finding her way in the ordination process as a person with mental health diagnoses. The tremendous gift of the Spirit, however, in that moment was that in Bailie's sharing of her own experiences, she became the mirror she had so desperately wanted all those years for Morrigan and her family. At only nine years old, and with her and her family not yet comfortable in sharing her diagnosis with others, Morrigan still saw herself as a leader in the context of a seminary in the business of forming theological leaders, simply because Bailie was willing to misfit and share her own experience.

There is absolutely no way I could have done any of this work on my own as an educator or a theologian: despite my own experiences of struggling to make it in the academy and in the church, when my students look at me, they largely see someone who fits, who fulfills the checklist of able-bodied Christian leadership. But this is precisely the problem. Disabled people are largely absent from classrooms, sanctuaries, and even coffee hours. This connotes a devastating lack of leadership and faithfulness in the church. It is a lack of leadership not only because disabled people are literally missing from seminary classrooms, seminary professorships, pews, and pulpits but because the unwillingness to recognize it as a problem on the part of able-bodied leaders perpetuates the status quo.

In bringing Morrigan and Bailie to the table that day, I took the tiniest step in uplifting and beholding the ministry and leadership of disabled people, and look what the Spirit did! What more transvaluative ministry

---

4   Email communication, March 31, 2020.
5   Email communication, April 1, 2020.

can the Spirit do if not just disabled leaders, but all Christian leaders embrace a leadership paradigm that values collaboration, disabled networking, and narrative ministry? Indeed, it is not just that the Clarkes need each other, that Rod and Lisa need each other, that Morrigan and Bailie need each other, but that the church needs them. The poverty of Christian leadership and the flailing ministry of the twenty-first-century church will not flourish without the ministry and leadership of disabled people. And the leadership of the church cannot flourish without a true reliance on the leadership of the Holy Spirit.

Sharon V. Betcher noted the work of the Spirit as transvaluing, but as this chapter shows, that transvaluing is not just capacious and creative but wildly destabilizing. In one of the very first conversations we had with Bailie, she talked about the intersections of her faith, having grown up Pentecostal and now pursuing ordination in the Presbyterian Church (U.S.A.). She talked about the vibrancy of her faith, especially her relationship with the Holy Spirit. "I think when Presbyterians talk about the Holy Spirit, they want to make the Spirit, like, gentle, motherly. I think the Spirit is motherly, too, but I think of the Spirit as having authority—like, the Spirit provokes you, the Spirit convicts you."[6] Describing the Spirit that day, Bailie pointed to some of the challenges and risks afoot for a church that truly abides by not just our image-bearing createdness, our callings to Jesus, but the provoking wisdom and authority of the Holy Spirit.

Could the Spirit be both motherly and authoritative? Bailie certainly thought so, but she knew the particular combination of those adjectives would be a hard pill for some to swallow. It would not be easy for a church so bent on perceiving authority in certain ways to receive guidance from marginalized and novel trailblazers. Her leadership would throw a wrench into the system that would not merely make more room at the table. Tables would be overturned, authority would be deconstructed, laws destroyed—and then what? Perhaps the hegemony of the church as we know it would crumble. Perhaps that would be the work of the Spirit, too.

---

[6] Fieldnotes, June 12, 2019.

9

Mirrors and Accomplices in the Kingdom of God

¹When the day of Pentecost had come, they were all together in one place. ²And suddenly from heaven there came a sound like the rush of a violent wind, and it filled the entire house where they were sitting. ³Divided tongues, as of fire, appeared among them, and a tongue rested on each of them. ⁴All of them were filled with the Holy Spirit and began to speak in other languages, as the Spirit gave them ability.

⁵Now there were devout Jews from every nation under heaven living in Jerusalem. ⁶And at this sound the crowd gathered and was bewildered, because each one heard them speaking in the native language of each. ⁷Amazed and astonished, they asked, "Are not all these who are speaking Galileans? ⁸And how is it that we hear, each of us, in our own native language? ⁹Parthians, Medes, Elamites, and residents of Mesopotamia, Judea and Cappadocia, Pontus and Asia, ¹⁰Phrygia and Pamphylia, Egypt and the parts of Libya belonging to Cyrene, and visitors from Rome, both Jews and proselytes, ¹¹Cretans and Arabs—in our own languages we hear them speaking about God's deeds of power." ¹²All were amazed and perplexed, saying to one another, "What does this mean?" ¹³But others sneered and said, "They are filled with new wine."

—Acts 2:1–13

INTRODUCTION

I woke up on Thursday morning, a day after my second COVID-19 vaccine shot, and came down into the dining room to meet and dismiss Lucia's nurse at 6 a.m. like I always do. As I stood there talking to him, a chilling, familiar feeling came over me: my stomach dropped, my vision began to get spotty, and I knew, because it had happened too many times in my life to count, that I was about to faint. I got my head between my knees, I got onto the floor, and though I was flushed and miserable, after ten to fifteen minutes, the feeling passed. Feeling weak, disheveled, and overwhelmed, I drank a glass of water and went back to bed.

The event was ordinary for me, because I've lived with a fainting disorder nearly my whole life. However, just a few months shy of my fortieth birthday, I began to realize something. Despite being told my whole life that this disorder was temporary, a nuisance of my youth, something I could even fix by eating breakfast, drinking more water, just being a bit more responsible, it was now undeniable that I had not outgrown this. Maybe I was not going to outgrow it. Maybe I was living with it.

It had never occurred to me, despite studying disability for a living, despite growing up with a mother who has multiple sclerosis, a grandfather with a spine injury, despite raising a daughter who has a neurological disease of the brain, that I, too, might be disabled. *The internalized ableism is strong with this one*, I thought, immediately ashamed that I had held this identity at arm's length for all these years. But being told by my lovely neurologist that this was both nothing to worry about and something I'd grow out of had been a slippery slope. I assumed that my experiences, the disruptions they caused—first in a busy high school that didn't have time for someone to rest, recuperate, and maybe return to class, next in an elite college that did not want to take on the liability of a student who couldn't remain upright, and finally in a grad program that sought to treat everyone the same—were personal, isolated, and insignificant. When I was told in college that I would not be allowed to go on the mission trip to Nicaragua because I was too much of a liability, I remember crying hot, bitter tears, more angry than sad, because something seemed very wrong.

When I connected recently with a group of women with whom I went to college, all of whom identify as disabled, I was reticent to share my experience. Was I making a mountain out of a molehill? Several of the women had visible, physical disabilities. They'd never had the luxury of passing. Would they think I was trite or insensitive for suggesting my experiences somehow fell into the same category as theirs? Instead, their collective responses were warm, genuine, soft, even. "How could you have known?" one of them empathized. "No one knew what disability was in the 2000s, the college administration didn't know how to deal with us, none of us knew what we know now." Still another said encouragingly that, despite being late to the game, my voice and my experience mattered.

When I queried my deepest fear in sharing my experiences, this phantom disappearance of my disorder, she responded, "Honestly, I think we need to think more about that in the disability community. Who's to say people who are born with club feet and have surgery shouldn't be part of the community? Who's to say who's in and who's out? If you grow out of something, wouldn't you still have something to contribute? That's all worth thinking about. Thank you for sharing that."

I am not sure where my experience fits, for my life, for my career, or even for this book, but I share it, because I realize that what I was lacking all those years wasn't Christian community. In fact, I had plenty of that. But what I didn't have in Christian community or the academy were the mirrors Bailie had talked about, mirrors that would have helped me to see myself more clearly and maybe even accept myself as I am. It was never the purpose of this research project, but were it not for the dozens of mirrors reflecting toward me, I'm certain I would never have caught a glimpse of myself.

Throughout this book I have impressed upon readers that it's not enough to proclaim that disabled people are made in God's image; rather, we must recognize that they are called by Jesus into ministry and transformed by the Spirit in leadership. But Bailie's call for mirrors kind of brings us full circle. The kind of mirrors Bailie has in mind reflect God's image by being who they are called to be in the world. They lead others to Christ by showing them how to be more themselves in a world that would too often demand otherwise. They lead disabled people to a Christ who doesn't demand of them compulsory able-bodiedness but instead offers them a life of freedom, flourishing, and resurrection in their very own skin. If disabled people are clear that what they need to thrive in ministry and leadership are more mirrors, then churches must work not only on tearing down the obstacles to letting those mirrors shine but on empowering disabled people to find mirrors and to lead the church to the mirrors that already work for them.

Simply put, churches cannot be mirrors for disabled people without disabled people. This is why disabled ministry and leadership are such vital steps for Jesus' work of justice in the church and society. If churches acknowledge the absence and necessity of disabled mirrors, they will seek to trust and amplify disabled leaders, and let disabled leaders lead them to disabled ministries inside or outside the church that are worth nurturing, thereby growing in their relationships with disabled people, their understanding of ableism and disability, and their work for justice.

But representation alone is not enough to alter the systems and structures that reproduce ableism. For Jesus' vision of the kingdom of God here on earth, the work of dismantling ableism becomes everyone's work. And it is risky work, because it requires skin in the game, not just from disabled folks but from their non-disabled allies, as well. Just because I hadn't had disabled mirrors growing up doesn't meant that I hadn't had accomplices—like my mother, who boldly encouraged me to share my experience of disability with people so that I could be safe and cared for in the communities I joined; the school administrator at Davidson College who let me rest on her couch after each time I fainted, even though that meant she took on the liability risk of my condition personally; and my husband, who has always accepted my fainting disorder as part of who I am, never making me feel like an inconvenience or a burden.

I borrow the term accomplice from autistic activist Reyma McCoy McDeid because it gets beyond the performative work of allyship to the risky work of what it means to work for justice alongside those who are disabled (McCoy McDeid as qtd. in Ladau 2021, 142). I think it is vital that Christians see ourselves as accomplices in working to usher in the kingdom of God, because in order to dismantle a prejudiced system, we will need to stand in radical opposition to what currently exists. We will need to speak up, and not just when it's convenient. We will need to take risks, risks that may cost not just disabled people but us, our churches, our families, ourselves. We may even need to break the law.

After all, the COVID-19 crisis has brought racism, capitalism, and ableism into full view for all to see, and yet so many of us have been bystanders to injustice. This kingdom of God of which Jesus speaks looks nothing like our prejudiced systems and our ableist leadership, and yet we settle for eking out a living in an ableist, capitalist, racist system as long as the impact on us and those we love is not too severe. Yet Jesus holds out not just the possibility of justice but the plural possibilities of more authentic, flourishing life in the Spirit that all of us need to embrace if we are to live as fully human beings in the twenty-first century. In this final chapter, drawing on Sharon V. Betcher, I alert the church to the way in which the Holy Spirit has been colonized as an instrument of normalcy and propriety. In response, I theorize the Spirit as advocate, calling the church away from the charity and oppression associated with ministries of inclusion and to a new holy role as accomplices with disabled people to pursue (disability) justice and the kingdom of God in the world. Drawing on Betcher's concept of Crip Nation, I argue that decolonization must pry itself away from the legacy of the oppressors, following the Spirit toward a radical new vision for fellowship and justice in the world.

DECOLONIZING SPIRIT

Alongside disabled theologians like Betcher, the church must reject readings of the healing narratives that interpret disability as a defect that needs to be divinely remediated by the Spirit. Just as with inclusion, such readings maintain disability as a problem, because they pivot and climax on its removal, and they disappear disabled persons by making them normal as a messianic sign. This is why Betcher argues that Spirit can function as an

> "ideology of normalcy"... hidden in our theological anticipations, espe-cially in relation to the healing of suffering and thus in our theologies of Spirit. Spirit, even in these "politics of compassion," has been con-flated with the scopic dynamics that generate the bourgeois—whole, individuated, and idealized—body. Spirit, in this vein, generates a zone of respectability, propriety, and civility. While such a subjective technology appears to be, perhaps intends to be, life-giving, it coin-cidently serves as a mechanism of containment against its own fears. Neither miraculous nor medical remediation, nor the physics of this version of social compassion, evade, but rather enforce, the cultural ideology of normalcy. (2006, np)

Indeed, throughout this book we have seen the ways in which the church purports to hold out life-giving inclusion to disabled people, when that inclusion actually demands conformity to normalcy in exchange for healing.

As an alternative to neoliberalism's stifling inclusionism of disabled persons, Betcher imagines a radical Crip Nation flaunting its "subver-sive living even within the belly of empire" and "transvaluing Spirit from guarantor of miraculous remediation towards the recognition of persons living the variability and vulnerabilities of bodies with real presence to life" (2006, np). Although Betcher's vision of Crip Nation remains relatively abstract, I wonder if we haven't glimpsed elements of it across these very pages. Prayers of the people that ardently assert the needs and the gifts of disabled people front and center in a worship service, another worship service that draws families with disabled children from across the state on Sunday afternoons to worship with freedom, a place on Friday nights for disabled people to be themselves, eat, and sing, Belser's elbows-out leadership, Bailie's authoritative voice for folks with mental illness, Lisa's all-or-nothing leadership. These ministries and leaders do not stifle but instead uplift the "variability and vulnerability of bodies with real presence to life," and the Spirit is evident in their particular, restless advocacy, and the way that advocacy critically requires and effects a transformation not just in themselves but in others, and in the church.

The trouble in the church, however, is that our paradigm for recognizing the Spirit is too narrowly restricted to one-off events like miracles or Pentecost, rather than the slow, painstaking work of advocacy for justice that often offends, offputs, and convicts the status quo and conventional leaders in unsettling ways. In this way, we still prefer a spirit of normalcy, because we prefer a life free from struggle, pain, and hardship. We often prefer miraculous remediation because it solves the problem of disability for us, leaving our comfortable systems and our fraught theologies intact.

DECOLONIZING PENTECOST

The story the church likes to tell when it comes to the Christian scriptures' radical vision for diversity and inclusion is Pentecost. At Pentecost, as the story goes at the beginning of this chapter and the second chapter of Acts, the Spirit suddenly filled Jews of all nationalities—Galileans, Parthians, Medes, Elamites, folks from Mesopotamia, Libya, Rome, and Asia—with each other's languages, but also with the ability to understand one another. It's a miraculous moment that has inspired the church for thousands of years, has even birthed ministries and denominations, so poignant is this witness and gift of God and our beholding of ourselves as beloved in all of our differences.

Yet, too often in Christian churches, teachings, and theologies, Pentecost is read out of context in order to announce Christian communion across difference, as if we have arrived when we are still very much on the way. For example, we are quick to celebrate stories of people who triumph over suffering and disability, the "supercrips," rather than accompany those whose disabled dignity demands reform from our systems and society. Supercrips expose ableism because they are often celebrated for meeting extremely low, dehumanizing expectations, or held to impossible standards that force them to deny, diminish, or overcome their disabilities (Kafer 2013, 90). And "supercrip" narratives require nothing from able-bodied people: in fact, they distance disabled and able-bodied people from one another, othering disabled narratives and perverting the Spirit.

As we know, Pentecost is not the end of the church but a mere beginning, a Spirit-filled moment in time that offers a vision of things as they could be or should be because of all that they are not. Rather, the book of Acts takes place under the civilizing mission of empire, in which the Jews live a fearful and displaced diaspora life (Jennings 2017, 19–21). As Willie James Jennings reminds us, the enjoining so powerfully envisioned in Pentecost among the Jews is hardly complete, because even Acts is a story in which "the Gentiles of Acts are on their way to communion with Jews while remaining Gentiles" (22). As Jennings so poignantly puts it,

> The book of Acts reminds us that to follow Jesus is already to be a betrayer of one's people. The betrayal is at the point of diaspora concern and imperial desire. The disciples of Jesus do not betray an identity but a destiny, not a history but how the story of my people will be used to dictate to me a future and plan my life projects. The imperial project of the Roman Empire also dies in the body of the disciple who has joined her or his body to the risen savior, Jesus. (2017, 23)

Jennings' thick description of Acts draws us out of Pentecost idolatry by complicating the Spirit's work as not just enjoining but disruptive, betraying, revealing political subterfuge. Indeed, all too often the story of Pentecost functions institutionally for the church as do the rhetoric and practices of diversity and inclusion for secular institutions (see chapter 1). Pentecost announces inclusion, thus disallowing space for those who still experience exclusion and effacing the role of the empire in colonizing, coopting, and civilizing. It also tends to minimize the complex politics of groups in Acts living under empire, in which the Jews were but one entity, or the intersectional, often fragmented experiences of being Jews or Gentiles in the early church, to which Jennings points above.

Although we can rejoice in the vision cast long by the spontaneous valorizing of difference alongside communion engendered at Pentecost, we must recognize that our sanitized interpretations of the story need to be decolonized as well. If the long story of Acts, as Jennings writes, compels followers of Jesus to be "betrayers of one's people" and "die" to life in Christ, how can the church pursue Jesus in today's complex context, in which disabled people are just one such group that lives in the shadow of empire?

A SPIRIT OF ADVOCACY AND TRUTH

Although the tendency will be to behold the Spirit's intervention primarily in Bartimaeus' overcoming of blindness, neither the circumstances of injustice, nor Bartimaeus' faith, nor his ministry is at all visible without a Spirit of advocacy and truth that runs through the narrative. This new vision of disabled justice, ministry, and leadership culminates in Bartimaeus following Jesus on the way, orienting us to the Spirit-led community work that would become the foundations of the early church. The old visions for leadership—those of able-bodied leadership, leadership from the center, leadership that ignores injustice—will have to die if the church is to be reborn from leadership on the margins as Christ intends, and they will have to suffer with those who suffer, even as he is resurrected and his Spirit lives on.

Given the Spirit's classic description as advocate in the Gospel of John, we can recognize the work of the Spirit not just in helping Bartimaeus to see but in giving him the courage to plead with Jesus in the first place. Were it not for Bartimaeus' cries, Jesus may have kept on walking past him on the roadside. Yet it is Bartimaeus' advocacy that invites everyone in the text to see him and the image of God in him more clearly, as he compels Jesus to a new standard in his ministry. It makes sense that what we do with the healing narratives is that we follow Jesus' turn of heart in listening to what it is that disabled people are truly saying. When the cries are cries of lament, we make space for those laments, even unto the form of rebuke, and repentance, in the church. Nurturing the ministry of disabled people by supporting and recognizing the importance of free spaces is something tangible that churches can also do. Finally, letting these free spaces and disabled leaders teach us new ways of ministry and leadership is also paramount.

"But what do we do next?" people always seem to be asking. "What is it when we are done listening, lamenting, and repenting that we are actually called to do?" On the one hand, it is important to recognize that listening, lamenting, repenting, and nurturing are actions—they just aren't the shiny, programmatic, transactional actions non-disabled people are used to taking in disability ministry. They are also actions that resist the control that churches, and especially non-disabled people, struggle to relinquish over ministry in the first place, which is why they are so difficult yet important if the ministry is to belong to God. However, if non-disabled people are able to listen, lament, repent, and learn from disabled people in their congregations, it is true that remaining bystanders to the ableism and injustices in our society and out institutions simply will not do. More is required in life in the Spirit.

ACCOMPLICES FOR THE KINGDOM

When Patty Berne, Mia Mingus, Leroy Moore, Eli Clare, Sebastian Margaret, and Sins Invalid, the Disability Justice Performing Collective of Patty Berne and Leroy Moore, planted the roots of the disability justice movement in the early 2000s, they looked like the ultimate betrayers of one's people. Radically rebuking the white, capitalist, heteronormative foundations of the disability rights movement in the United States, disability justice advocates made clear that there could be no justice without justice for all. This did not mean that they were opposed to collaboration with other groups to meet their goals. Rather, it meant that they wanted to harken back to the complexity of the history of the disability rights movement—that before there were whitewashed laws and legislators and white disability rights leaders, there were Black Panthers, indigenous people, queer people, disabled people who were incarcerated or houseless, who held their freedom in common but for whom freedom became about being more like what capitalism required them to be. This is why one of the ten principles of disability justice honors the leadership of the most impacted, such that the movement never acquiesces to requiring the most impacted to continue to sacrifice in the service of those who are less impacted.

Allegedly this is what we mean when we talk about the gospel, Jesus' command to serve the least of these, but we so often forget that the posture of servanthood means that someone else, not us, is always in leadership. We do not become great in doing unto the least of these as the world so often champions. Neither do we become great by demeaning the least of these by always making them lesser, objects, instruments, indentured servants to our help. In her book *Demystifying Disability,* disabled activist Emily Ladau draws on autistic activist Reyma McCoy McDeid to problematize the way in which those who seek to be allies often preserve their privilege by assuming those with whom they are allied are in need of help (Ladau 2021). Ladau writes that "the first step of being an ally is . . . recognizing that disabled people aren't in need of saving. We're in need of a world that recognizes our rights and our humanity without question" (2021, 142). McCoy McDeid offers a powerful reframing of allyship: "To be an ally is to help people who are marginalized in some capacity to make the most of their life in this unchanged system," whereas, "To be an accomplice, on the other hand, is to work side by side with people who are marginalized, to confront the system and contribute to shifting it accordingly" (McCoy McDeid as qtd. in Ladau 2021, 142). Not just at Pentecost, but throughout his entire ministry, Jesus is not just asking people to work within the system or the world that they have been given; rather, he is asking them to tear the system down and to create a new heaven and a new earth! Jesus is an agitator: he is deeply critical of the world's power and politics. But he is also wildly creative: because he believes in God's vision for justice, he calls for the current system to crumble in order to birth something new.

Yet being an accomplice for justice is not effortless or cheap. It is, as Jennings notes, an invitation not just to be unpopular but to become a traitor to one's people, to forgo the comforts and benefits of being able-bodied in a world that demands it and to join oneself with a Jesus who will be crucified and a Crip Nation that will only walk the earth bearing the scars of empire. Although the stories of mirrors in the kingdom of God are readily available in this book and in the disability justice work of so many, the stories of accomplices are few and far between. One reason for this is that they are still being called forth. They are still too fearful and too cowardly, too self-preserving and sheepish, to come into their ministry, and my hope is that this book will change that.

Another reason why there are few stories of accomplices is because they look to the world so like traitors and are so vilified this side of earth for their advocacy that they are rarely recognizable to the common eye. A case in point are the Black Panthers who supported the Section 504 protests in one of the first radical displays of disability justice (Piepzna-Samarasinha 2018, 22–23). Yet they, the Black Panthers, who were always highly visible, have been shockingly rendered invisible in this history. This is not accidental, but the clear politics of a white supremacy that would have disability activists believe that they can settle for a disability justice that excludes people of color, that pits marginalized groups against one another as a tactic for undermining freedom itself.

The same concern comes up in Jennings' critique of *The Christian Imagination* and the way in which Western theological education, even reconciliation, render invisible colonialism and whiteness at the heart of the Christian mission (2010). Jennings argues that Western Christianity is in crisis as it seeks a post-racial future yet carries within it a tragic, racist past that devalues and undermines the particular stories of Christians of color. In *After Whiteness* (2020), Jennings makes clear that the shape of whiteness in theological education is marked by mastery, control, and possession, thus allying himself with disability justice advocates who offer a vision of creative, collaborative leadership and care to foment the forces of capitalism, racism, and colonialism.

But does ableism as a feature of colonialism run so deep that even Jennings fails to recognize it? In *The Christian Imagination*, he argues persuasively and vehemently that Christian imagination is "diseased" and "deformed" by whiteness and colonialism (9–10). He writes,

> I anticipate some resistance to the fundamental claim of this work, that Christian social imagination is diseased and disfigured. In making such a claim, I am not saying that the church is lost, moribund, or impotent. Rather I want my readers to capture sight of a loss, almost imperceptible, yet articulated powerfully in the remaining slender testimonies of Native American peoples and other aboriginal peoples. This loss points not only to the deep psychic cuts and gashes in the social imaginary of western peoples, but also to an abiding mutilation of a Christian vision of creation and our own creatureliness. The loss is nothing less than the loss of the sense of our own creatureliness. I want Christians to recognize the grotesque nature of a social performance of Christianity that imagines Christian identity floating above the land, landscape, animals, place, and space, leaving such realities to machinations of capitalistic calculations and the commodity chains of private property. Such Christian identity can only inevitably lodge itself in the materiality of racial existence. (2010, 293)

In inverting the grotesque as that which is disconnected from earthly, creaturely forms, in positing disease and disfigurement as loss, Jennings appears to be critiquing what is upside down about Christianity on this side of heaven. However, the biting critique of Christian imagination also relies on the sublimation of disease, disfigurement, and disability to do its bidding. Critically, appreciating Jennings' challenging call for accomplices to be betrayers of the world, empire, capitalism, whiteness, and distorted Christian imagination by joining themselves with Christ cannot happen on the backs of disabled people. This is what disability justice leaders mean when they say no body can be left behind and they resolve to let those who are most impacted lead. Would that this broad, coalitional Crip Nation serve as a mirror for all of us of the ways we have been beguiled by ableism, and that the Spirit would call us all toward a creatureliness that leaves no creatures, even those with disabilities, without the possibility to flourish. In Crip Nation, in disability justice, in Jesus, we see a "least of these" who both talks back and serves, an ethic of collective caregiving and community that creates a new kingdom as it tears down the dividing walls among us.

THE KINGDOM OF GOD

I cannot help but hear echoes of the already-but-not-yet shape of Christian life in the vision for disability justice, but what also compels the vision is the way it is anchored in a particular time and place, particular injustices and struggles that make it impossible for their authors to settle for inclusion in an able-bodied world. Instead, they imagine more, even as they struggle together for a life that creates care webs, dignifies and expands access, and advocates tirelessly against the oppression of this very world. Willie James Jennings describes how the movement of the Spirit in Acts confronts, calls, and creates. He writes,

> The hierarchies nurtured by the Roman Empire are being undone by the Spirit, who will not release slave or free, Jew or Gentile, to their own self-interpretations, but who will relentlessly prod them to open themselves toward one another in a life that builds the common. Now in the Spirit the common is not the bottom, not the despised humble beginning, and not the launching pad into social and economic hierarchies. It is the goal of life together in God. (2017, 22–23)

Disability justice advocates "open themselves toward one another in a life that builds the common," evidencing the work of the Spirit in their midst. In their prophetic calls and practical activism, churches can listen intently, amplify their perspectives and protests, and show themselves to be thoughtful accomplices in tearing down the systems of oppression as we seek life together in the kingdom of God.

Importantly, the authors and the activists who seek disability justice note that it is not yet a broad-based popular movement; rather, "disability justice is a vision and practice of a yet-to-be, a map . . . a movement towards a world in which every body and mind is known as beautiful" (Piepzna-Samarasinha 2018, 29). It is also a movement that emerges from the edges, rather than the center, precisely because white activists have not valued the lives and perspectives of BIPOC, trans, and queer disabled activists. Therefore, it is vital that those of us who are at the center continue to embrace the disruptive, decentering work of the Spirit among us, that we not speak for or minister over those who have been most impacted in the disability justice movement, that our witness serve to amplify their ministry and leadership rather than our own voices. After all, we are not mirrors, the Bartimaeuses, but accomplices, the crowds and recipients, in Jesus' ministry. As we deny ourselves, and especially the myth of our able bodies, we offer more space for this vision for disability justice, this Crip Nation of leaders, this kingdom of God, to come to fruition. And in so doing, we are dispossessed of the very things we thought we needed and invited to taste true intimacy, care, freedom, and interdependence. Foretastes of the kingdom, glimmers of hope, disabled leadership, and a new vision for the church that is only and always following Jesus on the way toward justice.

Conclusion

When Lucia was about two years old, with most of the acute discomfort in terms of her seizures and her feeding difficulties finally behind her, it was as if she woke up to the world around her. Instead of screaming in discomfort, her smile lit up the room, her giggles bubbled forth unexpectedly, and she cocked her head sometimes in thought, her eyes sparkling. But at her preschool, a special education school filled with kids in need of attention, Lucia's newfound peace caused her to fade into the background. Her report cards stressed how pleasant she was, that she didn't have any "behaviors," rather than what she was learning or how she was growing.[1]

When she became old enough for kindergarten, we decided to move her into a local typical kindergarten, where she spent approximately half the day in special education classrooms and half the day in a regular kindergarten classroom. What we began to discover is that despite having no apparent verbal communication, Lucia could consistently nod her head yes and turn her head for no. And she had preferences and ideas just like everyone else, but waiting for her communication,

[1]   Portions of this chapter were derived in part from the following article, copyright Taylor & Francis: Erin Raffety and Stuart Carroll 2021, "From Charity to Classroom Co-Learning: Togetherness in the Spirit as a Model for Experiential Education with People with Disabilities," *Journal of Disability & Religion* 25, no. 3: 312–28, https://www.tandfonline.com/doi/full/10.1080/23312521.2021 .1895027.

perceiving, and receiving her communication required time and practice from people around her.

In the midst of a global pandemic in which mental health is deteriorating and relationships are crumbling, Lucia's communication is blossoming. Maybe it's because she's had to switch to one-on-one instruction and communication rather than going to school in the typical way. We've had to find new ways to communicate over Zoom or outside for safety. Everyone is experimenting, not just with communicating with her but with how to connect when the going gets tough. And it is her adaptability, her ingenuity, her resolve that have truly gotten so many of us around her through these dark days. This is the type of unexpected leadership that is often imperceptible when things are "as they should be." But if disabled people aren't contributing and leading, maybe things need to change. Maybe all our communication could use intention and reformation. Maybe Lucia was made for such a time as this.

. . .

In February of 2020, a group of master's students training to be pastors at Princeton Theological Seminary (PTS) and undergraduate students with intellectual and developmental disabilities (I/DD) from The College of New Jersey (TCNJ) set out to learn together about Christian theology, scripture, and ministry with people with disabilities. I had met Stuart Carroll through a mutual friend several months prior and learned about the Career and Community Studies (CCS) program for learners aged eighteen to twenty-five with I/DD at TCNJ and their model of "reverse inclusion," learning experiences designed with the CCS students in mind but in which typically matriculated TCNJ students also participated, not as mentors or assistants but fellow students. In addition, CCS students also take courses across the general core curriculum and graduate in four years. Together, Stuart and I created a Ministry and Disability course in which CCS and PTS students learned about disability and Christianity and, based on their learning, put together a worship service for the public. Seminarians elected to participate in the mini-course at TCNJ as one of several experiential learning tracks offered in a traditional course on Ministry with People with Disabilities at the seminary, one of which included what we called "co-learning" and worship leadership with students from TCNJ.

Although the initial classroom sessions at TCNJ went well and the students got to know one another through interactive activities, midway through the semester the COVID-19 pandemic forced both our institutions to put the rest of the coursework for the semester online. This seemed like too great a challenge for what was already an experimental course, and I initially wanted to give up. Yet Stuart urged me that the CCS students all wanted to continue with the course, and the majority of PTS students expressed interest as well. Still, the adjustments proved difficult. We had to scrap the worship service that the students were looking forward to and shift to an online, creative presentation regarding their interpretation of disability and scripture.

As we checked in with casual conversation at the beginning of class in late February and early March, it was apparent that the CCS and PTS students were undergoing, or at least articulating, their experiences with the COVID-19 pandemic fairly differently. Whereas the PTS students expressed some frustration, sadness, and fear, they were reserved and polished in their comments. Meanwhile, many of the CCS students wore their emotions on their sleeves: "It's not fair that this virus is keeping me at home! This is no fun! I can't see my friends," they lamented. One week a student expressed anger: "Why did that person in China have to eat a bat and make this virus start? I blame those people in China!" I remember yet another student expressing real fear over sick relatives, "She's really sick! What if she dies?" the student exclaimed.

These exclamations of raw emotion often came up during the prayer requests we took at the beginning of class. Rather than always praying myself, I often invited the students to pray. The CCS students typically declined, but the PTS students often solicited prayer requests from the large group and then incorporated them into an opening prayer as practice for future ministry. I remember in the second week of the online course, many of the CCS students communicated these raw, emotional prayer requests, and I watched the PTS student who was gathering them kind of stumble in his tracks. "You're right, it's not fair," he finally replied to one of his classmates. "Thank you for saying out loud what is really true, what so many of us feel, but don't want to admit." I could see in that moment that he realized he could not explain this virus away using theology, and that he was challenged and moved to have to meet his classmate in the throes of frustration and grief. Maybe ministry wasn't about fitting these classmates' prayers into the form of the prayers they had been taught; maybe their prayers had something to teach all of us.

As the PTS students were being challenged by their classmates' earnest prayers, they were not only faced with this very pressing challenge of doing ministry online with people who were socially isolated, but I think they started to recognize the value of some of their classmates' ministry among them and to them. These wild, emotional prayer requests, led by the CCS students, took the form of lament, a crying out to God in the face of injustice, which is a deeply faithful, biblical practice (Brueggemann 1986, 1978; Ellington 2008; Katongole 2017). In these seemingly peripheral moments that happened in the first few minutes of class, some of the power dynamics started to shift. The CCS students' prayers demonstrated a kind of boldness and faithfulness that PTS students weren't seeing at the seminary or even much in churches. In responding to their classmates in prayer, PTS students were being shaped by the CCS students' prayers and faith. The kernels of some kind of mutual formation first bubbled up through the movement of the Spirit in prayer: God was leading, even online, in a global pandemic.

But when we gave students the opportunity to work independently in groups to plan their projects, PTS students ended up taking over, fragmenting the group and doling out individual tasks. In the PTS students' anxiety to complete the assignment, especially in a new, online format, and do it well, they took control over the project, ceasing to be co-learners alongside the TCNJ students. After the breakdown of communication online between the PTS and CCS students during their unsupervised small-group meeting, a PTS student reached out to me to let me know that she was concerned about the way they were interacting. It became apparent that in wanting to "treat everyone the same," the PTS students were not paying attention to what their CCS classmates wanted to contribute, or felt that they could contribute, especially in trying to break down responsibilities "equally" and assigning portions of the project to complete. I wish I had asked them where this ethic of fairness, "treating everyone the same," came from, but what was important was that it had not come from the CCS students themselves. Rather, early on in the course the CCS students had clearly voiced their concerns and needs for additional classroom support to complete the course. Yet they had also made evident areas in which they had gifts and ideas they had for the final project.

Following this struggle, I reached out to the PTS students in the group and reminded them that the goal of the assignment was not really the final product but the learning involved in doing it together. I reminded them that they needed to pay attention and get to know one another well to work well together, even though this was really difficult online. And we advised the group of six to split into two smaller groups of three, with two PTS students to one CCS student, so that with fewer people, coordination of parts of the final project would be easier.

By reframing the goal of the project back toward learning and community, PTS students not only felt relieved of some of the burden of excelling in the project's outcome, but they were also reminded that ministry and discipleship, even in the service of theology education, cannot be transactional, proscribed, or efficient. Rather, co-learning as a model for discipleship means that learning is not just parallel but intertwined with learning from one another what it means to serve and glorify Jesus.

As we gathered for our final class period, CCS and PTS students were asked to share what they had learned in the course. Both groups of students emphasized, despite and sometimes even owing to the online format, the beauty and intimacy of forming relationships with people they would not have met had they not participated in the course. Many PTS students stressed that getting to know the CCS students helped them realize that the final assignment product and the plans they had made on their own paled in comparison to the challenge and gift of really listening well and working together, finding their way toward new interpretations of scripture together. It was particularly gratifying to hear the CCS students identify their gifts for ministry and say that they now see themselves as ministers and leaders, because their fellow students helped them to see these gifts more clearly.

As the groups presented their final assignments, largely in prerecorded video form over the internet that evening, the air was filled with anxious anticipation. Several of the CCS students reminded the class about how nervous they get; in this way, the online format provided several advantages. For one, it gave students the opportunity to prerecord their presentations so that they could present their best to their professors and their peers. But as we played the presentations and watched them together, it also allowed students to re-experience their best, freeing them up to witness their gifts for ministry and leadership coming alive!

The two presentations, each of which offered varied interpretations of disability scriptures, featured original worship songs, testimony, preaching, and biblical exegesis. The chat feature of the online platform rolled by with encouraging comments from one group to the other. "Preach, brother!" one PTS student commended her CCS classmate. "Praise God!" students exclaimed, as if they were in a worship service, offering not just praise of one another but thanksgiving to God for the gifts of one another. One CCS student who was anxious about even speaking in class sang alongside his PTS peers in virtually constructed harmony; another CCS student offered a four-minute sermon in his own singsong style, captivating his classmates. A CCS student gave an earnest testimony of her growth in faith, and yet another CCS student, shy to speak, opened up about a hurtful experience in the church in a dialogue with PTS peers.

Much as the CCS students' laments had led us toward different and more poignant practices of prayer earlier in the semester, the gifts of the CCS students were lifted up in these presentations as true instances of ministry and leadership. It was the CCS students whose contributions especially refused to be confined to the form of a classroom assignment. In those moments that evening, their gifts prompted the walls between the classroom and the sanctuary to come tumbling down online. Although we had given up the pursuit of putting together a final worship service for the public, I proclaimed at the end of the class period that that hadn't stopped God from being worshiped in powerful, novel ways that evening. God did a worship service among us.

In fall 2020, a dear friend of mine at a church in Atlanta reached out to me, asking if I would be willing to preach a sermon on disability for their online Advent sermon series. I was a bit hesitant to accept, since I prefer to recommend a disabled preacher for these invitations, but Jessica's request was a bit different: Would I be open to preaching with a congregational leader in their church named Martha, a woman with Down Syndrome? I had never preached a sermon with another preacher before, but Martha was an accomplished public speaker and disability advocate. It seemed like too good an opportunity to pass up!

Jessica introduced us over Zoom one afternoon, and the following week we met online to brainstorm our interpretations of the scripture we were preaching on. When I told Martha about my daughter, Lucia, she was eager to see pictures and hear more about her. She was instantly drawn to her. That afternoon as we talked about what we would share about the scripture, I told Martha that I was in the midst of a harrowing battle with Lucia's insurance company regarding coverage for her at the local children's hospital. It was so scary and upsetting that I could barely see straight. Martha's indignation over our struggles and her clarity about Lucia's value and her gifts moved me through the computer screen. When people hear that my family is struggling to access care and coverage for Lucia, they often seem to shrivel up. Maybe they don't want me to be political, because it's something they don't want to think about. Maybe they don't know what to say. But in that moment, Martha didn't hesitate, "Lucia's life matters!" she practically shouted through the screen. "She shouldn't be going through that. She's beautiful. She has so much to give the world! She's a child of God!"

Fittingly, the text we were preaching on that Advent was Mary's Magnificat, in which, in the midst of proclaiming her humility to give birth to the Christ child, Mary also testifies to God's vision for justice: "He has scattered the proud in the thoughts of their hearts. He has brought down the powerful from their thrones, and lifted up the lowly. He has filled the hungry with good things, and sent the rich away empty" (Luke 1:51b–53). Martha's soul also magnified the Lord to me, because she instantly saw Lucia as a child of God and the world that would treat her otherwise as a world in need of change.

* * *

As I wrap up this book, the world is entering year two of the pandemic, and we are all fatigued, disheartened, and frustrated. The stories I share above are not the stories I expected to be telling about disabled ministry and leadership, Christian congregations, or the world that needs them. And yet it is important to witness to how disabled Christian leaders and ministers are being used by God at such a time as this. The angst and the suffering witnessed in the pandemic remind us that the world is not as it should be, especially for disabled folks who have disproportionately been affected and endangered by, and died of, COVID-19.

And yet, God is still ardently pursuing justice, if we can only behold ministry and leadership in the new, adaptable, collaborative ways in which they come to us. I think about how disabled leadership in each of these instances—Lucia's communication, the TCNJ students' laments and invitations for help, and Martha's advocacy—are not solo acts but bids for intimacy, understanding, dignity, and collaboration in a world that so often doesn't make or have time for those things. Disabled leadership does not lift up the mighty and the powerful but makes a new way for dignity to replace agency, for our collective humanity to be affirmed, as we leave no one behind. In fact, in its defiant, collaborative, coalitional work, disabled leadership makes leadership accessible to all, undermining hierarchy, foregrounding relationship, and magnifying Jesus' kingdom for all.

I once worried in my heart of hearts as a parent that Lucia would not be able to give love as the world gives it. And she still can't. So I suppose she gives love in an extra-worldly way. Her love becomes the mirror I didn't know I needed. When her smiles radiate through her body so viscerally that she shakes with joy, I forget to worry about what I look like in response. When her healthcare and rights are threatened, I forget to care what anyone thinks of me or what it requires of me as I become an accomplice for justice in this world. And when she reminds me that being disabled offers insight, expression, justice, and dignity to God in a world so short on those things, I wonder if I can show up and embrace myself, too, just as I am.

After all, true love comes from God. It cannot be anything other than what it is in this world. The challenge for non-disabled people is to stop trying to get it to conform, so we can simply receive it. The challenge for disabled folks is to be dignified and amplified in the ways they give it so that others can also receive it. The challenge for us all is to journey toward justice with Jesus, even in a pandemic, even with the church in crisis, even when the world tells us otherwise. It can be done, but only if we do not leave one another behind.

Bibliography

Ahmed, Sara. 2012. *On Being Included*. Durham, N.C.: Duke University Press.

Akhtar, Nameera, and Vikram A. Jaswal. 2020. "Stretching the Social: Broadening the Behavioral Indicators of Sociality." *Child Development Perspectives* 14, no. 1: 28–33.

Annandale, Naomi H., and Erik W. Carter. 2014. "Disability and Theological Education: A North American Study." *Theological Education* 48, no. 2: 83–102.

Barnes, Colin, Geof Mercer, and Tom Shakespeare. 1999. *Exploring Disability: A Sociological Introduction*. Oxford: Polity Press.

Bauman, H-Dirksen L., and Joseph J. Murray, eds. 2014. *Deaf Gain: Raising the Stakes for Human Diversity*. Minneapolis: University of Minnesota Press.

Belser, Julia Watts. 2019. "God on Wheels: Disability Liberation and Spiritual Leadership." YouTube video, 1:13:57. October 25, 2019. https://www.youtube.com/watch?v=tjq7sWgwsQk.

Bendroth, Norman B., ed. 2015. *Transitional Ministry Today*. Lanham, Md.: Rowan & Littlefield.

Betcher, Sharon V. 2006. "Saving the Wretched of the Earth." *Disability Studies Quarterly* 26, no. 3. https://dsq-sds.org/article/view/721/898.

———. 2007. *Spirit and the Politics of Disablement*. Minneapolis: Augsburg Fortress.

Black, Kathy. 1996. *A Healing Homiletic*. Nashville: Abingdon.

Block, Jennie Weiss. 2002. *Copious Hosting: A Theology of Access for People with Disabilities*. New York: Continuum.

Bolsinger, Tod E. 2015. *Canoeing the Mountains: Christian Leadership in Uncharted Territory*. Downers Grove, Ill.: IVP Books.

Bowman, Daniel, Jr. 2021. *On the Spectrum: Autism, Faith, and the Gifts of Neuro-diversity*. Grand Rapids: Brazos.

Branson, Mark Lau, and Juan F. Martinez. 2011. *Churches, Cultures and Leadership: A Practical Theology of Congregations and Ethnicities*. Downers Grove, Ill.: IVP Academic.

Brisenden, Simon. (1986) 1998. "Independent Living and the Medical Model of Disability." In *The Disability Studies Reader*, edited by Tom Shakespeare, 20–27. New York: Cassell.

Brock, Brian. 2020. "Disability Is Not a 'Problem' to Be Solved." *Faith & Leadership*, June 23. https://faithandleadership.com/disability-not-problem-be-solved.

Brown, Lyn Mikel, and Carol Gilligan. 1992. *Meeting at the Crossroads: Women's Psychology and Girls' Development*. Cambridge, Mass.: Harvard University Press.

Brueggemann, Walter. (1978) 2018. *The Prophetic Imagination*. 40th anniversary edition. Minneapolis: Fortress.

———. 1986. "The Costly Loss of Lament." *Journal of the Study of the Old Testament* 36: 57–71.

Burke, Minyvonne. 2020. "Church Denied 8-Year Old Boy First Communion because He's Autistic, New Jersey Family Says." *NBC News*, February 27. https://www.nbcnews.com/news/religion/church-denied-8-year-old-boy-first-communion-because-he-n1144341.

Cameron, C. 2007. "Whose Problem? Disability Narratives and Available Identities." *Community Development Journal* 42, no. 4: 501–11.

———. 2011. "Not Our Problem: Impairment as Difference, Disability as Role." *Journal of Inclusive Practice in Further Higher Education* 3, no. 2: 10–25.

Carey, Allison, Pamela Block, and Richard Scotch. 2020. *Allies and Obstacles: Disability Activism and Parents of Children with Disabilities*. Philadelphia: Temple University Press.

Carter, Erik W. 2007. *Including People with Disabilities in Faith Communities: A Guide for Service Providers, Families, and Congregations*. Baltimore: Brookes.

Carter, Erik W., Thomas L. Boehm, Naomi H. Annandale, and Courtney E. Taylor. 2015. "Supporting Congregational Inclusion for Children and Youth with Disabilities and Their Families." *Exceptional Children* 82, no. 3: 372–89.

Carter, Erik W., Harold L. Kleinert, Tony F. LoBianco, Kathleen Sheppard-Jones, Laura N. Butler, and Milton S. Tyree. 2015. "Congregational Participation of National Sample of Adults with Intellectual and Developmental Disabilities." *Intellectual and Developmental Disabilities* 53, no. 6: 381–93.

Chow, Rey. 1993. *Writing Diaspora: Tactics of Intervention in Contemporary Cultural Studies*. Bloomington: Indiana University Press.

Conner, Benjamin T. 2012. *Amplifying Our Witness: Giving Voice to Adolescents with Developmental Disabilities*. Grand Rapids: Eerdmans.

———. 2018. *Disabling Mission, Enabling Witness: Exploring Missiology through the Lens of Disability Studies*. Downers Grove, Ill.: IVP Academic.

Creamer, Deborah Beth. 2008. *Disability and Christian Theology: Embodied Limits and Constructive Possibilities*. New York: Oxford University Press.

Cushing, Pamela. 2010. "Disability Attitudes, Cultural Conditions, and the Moral Imagination." In *The Paradox of Disability*, edited by Hans S. Reinders, 75–93. Grand Rapids: Eerdmans.

Davis, Ellen F. 2001. *Getting Involved with God: Rediscovering the Old Testament*. Cambridge, Mass.: Cowley Publications.

Davis, Lennard J. 1995. *Enforcing Normalcy: Disability, Deafness, and the Body*. London: Verso.

———. 1997. "Constructing Normalcy: The Bell Curve, the Novel, and the Invention of the Disabled Body in the Nineteenth Century." In *The Disability Studies Reader*, edited by Lennard J. Davis, 9–28. London: Routledge.

Dingle, Shannon. 2018. "Resisting Ableism in the American Church." *Sojourners*, November 7. https://sojo.net/articles/resisting-ableism-american-church.

Dolmage, Jay T. 2017. *Academic Ableism*. Ann Arbor: University of Michigan Press.

Eiesland, Nancy. 1994. *The Disabled God: Toward a Liberatory Theology of Disability*. Nashville: Abingdon.

Eklund, Rebekah. 2015. "Empires and Enemies: Re-Reading Lament in Politics." In *Reading Scripture as a Political Act*, edited by Matthew A. Tapie and Daniel Wade McClain, 19–35. Minneapolis: Fortress.

Elbow, Peter. 1973. "The Pedagogy of the Bamboozled." *Soundings: An Interdisciplinary Journal* 56, no. 2: 247–58.

Ellington, Scott A. 2008. *Risking Truth: Reshaping the World through Prayers of Lament*. Eugene, Ore.: Pickwick.

Evans, Sara. 1979. *Personal Politics*. New York: Vintage Books.

Evans, Sara, and Harry C. Boyte. 1986. *Free Spaces: The Sources of Democratic Change in America*. New York: Harper Row.

Fadiman, Anne. 1997. *The Spirit Catches You and You Fall Down*. New York: Farrar, Strauss, and Giroux.

Fineman, Martha Albertson. 2005. *The Autonomy Myth: A Theory of Dependency*. New York: New Press.

———. 2008. "The Vulnerable Subject: Anchoring Equality in the Human Condition." *Yale Journal of Law and Feminism* 20, no. 1: 1–23.

Finkelstein, Vic. 1975. "To Deny or Not to Deny Disability—What Is Disability?" Independent Living Institute. https://www.independentliving.org/docs1/finkelstein.html.

Fox, Bethany McKinney. 2019. *Disability and the Way of Jesus: Holistic Healing in the Gospels and the Church*. Downers Grove, Ill.: IVP Academic.

Freire, Paulo. (1986) 1993. *Pedagogy of the Oppressed*. Translated by Myra Bergman Ramos. New York: Continuum.

Friedman, Edwin H. (1985) 2011. *Generation to Generation: Family Process in Church and Synagogue*. New York: Guilford Press.

Garland-Thomson, Rosemarie. 2011. "Misfits: A Feminist Materialist Concept." *Hypatia* 26, no. 3: 591–609.

Goldingay, John. 2016. "Psalms of Lament." Fuller Studio, April 25. Video, 11:43. https://fullerstudio.fuller.edu/john-goldingay-lament/.

———. 2020. "Praying for Justice." Fuller Studio, July 16. Video, 15:11. https://fullerstudio.fuller.edu/video/john-goldingay-on-praying-for-justice/.

Gosbell, Louise A. 2018. *The Poor, the Crippled, the Blind, and the Lame: Physical and Sensory Disability in the Gospels of the New Testament*. Tubingen: Mohr Siebeck.

Hart, Brendan. 2014. "Autism and Parents and Neurodiversity: Radical Translation, Joint Embodiment and the Prosthetic Environment." *Biosocieties* 9: 284–303.

Heifetz, Ron, and Marty Linsky. 2002. *Leadership on the Line: Staying Alive through the Dangers of Leading*. Boston: Harvard Business School Press.

Jacober, Amy. 2010. "Youth Ministry, Religious Education, and Adolescents with Disabilities: Insights from Parents and Guardians." *Journal of Religion, Disability & Health* 14, no. 2: 167–81.

Jacobs, Naomi Lawson. 2019. "The Upside-Down Kingdom of God: A Disability Studies Perspective on Disabled People's Experiences in Churches and Theologies of Disability." PhD diss., SOAS University of London. http://eprints.soas.ac.uk/32204.

Jaswal, Vikram K., and Nameera Akhtar. 2019. "Being versus Appearing Socially Interested: Challenging Assumptions about Social Motivation in Autism." *Behavioral and Brain Sciences* 42: 1–14.

Jennings, Willie James. 2010. *The Christian Imagination: Theology and the Origins of Race*. New Haven: Yale University Press.

———. 2017. *Acts: A Theological Commentary on the Bible*. Louisville: Westminster John Knox.

———. 2020. *After Whiteness: An Education in Belonging*. Grand Rapids: Eerdmans.

Johnson, Patrick W. T. 2017. "Jesus, Racism, and the Canaanite Woman." *Patrickwtjohnson.com*, August 14. https://patrickwtjohnson.com/2017/08/14/jesus-racism-and-the-canaanite-woman/.

Kafer, Alison. 2013. *Feminist, Queer, Crip*. Bloomington: Indiana University Press.

Katongole, Emmanuel. 2017. *Born from Lament: The Theology and Politics of Hope in Africa*. Grand Rapids: Eerdmans.

Kessler, Volker, and Louise Kretzschmar. 2015. "Christian Leadership as a Trans-Disciplinary Field of Study." *Verbum Et Ecclesia* 36, no. 1: 1–8.

Kingsbury, Jack Dean. 1976. "The Title 'Son of David' in Matthew's Gospel." *Journal of Biblical Literature* 95: 591–602.

Knudson-Martin, Carmen. 1994. "The Female Voice: Applications to Bowen's Family Systems Theory." *Journal of Marital and Family Therapy* 20, no. 1: 35–46.

———. 1996. "Differentiation and Self-Development in the Relationship Context." *Family Journal* 4, no. 3: 188–98.

Ladau, Emily. 2021. *Demystifying Disability: What to Know, What to Say, and How to Be an Ally*. Berkeley, Calif.: Ten Speed Press.

Lerner, Harriet. 1983. "Family Dependency in Context: Some Theoretical and Technical Considerations." *American Journal of Orthopsychiatry* 53: 697–705.

———. 1988. "Is Family Systems Theory Really Systematic? A Feminist Communication." In *A Guide to Feminist Family Therapy*, edited by Lois Braverman, 47–63. London: Harrington Park Press.

Lewis, Hannah. 2007. *Deaf Liberation Theology*. Burlington: Ashgate.

Linton, Simi. 1998. *Claiming Disability*. New York: New York University Press.

Luepnitz, D. 1988. *The Family Interpreted: Psychoanalysis, Feminism, and Family Therapy*. New York: Basic Books.

McGoldrick, Monica, ed. 1998. *Re-visioning Family Therapy: Race, Culture, and Gender in Clinical Practice*. New York: Guilford Press.

McRuer, Robert. 2006. *Crip Theory: Cultural Signs of Queerness and Disability*. New York: New York University Press.

Metzger, James. 2010. "Disability and the Marginalisation of God in the Parable of the Snubbed Host (Luke 14:15–24)." *The Bible and Critical Theory* 6, no. 2: 23.1–23.15.

Mitchell, David, and Sharon Snyder. 2020. "Disability, Inclusionism, and Non-Normative Positivism." In *Neoliberalism in Context: Governance, Subjectivity, and Knowledge*, edited by David Mitchell and Sharon Snyder, 177–93. Cham: Palgrave MacMillan.

Monro, A. 1994. "Alterity and the Canaanite Woman: A Postmodern Feminist Theological Reflection on Political Action." *Colloquium* 26: 32–43.

Newman, Barbara J. 2016. *Accessible Gospel, Inclusive Worship*. CreateSpace Independent Publishing Platform.

Northway, Ruth, Joyce Howarth, and Lynne Evans. 2014. "Participatory Research, People with Intellectual Disabilities and Research Approval: Making Reasonable Adjustments to Enable Participation." *Journal of Clinical Nursing* 24, nos. 3–4: 573–81.

Peterson, Eugene. 1993. *Where Your Treasure Is: Psalms That Summon You from Self to Community*. 2nd ed. Grand Rapids: Eerdmans.

Piepzna-Samarasinha, Leah Lakshmi. 2018. *Care Work: Dreaming Disability Justice*. Vancouver: Arsenal Pulp Press.

Polletta, Francesca. 1999. "'Free Spaces' in Collective Action." *Theory and Society* 28, no. 1: 1–38.

Pope John Paul VI. 1963. "Constitution on Sacred Liturgy (Sacrosanctum Concilium)." Documents of the Second Vatican Council, December 4. https://www.vatican.va/archive/hist_councils/ii_vatican_council/documents/vat-ii_const_19631204_sacrosanctum-concilium_en.html.

Portolano, Lana. 2020. *Be Opened! The Catholic Church and Deaf Culture*. Washington, D.C.: Catholic University of America Press.

Raffety, Erin. 2016. "I'm Not Sorry." *HuffPost Life* (blog), February 16. https://www.huffpost.com/entry/im-not-sorry_b_9040994.

———. 2018. "The God of Difference: Disability, Youth Ministry, and the Difference Anthropology Makes." *Journal of Disability & Religion* 22, no. 4: 371–89.

———. 2020a. "From Depression and Decline to Repentance and Transformation." *Theology Today* 77, no. 2: 117–23.

———. 2020b. "From Inclusion to Leadership: Disabled 'Misfitting' in Congregational Leadership." *Theology Today* 77, no. 2: 198–209.

———. 2021a. "2nd Sunday of Lent." *Disabling Lent: An Anti-Ableist Devotional*, published online in *Unbound: An Interactive Journal on Christian Social Justice*, February 5. https://justiceunbound.org/2nd-sunday-of-lent/.

———. 2021b. "Listening Even unto Rebuke." Invited Commentary. *Canadian Journal of Theology, Mental Health, and Disability* 1, no. 2: 117–21.

Raffety, Erin, and Stuart Carroll. 2021. "From Charity to Classroom Co-Learning: Togetherness in the Spirit as a Model for Experiential Education with People with Disabilities." *Journal of Disability & Religion* 25, no. 3: 312–28.

Raffety, Erin, Kevin Vollrath, Emily Harris, and Laura Foote. 2019. "Lonely Joy: How Families with Nonverbal Children with Disabilities Communicate, Collaborate, and Resist in a World That Values Words." *Journal of Pastoral Theology* 29, no. 2: 101–15.

Rah, Soong-Chan. 2015. *Prophetic Lament: A Call for Justice in Troubled Times*. Downers Grove, Ill.: IVP Books.

Rasmussen, Erica. 2021. "Inclusive Prayer Service for People with Disabilities Marks 30th Anniversary of the ADA." *America: The Jesuit Review*, November 27. https://www.americamagazine.org/faith/2020/11/27/disabilities-prayer-service-god-ability-xavier-ada-239345.

Ravaud, Jean-Francois, and Henri-Jacques Stiker. 2001. "Inclusion/Exclusion: An Analysis of Historical and Cultural Meanings." In *Handbook of Disability Studies*, edited by Gary Albrecht et al., 490–514. Thousand Oaks, Calif.: SAGE Publications.

Reeve, D. 2012. "Psycho-Emotional Disablism: The Missing Link?" In *Routledge Handbook of Disability Studies*, edited by Nick Watson, Alan Roulstone, and Carol Thomas, 78–92. New York: Routledge.

Reinders, Hans. S. 2008. *Receiving the Gift of Friendship: Profound Disability, Theological Anthropology, and Ethics*. Grand Rapids: Eerdmans.

Rendle, Gil. 2010. *Journey in the Wilderness: New Life for Mainline Churches*. Nashville: Abingdon.

Reynolds, Thomas. 2008. *Vulnerable Communion: A Theology of Disability and Hospitality*. Grand Rapids: Brazos Press.

———. 2012. "Invoking Deep Access: Disability beyond Inclusion in the Church." *Dialog: A Journal of Theology* 51, no. 3: 212–23.

Saliers, Don. 1998. "Introduction: Toward a Spirituality of Inclusiveness." In *Human Disability and the Service of God*, edited by Nancy L. Eiesland and Don E. Saliers, 19–32. Nashville: Abingdon.

Schipper, Jeremy, and Candida Moss, eds. 2011. *Disability Studies and Biblical Literature*. New York: Palgrave MacMillan.

Scott, J. M. C. 1996. "Matthew 15.21–28: A Test-Case for Jesus' Manners." *Journal for the Study of the New Testament* 63: 21–44.

Shildrick, Margrit. 2009. *Dangerous Discourses of Disability, Subjectivity, and Sexuality*. Basingstoke, UK: Palgrave Macmillan.

Silverman, Arielle M., Jason D. Gwinn, and Leaf Van Boven. 2014. "Stumbling in Their Shoes: Disability Simulations Reduce Judged Capabilities of Disabled People." *Social Psychological and Personality Science* 6, no. 4: 464–71.

Spies, Miriam. 2021. "From Belonging as Supercrip to Misfitting as Crip: Journeying through Seminary." *Journal of Disability & Religion* 25, no. 3: 296–311.

Steinke, Peter L. 2006. *Congregational Leadership in Anxious Times: Being Calm and Courageous No Matter What*. Herndon, Va.: Rowman & Littlefield.

Swinton, John. 2007. *Raging with Compassion: Pastoral Responses to the Problem of Evil*. Grand Rapids: Eerdmans.

———. 2011. "Who Is the God We Worship? Theologies of Disability: Challenges and New Possibilities." *International Journal of Practical Theology* 14, no. 2: 273–307.

———. 2012. "From Inclusion to Belonging: A Practical Theology of Community, Disability, and Humanness." *Journal of Religion, Disability & Health* 16, no. 2: 172–90.

———. 2016. *Becoming Friends of Time: Disability, Timefullness, and Gentle Discipleship*. Waco, Tex.: Baylor University Press.

———. 2020a. "Disability, Vocation, and Prophetic Witness." *Theology Today* 77, no. 2: 186–97.

———. 2020b. *Finding Jesus in the Storm*. Grand Rapids: Eerdmans.

Swinton, John, and Erin Raffety. 2021. "Disability and Christianity." In *Christianity & Psychiatry*, edited by by J. R. Peteet, H. S. Moffic, A. Hankir, and H. G. Koenig. Cham: Springer International Publishing.

Thomas, Carol. 1999. *Female Forms: Experiencing and Understanding Disability*. Buckingham, UK: Open University Press.

Titchkosky, Tanya. 2011. *The Question of Access: Disability, Space, Meaning*. Toronto: University of Toronto Press.

United States Department of Justice, Civil Rights Division. 1990. *Americans with Disabilities Act*. https://www.ada.gov/ada_intro.htm.

Webb-Mitchell, Brett. (1994) 2009. *Unexpected Guests at God's Banquet: Welcoming People with Disabilities into the Church*. Eugene, Ore.: Wipf and Stock.

———. 2010. *Beyond Accessibility: Toward Full Inclusion of People with Disabilities in Faith Communities*. New York: Church Publishing.

Wendell, Susan. 2010. "Toward a Feminist Theory of Disability." In *The Disability Studies Reader*, 3rd ed., edited by Lennard J. Davis, 336–52. New York: Routledge.

Westermann, Claus. 1974. "The Role of Lament in the Theology of the Old Testament." *Interpretation* 28, no. 1: 20–38.

Whitehead, Andrew L. 2018. "Religion and Disability: Variation in Religious Attendance Rates for Children with Chronic Health Conditions." *Journal for the Scientific Study of Religion* 57, no. 2: 377–95.

Whitmore, Todd. 2021. "The Confession as Retrospective Narrative: A Genre for Ethnographically-Driven Theology." *Ecclesial Practices* 8: 73–88.

Wigg-Stevenson, Natalie. 2018. "Just Don't Call It Ethnography: A Critical Ethnographic Pedagogy for Transformative Theological Education." In *Qualitative Research in Theological Education*, edited by Mary Clark Moschella and Susan Willhauck, 100–117. London: SCM Press.

Yan, Eric G., and Kerim M. Munir. 2004. "Regulatory and Ethical Principles in Research Involving Children and Individuals with Developmental Disabilities." *Ethics and Behavior* 14, no. 1: 31–49.

Yong, Amos. 2011. *The Bible, Disability, and the Church: A New Vision of the People of God*. Grand Rapids: Eerdmans.

Index of Names and Subjects

Index of Scripture

Also Available in the SRTD Series

*Prophetic Disability: Divine Sovereignty and Human Bodies
in the Hebrew Bible*
Sarah J. Melcher

*Becoming the Baptized Body: Disability and the Practice of
Christian Community*
Sarah Jean Barton

The Cerulean Soul: A Relational Theology of Depression
Peter J. Bellini

Accessible Atonement: Disability Theology and the Cross of Christ
David McLachlan

Formed Together: Mystery, Narrative, and Virtue in Christian Caregiving
Keith Dow

Wondrously Wounded: Theology, Disability, and the Body of Christ
Brian Brock

Disability and Spirituality: Recovering Wholeness
William C. Gaventa

Crippled Grace: Disability, Virtue Ethics, and the Good Life
Shane Clifton

The Bible and Disability: A Commentary
Edited by Sarah J. Melcher, Mikeal C. Parsons, and Amos Yong

Pastoral Care and Intellectual Disability: A Person-Centered Approach
Anna Katherine Shurley

*Becoming Friends of Time: Disability, Timefullness, and Gentle
Discipleship*
John Swinton

Disability and World Religions: An Introduction
Edited by Darla Y. Schumm and Michael Stoltzfus

Madness: American Protestant Responses to Mental Illness
Heather H. Vacek

Disability, Providence, and Ethics: Bridging Gaps, Transforming Lives
Hans S. Reinders

Flannery O'Connor: Writing a Theology of Disabled Humanity
Timothy J. Basselin

Theology and Down Syndrome: Reimagining Disability in Late Modernity
Amos Yong

CPSIA information can be obtained
at www.ICGtesting.com
Printed in the USA
LVHW100802270922
729372LV00003B/386